*Emergent Literacy
and Dramatic Play
in Early Education*

Emergent Literacy and Dramatic Play in Early Education

Jane Ilene Davidson

Master Teacher
University of Delaware Laboratory Preschool
Lecturer

Individual and Family Studies
University of Delaware

Delmar Publishers
I(T)P˙ An International Thomson Publishing Company

Albany • Bonn • Boston • Cincinnati • Detroit • London • Madrid
Melbourne • Mexico City • New York • Pacific Grove • Paris • San Francisco
Singapore • Tokyo • Toronto • Washington

NOTICE TO THE READER

Cover Design: The Color Shop

Delmar Staff
Publisher: Diane L. McOscar
Administrative Editor: Jay S. Whitney
Associate Editor: Erin J. O'Connor
Project Editor: Colleen A. Corrice
Production Coordinator: James Zayicek
Art and Design Coordinator: Timothy J. Conners
Editorial Assistant: Glenna Stanfield

COPYRIGHT © 1996
By Delmar Publishers
A division of International Thomson Publishing Inc.

I(T)P The ITP logo is a trademark under license

Printed in the United States of America

For more information, contact:

Delmar Publishers
3 Columbia Circle, Box 15015
Albany, NY 12212-5015

International Thomson Publishing Europe
Berkshire House 168-173
High Holborn
London, WC1V7AA
England

Thomas Nelson Australia
102 Dodds Street
South Melbourne, 3205
Victoria, Australia

Nelson Canada
1120 Birchmount Road
Scarborough, Ontario
Canada M1K 5G4

International Thomson Editores
Compos Eliseos 385, Piso 7
Col Polanco
11560 Mexico D F Mexico

International Thomson Publishing Gmbh
Königswinterer Strasse 418
53227 Bonn
Germany

International Thomson Publishing Asia
221 Henderson Road
#05-10 Henderson Building
Singapore 0315

International Thomson Publishing – Japan
Hirakawacho Kyowa Building, 3F
2-2-1 Hirakawacho
Chiyoda-ku, 102 Tokyo
Japan

    4 5 6 7 8 9 10 XXX 01 00

Library of Congress Cataloging-in-Publication Data

Davidson, Jane Ilene, 1948-
    Emerging Literacy and Dramatic Play in Early Education / Jane I. Davidson
        p. cm.
    Includes bibliographical references and index.
    ISBN 0-8273-5721-4
    1. Drama in education. 2. Play. I. Title.
    PN3171.D29 1996
    372.13'32—dc20   94-36276
                                                          CIP

Contents

Foreword   *ix*

Preface   *xi*

Acknowledgments   *xiii*

CHAPTER 1 **Let's Play Pretend   1**
The Value of Dramatic Play   3
Providing Time and Space for Dramatic Play   8
A Preview   10
A Step Further: Can I Replicate the Olden Times? Sesame Street Play in My Room?   10

CHAPTER 2 **What Is Dramatic Play?   11**
Defining Dramatic Play   11
Developmental Differences in Children's Pretend Play   15
Master Players   20
Processes Needed for Dramatic Play   20
Social Development and Dramatic Play   21
A Step Further: Playing Firestation with Dispatchers   25
Cognitive Development and Dramatic Play   31
Language Development and Dramatic Play   37
Stretching Development to Enhance Dramatic Play   38
Observing the Differences in Children   40

CHAPTER 3 **What Do Teachers Do When Children Are Pretending?   41**
To Enter or Not to Enter   41
A Step Further: What Else Could the Teacher Have Said?   46
Adult Roles in Children's Pretend Play   47
How Do You Get Started?   69
Common Questions Adults Ask   72

CHAPTER 4 **Emergent Literacy: Children Construct Understandings of Written Language   78**
What Is Emergent Literacy?   79
Oral Language: The Beginning of Emergent Literacy   79

A Step Further: When to Teach and When to Listen   85
Language as a Social Symbol System   86
The Development of Written Language   87
A Step Further: Patrick Discovers He Can Write the Whole
   Alphabet   95
Supporting Children's Emerging Literacy   98

CHAPTER 5   **From All-Encompassing to Incidental: Different Modes for Integrating Literacy into Dramatic Play   105**
Assessing the Literacy in This Dramatic Play   106
How Should Literacy Be Integrated into Dramatic Play?   106
Different Modes for Integrating Literacy into Dramatic Play   106
A Step Further: Comparing Written and Oral Language   109
Which Is the Best Mode of Integrating Literacy into
   Dramatic Play?   128

CHAPTER 6   **Variations on Dramatic Play Themes: Many Faces of Restaurant Play and Other Themes   129**
Objectives for Restaurant Play   131
Selecting the Best Form of Restaurant Play   133
And Still More Restaurants   134
Evaluate What Really Happens   140
Many Other Themes   141
A Step Further: Are Literacy Props Different from Other Dramatic Play
   Props?   141
Putting This List in Perspective   155

CHAPTER 7   **Pretend Play beyond the Dramatic Play Area   156**
Facilitating Pretend Play in Many Different Forums   158
Similarities between Pretend Play in the Dramatic Play Area and
   Beyond   158
Differences between Pretend Play in the Dramatic Play Area and
   Beyond   161
Pretending in the Block Area   165
A Step Further: Using Props to Extend Pretend Play in the Block
   Area   169
A Step Further: Beyond Traffic Signs   172
Pretending with Art Media   179
Pretending with Manipulatives   183

Dramatic Play Outside   186
Playing Pretend in Other Contexts   188

CHAPTER 8   **Children's Books: A Gateway to Emergent Literacy   189**
Reading at Home   190
Story Reading in Childcare Settings   194
Rereading Books   194
A Step Further: Making Story Pieces   197
A Step Further: *The Very Hungry Caterpillar* Puppet Story   198
A Step Further: *Too Much Noise* Story Box   200
A Step Further: Books with Searching Games   203
Creating Warm Shared Experiences around Reading Books   206
Children Actively Participating in Book Sharing   206
Creating a Group Book Culture   207
Encouraging Pretend Play around Books   211
A Step Further: Resources on Playing about Books   211
A Step Further: Moving Day   221
A Step Further: *Too Much Noise* Reenactment   225
Building a Love for Books   226

CHAPTER 9   **Creating a Literacy-Rich Environment   227**
Should All Early Childhood Settings Have Message Boards?   229
How Is This Literacy-Supporting Atmosphere Created?   230
Seeing This Philosophy in Action   235
A Step Further: Preparing Mom for the Letter   235
Creating an Environment to Support This Philosophy   239
A Step Further: Becoming Someone Else   241
A Step Further: Keeping the Joy in Rhyming Games   251
Weaving Literacy and Dramatic Play into Other Areas of
    Learning   252
A Step Further: Each Child Will Approach Activities in Individual
    Ways   257
Even with a Supporting Literacy Atmosphere, No Activity Is
    Magical   261

CHAPTER 10   **Creating Continuity   262**
Why Is Continuity Needed?   264
Impediments to Continuity between Home and School, Classroom and
    Classroom   266
Ingredients for Building Strong Teacher/Parent Partnerships   270

Formats for Communicating   275
A Step Further: Possible Literacy Information to Share   276
A Step Further: A Newsletter   278
A Step Further: "What I Did Today" Notes   281
Building Partnerships with Administrators and Other
    Professionals   284
Isn't This Continuity a Frill?   287

Glossary   289

References   294

Bibliography of Children's Books and Software   304

Subject Index   307

Author Index   311

Author Index-Children's Books   313

Delmar Publishers' Online Services

To access Delmar on the World Wide Web, point your browser to:
http://www.delmar.com/delmar.html
To access through Gopher: gopher://gopher.delmar.com
(Delmar Online is part of "thomson.com", an Internet site with information on
more than 30 publishers of the International Thomson Publishing organization.)
For information on our products and services:
email: info@delmar.com
or call 800-347-7707

Foreword

Patricia Monighan Nourot, Ph.D.*
Sonoma State University*
Rohnert Park, CA*

Jane Davidson writes about young children and their teachers with care and authenticity. In focusing specifically on children's dramatic play and its links to literacy, she addresses many of the concerns I hear voiced by the beginning teachers I teach: What does the link between literacy and play look like in daily classroom life? And what can I as a teacher do to support children's symbolic thinking and ability to create "story?"

Davidson uses rich and detailed anecdotes of play and literacy events to illuminate the developmental course of play and to articulate the instrumental value of educational play in classrooms for young children. She paints portraits of life in preschool classrooms in which teachers are keen and sensitive observers of children's play, respectful and supportive of their imaginations, and clear in their thinking about how the teacher's involvement in play serves development and learning. We come to see that not only the *what*, but the *why* of orchestrating play is of prime importance.

Throughout the book, Davidson scaffolds her very practical suggestions with a framework of theory and research, explicating principles for articulating a rationale for play-based literacy learning in simple and direct forms. She offers suggestions to teachers for providing accessories for children's play that promote expression and communication of ideas, as well as guidelines for decisions about when children are best served by teachers watching their play and when teachers might fruitfully and appropriately participate in play events.

This aspect of monitoring one's intervention in children's play and literacy events comes across to me as the most powerful and valuable feature of *Emergent Literacy and Dramatic Play in Early Education*. In each chapter Davidson emphasizes teachers' self-reflective processes in their work with children. She describes a kind of dance through which the teacher consistently views the situation from the child's viewpoint, and then factors in her own perspective. The willingness for a teacher to say "I could have done this better, or in a different way" is modeled throughout the text, painting a picture of thoughtful engagement and flexibility in the art of teaching.

In addition to accessories and strategies for enhancing literacy in children's play, Davidson has written a very practical chapter describing the use of children's literature to stimulate and extend dramatic play experiences, modeling the creation of thematic curriculum in the process. She describes how children's growing understanding of the use of story brings them into the literacy community through their play.

Finally, Davidson does not stop with her discussion of school literacy and dramatic play, but extends her lively anecdotes and interpretive framework to children's play with language and literacy in their homes. She stresses the importance of teachers' communication with parents around their children's development, and presents strategies for promoting parental understanding of both emergent play and literacy. She touches on the importance of cultural sensitivity and awareness in communicating with parents about their values and expectations for their children's learning.

In discussing continuity, Davidson also brings in strategies for teachers who understand and utilize the power of play in early childhood curriculum to communicate with their colleagues about the importance of play-centered and literacy-rich environments for young children.

I can already anticipate the lively discussions among the beginning teachers I teach as they read and discuss Davidson's lively descriptions of both children and teachers fully exploring their capacity to make story through play and literacy. I believe that experienced teachers as well will see themselves in the stories of classroom life that Davidson writes, and will gain food for thought about their own practices.

Preface

How does one create an early childhood environment where play and literacy flourish? *Emergent Literacy and Dramatic Play in Early Education* answers this crucial question.

The best way to help teachers understand the atmosphere of early childhood environments that are rich in play and literacy is to spend time in these settings. Since this is not always possible, this book offers vicarious visits through numerous anecdotes from early childhood classrooms. The stories about children are compiled from observations of a number of classrooms. The classrooms include inner-city childcare centers, family childcare homes, a half-day laboratory preschool, small private childcare centers, public school classrooms and special education settings, and a corporate childcare.

The children observed range from eighteen months to eight years old, in both age-segregated and cross-aged classrooms. Many of the observations come from my own classrooms. At times they have been abbreviated, combined, or modified to make them easier to tell without losing the flavor of the incident. The names of teachers and children have been changed. Incidents have been varied at times to maintain the anonymity of those observed.

Chapter 1 presents an overview of the nature and value of dramatic play, and its connection with emergent literacy. The nature of dramatic play and how it varies by age and developmental level is explored in Chapter 2. Chapter 3 discusses the teacher's role in facilitating pretend play. Chapter 4 explores the nature of emergent literacy—what it is, how it develops, and the connections between dramatic play and emergent literacy. The ways emergent literacy can be integrated into a wide variety of pretend play themes, at many different levels is examined in Chapter 5.

Chapter 6 takes a specific theme and demonstrates how adults can design that theme to best meet the needs of their particular groups of children. Each dramatic play theme can be implemented in a variety of ways depending on the children's needs and the adult's goals.

Although we often think of dramatic play as happening in the "house corner" or dramatic play area, pretend play in fact occurs all around the room. Chapter 7 discusses how to facilitate dramatic play in all areas of the room. Pretend play can engender use and exploration of written language, but the reverse is also true. Often pretend play evolves from favorite books and characters. Chapter 8 examines ways that adults can use literature to promote pretend play.

Chapter 9 describes a language-rich early childhood setting in which emergent literacy may flourish. Unfortunately, many parents and adults do not feel that children are learning unless they are engaged in group activities or completing worksheets. This chapter presents more child centered alternatives.

Chapter 10 explores ways of educating other adults so they can see the tremendous learning that occurs in a developmentally appropriate early childhood program where dramatic play and literacy flourish. Once they understand the learning that is occurring, parents can offer play opportunities at home as well. This chapter presents some ways to encourage and support parents who wish to supplement the learning from the early childhood setting with similar activities at home; and some suggestions for dealing with administrators and colleagues who do not yet see the value of play and the true nature of emergent literacy.

Throughout the book there are sections entitled "A Step Further." These offer additional descriptions of the ideas implemented in early childhood classrooms as well as resources for teachers. Boldface type highlights words that are defined in the glossary.

I wrote this book to enable other teachers to share my joy in children's play and emerging literacy. For some teachers, the book will serve as an introduction to emergent literacy or to dramatic play. For other teachers, the book will support and extend what is already happening in their classrooms. The book can be used as a text for courses on emergent literacy, language arts, play, and as supplemental reading in an early childhood curriculum course.

Jane Ilene Davidson

Acknowledgments

This book would not have been completed without the support and encouragement of many people. I am grateful to my colleagues in the University of Delaware Department of Individual and Family Studies and at the Laboratory Preschool for their support, especially Marilou Hyson, Alice Eyman, Nancy Edwards, and Nadine Heim.

I am indebted to the children and teachers at St. Michael's Day Nursery, Newark Day Nursery, Delaware Curative Workshop, Great Expectations, and Eyman Children's Center for allowing me to observe their play and literacy, and to share it with readers through stories and photographs. I especially want to thank the children at the University of Delaware Laboratory Preschool and their families. It was the excitement of watching them play and grow that motivated me to share these ideas with others.

I would like to thank my family and many friends who were willing to listen as I tried out ideas on them. Finally, thank you to my parents who helped me into the world of literacy.

CHAPTER 1

Let's Play Pretend

Four-year-old Michael and seven-year-old Lily are at their family childcare home setting up a let's pretend game. Michael spreads out a towel and begins arranging stuffed Sesame Street characters around the edge. He places a plate at each corner saying "Let's pretend we're having breakfast." He places a plastic teapot on top of an upside down cardboard box proclaiming, "This is the stove."

"Okay!" says Lily, "Then after breakfast let's pretend they are going to school." Lily arranges a row of pillows for desks. She designates a corner as the principal's office and begins arranging a table with pencils, paper, and a toy typewriter.

The play continues constructively for another fifteen minutes, at which point Lily finds a long feather among her things. "I know! Let's pretend long ago like Little House in the Big Woods (Wilder, 1932). I'll be Laura and you can be Pa. I'll use this to write when I go to school." Michael doesn't like this idea—he still wants to play Sesame Street. An argument grows with such cries as, "How come we always have to play your games?" "Your games are too babyish," and "Well, if you won't do my idea, you can't use my puppet."

Jane, the family care provider, interrupted from feeding a baby, comes to quiet the din. She suggests taking turns choosing the plot, but the anger has escalated too much to allow this. She suggests picking a new plot altogether, but both children are now so determined to do THEIR thing that they find something wrong with each suggestion. Finally Jane suggests a compromise that will use both ideas. "Why don't you pretend that the Sesame Street characters travel in a time machine back to long ago and they meet Laura?" After a moment's reflection this idea is enthusiastically accepted.

The children begin negotiating the details of the plot. They decide to have a long-ago house and a long-ago school. Michael will work in the school. During the discussion they rearrange the props to signify long ago. The toy typewriter has been removed, the box Michael had been using as a stove is turned on its side to make a fireplace. The teapot is now in the fireplace rather than on the stove.

Michael goes off to work at school. "Where's the typewriter?" he asks with a put-upon tone. His annoyance that a favorite toy is missing may derail the new game. But Lily saves it by asking, "What is a typewriter? I have never heard of that." Michael quickly picks up on this new turn in the play. "It's like a computer," he explains. "But what is a computer?" the olden-days Lily asks. Michael goes on to explain how it has keys, you plug it in, it makes letters on a screen, and it can print out words. Lily pretends to suddenly comprehend that it is a writing implement he is looking for. She offers him the feather. He asks what it is for. She then explains what a quill pen was in olden days.

Michael and Lily are **master players**—children who are skilled at playing pretend. Master player is a term used in *The Play's the Thing* (1992) by Betty Jones and Gretchen Reynolds to describe children who are skilled at playing pretend. The term is also used by Greta Fein (1986). They are able to create characters, define plot, and devise **props**. They can integrate a variety of **scripts**—cooking, school, Sesame Street, and long ago—into a complex pretend game. They are able to take a small suggestion or idea and elaborate it into a longer, more involved, script. For the most part they are able to negotiate differences and keep the play going in ways that satisfy both of them.

Creating and enacting pretend stories is a common activity of young children. Haight and Miller (1993), in a study of children's pretend play at home, found that children "spent a significant amount of time engaged in this activity, which served simultaneously as a mode of relating to significant others and as a vehicle for expressing individuality" (p. 118). Not all children have reached the skill of Michael and Lily. Some children's play is simpler and more repetitive. With experience and support from adult and peers, these children will also grow to be skilled pretenders who can weave and sustain complex play.

The Value of Dramatic Play

It is clear that this play has a great deal of meaning and value for both children, as does **pretend play** for children at all levels of experience. Vygotsky (1967) suggested that pretend play may allow children to function at their highest level of competence. **Dramatic play** fosters development in all areas. (For more information, extensive discussions of many aspects of play, and a detailed look at the research on the value of play, see also Bergen, 1988; Dimidjian, 1992; Fein, 1981; Fein & Rivkin, 1986; Gottried & Brown, 1986; Klugman & Smilansky, 1990; Rogers & Sawyers, 1988; Rubin, Fein, & Vandenberg, 1983.)

Fosters Social Emotional Development

Dramatic play fosters social emotional development in a number of ways (Curry & Bergen, 1988; Saltz & Saltz, 1986). Young children have little power in the world. Dramatic play puts the children in charge. They can design a world of their choosing, where they can be in control of what happens (Rogers & Sharapan, 1992). Dramatic play allows children to try on the roles of important people in their lives—Mom, Dad, Big Sister—as well as other roles that hold value to them: favorite characters from TV or books, dogs, driver, or superheroes.

As the play above unfolds, Lily and Michael must negotiate the direction of the story. This requires them to understand the perspective of the roles they are portraying and to listen to and understand the other child (Fein & Schwartz, 1986; Rubin & Howe, 1986). The direction of the play is set by each child's adding bits to the story line. Michael suggests making breakfast. Lily adds school to this. The play is important enough to them that they are willing to work to resolve disputes that arise. When Michael is upset about the missing typewriter, Lily incorporates the absent prop in the conversation by pretending she does not know what a typewriter is. This new, interesting turn to the play negates the immediate need for a typewriter.

There are times when children cannot find a way to resolve differences, and adult support is needed in order to solve the problem. Jane stepped in to offer a solution when Lily and Michael were arguing over what game to play. With Jane's help a compromise was found that both

FIGURE 1-1 Trying on important roles like "driver"

could accept. This process helps children to see that conflicts can be resolved, and that there are often more alternatives than are obvious at first (Wittmer & Honig, 1994).

Dramatic play also allows children to explore distressing events in more manageable ways (Beckwith, 1986; Fein, 1986).

> *One-year-old Lisa falls and bumps her head on the coffee table. She cries and is comforted by Mom. A few minutes later she walks over to the corner and lowers her head carefully so she just touches the dangerous corner with her forehead. She repeats this five or six times, then smiles and moves on to other play.*

By reenacting the fall Lisa was able to come to terms with a scary event. In her reenactment she was in control of her interaction with the table. She was able to move around the table without it hurting her. Unfortunately many children are increasingly exposed to violence, both in their own homes and in their community. Play becomes a powerful tool for coming to terms with these overwhelming experiences.

Fein (1986) suggested that pretend play offers the child an opportunity to play out both positive and negative emotions, thus allowing for the regulation of emotions with regard to "children's changing emotional preoccupations" (p. 40).

Presents a Forum for Cognitive Development

Dramatic play also offers children a forum for cognitive development (Johnson, 1990; Athey, 1988) provided reviews of research on the relation between dramatic play and cognitive development. Dramatic play allows children to explore their understandings of events, characters, and objects in a manageable context. Lily and Michael are exploring the events of breakfast, school, and family life long ago. Enacting a role or event requires children to synthesize what they know about that role or event to create an enactment that will communicate what they are doing to themselves and others. This process helps children to clarify concepts about people and the world.

Bretherton (1986) suggested that children create a mental picture or schema of events (such as shopping) after repeated experience. Once created, this mental picture of shopping will help children to understand future experiences. But the schema is not static—it continues to expand

FIGURE 1-2 Acting out the negative emotions of the "bad guy"

FIGURE 1-3 In play, children can explore what it feels like to be a writer

and change with additional shopping experiences. In dramatic play children reenact and adapt their schema, or concepts, about the events they are enacting.

Encourages Language Development

Dramatic play encourages children to use rich, elaborate language (Athey, 1988; Pelligrini, 1986). According to Rogers and Sawyers (1988), researchers have recognized that the development of symbols is similar in language and in pretend play. "Although play is not a necessary condition for learning language and literacy skills, play is probably the best environment for these abilities to thrive" (Rogers & Sawyers, 1988, p. 64).

While playing, children use language to set the stage and negotiate the direction for the play, as when Michael says, "Let's pretend we are having breakfast" and "This is the stove." Children also use language within the context of their pretending, as when Lily as a character in the story says, "What is a typewriter? I have never heard of that." According to Giffin (1984), children have many techniques for setting the direction of the play without stepping outside of their roles. Instead of stepping outside of the play to suggest breakfast, Michael might have signaled his idea by asking, "Is it breakfast time?" Giffin provided a detailed discussion of the variety and complexity of the language that children use in their dramatic play.

Dramatic play can also facilitate children's emerging literacy (Christie, 1991). In this particular episode Michael and Lily are increasing their understanding of written language. They are trying out the role of writer, exploring the properties of writing tools, and expanding on characters and events they have met in books. All these activities allow children to explore literacy. Although they cannot yet read or write conventionally, in their play they are able to explore what it feels like to be a writer and to use the tools that writers use (Neuman & Roskos, 1991; Strickland & Morrow, 1989). By using themes from books in their play, these children are enriching their understanding of the characters and events, bringing deeper meaning and appreciation to these books.

Assists Physical Development

Children's dramatic play offers many opportunities for practicing both large and small muscle skills. When children dress up, they practice using a variety of fasteners: buttons, snaps, zippers, and ties. Many actions require careful hand control: typing, cooking breakfast, arranging the blanket on the floor, and writing with the quill pen. Children exercise large muscles as they walk in adult dressup shoes, carry around heavy props, enact roles requiring special motions (such as dogs), and do other tasks such as sweeping, making the bed, or taming the bad guy.

Contributes to Development

The multidimensional learning that occurs is a natural component of children's pretend play, whether the children are skilled pretenders or beginning players. Some suggest that for children with language impairments, and for those with developmental delays, this type of play is particularly important. Because dramatic play is child-directed, and child-selected, it often motivates children to stretch their skills in order to keep the play going.

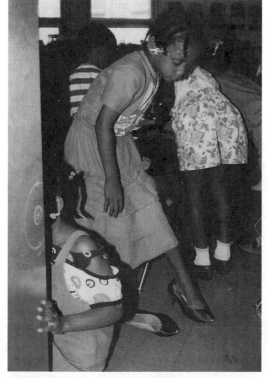

FIGURE 1-4 Walking in high heels exercises large muscle skills

FIGURE 1-5 Pretend play is common in early childhood

Providing Time and Space for Dramatic Play

"Let's pretend" play is common in early childhood. It occurs wherever there are children, sometimes in the elaborate version as described above, sometimes more simply when a child adds noises while zooming a toy car along a pretend road.

Dramatic Play Is Often Missing

Pretend play can and should be common in early childhood centers—but this does not always happen. Unfortunately, time and space for pretend play is less prevalent in kindergarten than in preschool, and extremely rare in first grade (Hatch & Freeman, 1988).

In some schools* the **dramatic play area** is only "open" for short periods of time, making it difficult for children to develop and expand their play themes (Jones & Reynolds, 1991). Adults observing such brief play are unlikely to see the richness that is possible in pretend play. This may reaffirm their belief that pretend play is not important. (The term "dramatic play area" describes the part of the room where children can take on and enact roles in pretend play. Some refer to this area as the "housekeeping area," but since it can be set up to support themes other than house play—such as grocery store or firestation—the use of housekeeping area is misleading).

Some teachers** find it difficult to deal with the squabbles and wildness that pretending may engender. Some early childhood programs may place such strong emphasis on the more school-like, academic tasks that the dramatic play area is ignored by the adults (Bowman, 1990), sending a message to the children that such play is not important, and depriving children of the guidance that could lead the play to a more complex level.

With the great pressure that early childhood programs put on adults to be accountable for what they teach and to cover a certain amount of information, it is easy to see why dramatic play, which appears "fun," will be put aside by the teacher who has many seemingly more urgent demands.

---

*Young children are cared for in many different settings—schools, childcare centers, family childcare homes, kindergartens, and nursery schools, to name a few. As there is no good term that encompasses all early childhood settings, I will use a variety of terms. The suggestions in the book are applicable to ALL early childhood settings.

**There is no convenient term that encompasses all adults who work with young children—I use the term "teacher." Young children are growing and developing. The adults who are with them facilitate this growth and thus are teachers.

Dramatic Play Is Used to Facilitate Learning

Although pretend play may look insignificant to the casual observer, there is enormous learning occurring—learning that can be expanded when the adult provides appropriate props, space, time, and guidance. Not only does the above scenario allow the children to stretch their language, cognitive, and social skills, it also is a means by which they can explore literacy. The theme of the play is a reworking of stories and characters in books. The typewriter and the quill pen were important to Lily's and Michael's play. As children integrate written language into their play, they are building an understanding of its purposes, and beginning to define themselves as people who can use written language.

Pretend play is self-motivated and self-directed. Children can explore in depth the ideas most relevant to their developmental levels and their personal concerns and interests. The childcare worker who avoids dramatic play because of the "academic" things that need to be learned may find that dramatic play is, in fact, a powerful tool for teaching many "academic" skills as well as promoting development in general.

With a little practice, adults can learn to encourage and expand on the learning that occurs while children are playing pretend. Without props, time, and a place to play, Lily and Michael could not have developed their "story." Adult help at the right time facilitated problem solving, and raised the play to a higher, more complex level by providing a new theme. With

FIGURE 1-6 In play, children can begin to define themselves as people who use written language

adult facilitation, dramatic play is less likely to degenerate into wild and disruptive play. However, the adult's role in dramatic play is a delicate one. Too much direction will stop the play from being play, while ignoring the play may prevent it from reaching its potential richness.

A Preview

The remainder of this book explores the strong connection between dramatic play and children's understanding of written language. It describes both the nature and value of showing teachers how to create an atmosphere in their early childhood setting where emerging literacy and dramatic play can flourish. Chapters 2 and 3 illustrate the nature of dramatic play and the teacher's role in facilitating pretend play. Chapters 4 and 5 explore the nature of **emergent literacy** and its connections with dramatic play. Chapters 6 and 7 show the variety of options present in the dramatic play area and in other parts of the early childhood setting.

Pretend play can engender use and exploration of written language, but the reverse is also true. Literature as a prompt for pretend play is the topic of Chapter 8. Dramatic play is not the only forum for emergent literacy: Chapter 9 describes the many other supports for emergent literacy in language-rich early childhood settings. How can we help other adults, parents, and administrators to perceive the tremendous learning that occurs in a developmentally appropriate early childhood program where dramatic play and literacy flourish? Chapter 10 will answer this question by presenting ways of building a strong partnership with parents and colleagues.

A STEP FURTHER   *Can I Replicate the Olden Times?*
Sesame Street Play in My Room?

Throughout the book there are many examples of children, and sometimes adults, involved in dramatic play. This allows you to vicariously visit childcare facilities where wonderful things are happening. These examples create a picture of play in action. Do not expect the play in your setting to replicate the play in the examples. Play will look different depending on the ages, interests, experiences, and skills of the children. What forms the center of the play in one room may not be of interest to another group of children.

The examples are NOT meant as a recipe to be slavishly followed in your classroom. Rather, they are intended to give you the flavor of the types of play that may occur.

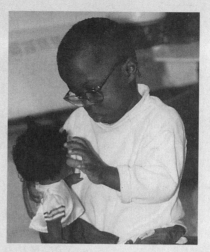

CHAPTER 2

What Is Dramatic Play?

Binta holds one end of a long chain she has constructed from play links. She wiggles the chain along the floor behind her making hissing noises.

* * *

Xavier tucks his doll into the crib and pats its back. "Shhh! My baby is sleeping," he informs the children who are noisily packing their suitcases for the beach.

Defining Dramatic Play

It is clear that both of these children are playing pretend, but coming up with an exact definition for pretend play has been difficult. Theorists and researchers who study play have written pages trying to define what is meant by pretend play and debating which term best encompasses the definition. To come up with a working definition one must first explore the current terms. Imaginative play, **symbolic play**, dramatic play, and **sociodramatic play** are a few of the terms that have been used.

Smilansky's Sociodramatic Play

Sara Smilansky (1968) coined the term sociodramatic play to define pretend play in a social context. By her definition, sociodramatic play involves six characteristics.

1. Taking on a make-believe role (for example, acting as a mother, dog, or a Ninja Turtle)
2. Making believe with regard to objects (for example, using a curved block as a steering wheel or covering a doll with an imaginary blanket)
3. Making believe with regard to situation or action (for example, pretending to make dinner, or pretending that you are all on a spaceship headed out to find the bad guys)
4. Persistence (play that continues at least for ten minutes)
5. Using language to communicate the context of the play
6. Interacting socially while playing

According to Smilansky, dramatic play includes the first four elements, but not the last two. By her definition, both dramatic play and sociodramatic play involve the child enacting a role, as opposed to play where the child uses a doll, car or some other object as the actor in the play. Binta's play where the play link snake becomes the actor would not be considered dramatic play under this definition.

Qualities of Play Behavior

Smilansky defined pretend play by looking at its component parts. Others consider the qualities exhibited in play behavior. Garvey (1990) mentioned four descriptive characteristics of play "which are widely cited as critical to the definition of play" (p. 4).

1. Play is pleasurable.
2. Play does not have extrinsic goals. Its motivations are intrinsic and it is enjoyed more for its process than for its end result.
3. Play is voluntary.
4. Play involves active engagement on the part of the player.

Although these are characteristics of play in general, they are also characteristics of pretend play.

Play versus Exploration

In attempting to define play there is often debate about the difference between "play" and "exploration." Piaget (1962) describes three levels of play. The first level is functional play—exploration or practice play, when children explore materials and use them in functional ways. The second level is symbolic play, where children play imaginatively, using actions and props to symbolize things in the environment. The third level is games with rules (Vandenberg, 1986). Manipulating an object to learn about it is **exploration**. A child who puts a hand in a cup, rolls it along the table, and bangs it against the tabletop is exploring the cup's properties. On the other hand, when the child uses the cup to further some purpose, this is considered play behavior. A child who pretends to fill a cup at the toy sink, and then drinks from the cup is "playing." Hutt (1971) summarized the difference nicely. "In play the emphasis changes from the question of 'what does this *object* do?' to 'what can I do with the object?'" (p. 246).

Children often move back and forth between exploration and play, making the distinction hard to see. A child who is pressing the keys on a cash register and taking the money in and out may be exploring the register's properties, pretending to be a cashier, or perhaps doing a bit of each. It is not necessary that teachers tease out the precise boundary between exploration and play, but it is important for adults to realize that hitting the keys on a toy cash register does not guarantee that a child is playing imaginatively. Adults will want to observe each child's play carefully to see if the child is using props imaginatively as well as exploring them.

FIGURE 2-1 Twos often play familiar themes like eating

Dramatic Play versus Constructive Play

There is also a difference between **constructive play** and dramatic play. Smiliansky listed constructive play, where children use materials to construct a representation of something, as one of Piaget's levels of play. Van Hoorn, Nourot, Scales, and Alward (1993) listed this as the first level of symbolic play. Smith and Vollstedt (1985) felt that Smilansky misinterpreted Piaget by adding constructive play as a distinct level; however, so much research and later work have been based on these categories that it is important to understand them (Rogers & Sawyers, 1988). Constructive play occurs when children use materials to construct, build, or create something, such as constructing a building with blocks, creating a painting of something at the art table, or stacking sand into a castle in the sandbox.

Often children's constructive play and imaginative play will overlap. They may take on a role—for example, the construction worker—as they are building. They may involve toy people as construction workers in their endeavor.

> *Four-year-old Robbie makes an enclosure with blocks. He opens one side and pulls his truck into the enclosure saying, "This is my garage." He then drives the truck around the block area as he goes to work, captures the bad guys, and returns to his garage again. He spends the next ten minutes building a roof over the garage and adding decorations to the top of the roof. "I'm in jail now," he says. When the teacher asks how he will get food in jail, he makes a small hole in the roof. He places a small wooden person in a truck, and collects colored cubes, which he drops into the hole to feed the captive.*

Robbie moves between constructive play and dramatic play. He begins with just building, takes on the role of construction work as he builds, then moves to just pretending (driving around). He returns to just building as he puts the roof on his garage, and ends by just pretending (feeding the prisoners). It is true that at times children will just build, while at other times it is clear that they are using their building as a site for dramatic play. There are many times when children move back and forth between dramatic play and constructive play. The exact boundaries between constructive play and dramatic play are not important for teachers, as long as they realize that when a child builds with blocks, dramatic play can, but does not automatically, occur.

A Working Definition for Teachers

Precise definitions are important when doing research. In order to recognize a specific behavior, the observer must know exactly what that behavior involves. For the purposes of teachers in the field and this book, a much broader definition will be more helpful. The terms pretend play and dramatic play are used interchangeably to describe any time a child uses props, actions, and/or language to represent realistic or imaginary experiences. We will be using the terms more broadly than Smilansky does. This definition of dramatic play encompasses Binta's play, where she uses the chain snake as the actor in her pretend story—the incident does not need to be lengthy to be called dramatic or pretend play.

Developmental Differences in Children's Pretend Play

Observing children of different ages involved in dramatic play is a good way to highlight the significant developmental differences that occur in the pretend play of children as they mature. What most two-year-olds do in the house area will be significantly different from what most five-year-olds do in the same place. Of course, one must always keep in mind that even within an age group the developmental levels often vary significantly.

Two-Year-Olds at Play

Mary picks up the phone. She holds it upside down and talks softly into the receiver. After hanging up the phone, Mary pretends to wash her hands in the play house sink. She dries her hands on an imaginary towel and begins putting plates on the table. "Mary's making us dinner," teacher Christine comments to the children sitting with her on a pretend bus. Kathy, one of the bus riders, notices what Mary is doing, and sits down at the table. Mary picks up a lunch box from the floor. She unpacks plastic fruit, putting a piece on each plate. Kathy moves her fruit around on the plate. Mary pretends to eat her apple. Kathy watches and then imitates Mary. Mary puts her fruit back in the lunch box on the floor. Kathy brings her fruit to Mary to put in the lunch box. Mary latches the lunch box. They tell each other goodbye.

The play of these two-year-olds is simple. It revolves around the familiar theme of eating. The children enact pretend actions, but do not seem to have adopted pretend roles. The events are symbolized by single actions. Eating is one pretend bite of an apple. The children seem to recognize and enjoy each other's presence, although little interaction occurs. Mary's presence and actions did influence Kathy's actions once the teacher drew Kathy's attention to Mary's play. Little language is involved in the play.

Three-Year-Olds at Play

The house area is crowded. The teacher is sitting at the table. A number of the children are making and giving food to the teacher. A child under the table is barking. Holly is dressed in a pink negligee and a floppy rimmed black hat. She carries on a running dialogue with the dolls as she dresses them and wraps them in blankets. "It is cold. You need lots of blankets. Mommy's not going to drive to the park. We are going to walk. Go to sleep now." "I am the Mommy cause I have a hat," Holly explains to Mark as he walks by.

"I am a Mommy, too. I have a hat," proclaims Mark pointing to his baseball cap.

Holly gives Mark one of the dolls and tells him, "I am playing in my Mommy house." Both children put the dolls into beds made of small boxes. Holly continues preparing the dolls for a trip to the park, as Mark wanders over to the teacher.

"I am a cowboy," he tells the teacher, exchanging his cap for a large straw hat. The other children are giving the teacher various condiments for her hamburger. They have "run out of mustard," so they are giving her silly things such as eggs, cocoa, and peas to put on the hamburger. Mark gives her some applesauce, then walks back and picks up his doll.

"I will be the Daddy," declares Holly.

"I will be the Mommy," says Mark.

Holly continues to get the dolls ready. She then pushes the box of babies to the other side of the room saying, "We're at the park." She takes the dolls out of the box, and puts them on the ground to play. When she is ready to return she repacks the dolls into the box. It is caught behind the leg of a table and she cannot get the box to move. "Mommy, help take the babies home," she calls to Mark. He comes over and helps to push the box back to the house.

He stays to change his baby's diaper. "It's stinky," he says, holding his nose with one hand and the pretend diaper with the other.

The play of these three-year-olds is more elaborate than that of the twos. The themes still revolve around the home, but the play involves more detail. They are now taking on roles, although these roles are fluid, shifting quickly to fit the moment. Language has become a more important part of the play. The children use it to define their play. They tell each other the roles they have chosen. Holly tells Mark what he needs to do next in the play. Holly also uses language within the play to enact the role of Mommy and to define for herself the context of the play. In telling the "babies" about the cold and the walk, she is creating the story that she is enacting. A great deal of her talk is to herself.

A number of different themes are being enacted in the same space: A group is playing "mealtime" with the teacher, another child is playing "pet," while Holly and Mark are playing "family." The meal group is large and remains focused on the food theme for a long time. The teacher who is central to the play keeps it going. Holly and Mark interact with each other as they play, but the interactions are brief. It is important to both of them to have another parent for their children, but once the parentage is established, their games move independently, only coming together now and then to restate their bond.

Four-Year-Olds at Play

Willie and Hannah enter the house area. Willie announces that he is the brother. Hannah claims she is the sister. Benje enters right behind them, saying, "Then I will be the dog. Okay?" As he climbs under the table Hannah tells him, "No, you need to be the cat."

Willie and Hannah sit on a bed reading the newspaper and discussing it. "Here is who voted." "Look, that's about a sex dude," says Hannah pointing out an underwear advertisement. "Look. Here is a map." Benje, the cat, comes out to look. "NO, CAT," scolds Willie. Benje hangs his head and scurries back under the table.

"Honey, do you want some tea?" inquires Willie.

"Yes, dear," she replies. They both get up to get plastic cups and Willie also gets some empty soda cans. Hannah starts drinking from the empty cup.

"Wait," Willie cautions, "I've got some tea. Oh, it's soda."

Benje crawls out from under the table to get some soda. "No, cat. Get." Willie says, shooing Benje back under the table. Benje takes a bowl and some soda with him.

Hannah tells Willie to "hold this," as she hands him the cups. She then pours some Sprite into both cups. They continue reading the paper as they sip their soda.

Willie points excitedly at a car ad in the newspaper. "Look, look! We have to go. That's the car place. We have to go to here, to that spot." He begins driving with an imaginary steering wheel. Hannah also drives.

Benje collects cans, papers, and other things in a paper bag. He announces, "Guys, I am gonna be the recycle man and put these out. Who wants soda?" Willie and Hannah ignore him. He repeats the question three times without getting a response. He then puts the cans in recycling bins that were added to the house for a conservation unit.

Willie shows the newspaper map to Hannah saying, "We have to go to Disney World." Willie puts the newspaper in front of him saying, "This is a seat belt." Hannah takes a piece of paper for her seat belt. When Benje crawls over, they give him a paper for a seat belt, too.

This play is more social. Willie and Hannah develop the story jointly, building on each other's ideas. The interaction is maintained for a long period of time with both children taking an active role in the play. Benje remains on the fringe of the play. It is unclear if this is because he does not know how to enter their play, or because they prefer to play as a pair. Many fours tend to play in pairs. Building on each other's ideas is easier when there are just two players.

The theme in this play is still a familiar one, but there is more elaboration, and the game continues longer. The trip now involves maps, drinks, seat belts, and a variety of destinations. Fours will often move beyond the house themes to such things as dating, robberies, jail, superheroes, movie stories such as Beauty and the Beast, hurricanes, and animal families. The spontaneous way in which these children integrate literacy into their pretend play can be seen at all ages. Chapter 4 will explore the partnership between emergent literacy and dramatic play in more detail.

FIGURE 2-2 Fours often play in pairs

For the two main players, language definitely sets the direction of the play. They are less physically active, using language to advance their story. Although Benje also uses language, his play is more physical. Both of these styles are common in a four-year-old class.

Five-Year-Olds at Play

The dramatic play area in this kindergarten class is set up as a garden shop. A small booth with a window is the store, a bench holds things to purchase, a table has paper for making shopping lists, and two shopping carts stand nearby.

Sung-Jin sits in the store booth counting money as he talks on the phone. Nancy loads items into her cart. Jeannine dresses to go to the store. She frantically searches her purse and pockets. "I only got two moneys. I don't know where my other moneys are." Sensing her friend's distress, Nancy interrupts her shopping to find Jeannine a purse that has some money. The two then continue loading their carts with merchandise. Nancy is methodical. She groups all the buckets in one spot, she carefully nests objects so the smaller ones fit inside the larger ones. They talk about what they are buying and what they will do with the various things at the beach.

Jeannine unloads her cart's contents onto the counter. Sung-Jin picks up each item, names it as he pushes some keys on the cash register, and says a price. When he gets to the bucket, he ponders, "How much is this?"

Nancy goes to look at the price chart on the side of the booth. "2 cents," she announces.

"Two cents," repeats Sung-Jin as he rings it up on the cash register. "Is that it?" Sung-Jin asks. Jeannine nods. He pushes some more keys and says, "25 cents." She hands him some paper money informing him, "Now you have to give me change." The change is deposited safely in her purse, and she takes

the bag of purchases that Sung-Jin hands her. Jeannine then unpacks her bag, arranging the items on the bench again. Soon she begins to shop again. The game continues in this way with the girls expanding the play to include a doll who wants something at the store, and to change clothes before shopping again.

These fives have elaborate, extended pretend play. The three children take on distinct roles that depend on each other for the game to continue. The shoppers require a cashier in order to buy things, and the cashier requires customers in order to do his job of selling things. These children easily maintain a three-person play episode. Fives are able to incorporate more children and more diverse roles into their play.

They move easily between speaking in their pretend roles—"How much is this?", and speaking as organizers of the play, "Now you have to give me the change." They are able to deal with small problems, like the missing money, and still keep the play going. The shopping theme is familiar to the children, though they may never have been to a garden store. Fives will often develop fantasy themes that are further from reality. Their themes can be quite detailed, involving many actors, and often continuing from day to day.

A Look at Some Other Fives

Not all five-year-olds have such rich elaborate play. Later in the day other children in the class complain that they have not had a chance in the store. The current players are asked to leave and four new children enter the store.

Joshua begins piling everything he can see into his cart. Carly searches for things to buy. She sees Joshua's heaping basket and complains, "He's got all the stuff." Looking for more things Joshua spies a bucket in Carly's basket and takes it. "Stop it!" shrieks Carly. Joshua returns the bucket, but later when she is not looking he removes two cups from her basket.

"The store is closed," declares Ryan, the new shopkeeper, as he closes the store's window.

Kirshnan shouts, "No, it's open." The window remains closed so Kirshnan pushes it open and throws cups and shoes into the store. Ryan attempts to close the window as he throws the merchandize back at Kirshnan.

The teacher hears the commotion and enters the area. "I am giving you the opportunity to play here. You need to think about your behavior. Is it something you will be proud of?" The boys mumble a response and the teacher moves on. For a few minutes they quietly move props around. Then, in an effort to get Ryan's attention, Kirshnan climbs onto the window shelf and begins tickling Ryan. Ryan tries to push Kirshnan away as Carly lifts her shopping cart, dumping the contents over the counter onto the floor of the booth. Ryan picks items up and tosses them randomly out of the booth. Joshua finds a hat and places it on Carly's head. She takes it off, adding it to the pile of stuff on the floor.

The dramatic play in these two episodes looks significantly different. The children in the first episode are deeply involved in their play. They are able to move in and out of their roles easily as they negotiate problems that arise. The children in the second episode wander aimlessly among the props. They are having trouble selecting roles, finding a pretend context for using the props, and organizing joint action.

Master Players

Although one can see certain trends in the children's play as they get older, there is still wide variation in play within each age group. Some of the children in each example seem in charge of their play. Two-year-old Mary, three-year-old Holly, four-year-olds Willie and Hannah, and five-year-olds Sung-Jin and Nancy were all able to develop and enact their play, often providing a leadership role for other children in the area. Jones and Reynolds (1992) call these children "master players." They "are skilled at representing their experiences symbolically in self-initiated improvisational drama"(p. 1). What is the difference between these more skilled master players and their less skilled peers? How can adults help all children to grow into master players? To answer these questions, it is necessary to delineate the skills and processes needed for dramatic play.

Processes Needed for Dramatic Play

There are three important overlapping areas of development which affect children's dramatic play: social development, cognitive development, and language development. How does children's development in each of these areas affect their dramatic play? What are the implications of this for how adults facilitate play?

Social Development and Dramatic Play

When looking at the social development of children, it is obvious that two-year-olds relate to each other in different ways than do five-year-olds. These two groups vary in several ways: (1) in their level of interactions with other children; (2) in their ability to adopt the perspective of others and negotiate the rules and direction of play; and (3) in their skills at initiating and entering play.

Level of Social Interaction with Peers

Parten (1932) described how children's manner of interaction changes as they develop. She describes four different levels of play interaction.

1. **Solitary play** occurs when children are engaged in their own activities with little regard for others. A child who is playing mother feeds her baby without noticing other children around her.
2. **Parallel play** describes play where children are engaged in the same activity next to each other. Children put food on the table together, enjoying the presence of the other child, and perhaps imitating each other's actions. Mary and Kathy are involved in parallel play in the example on page 15. At this stage, although the children are aware of each other's presence, the play is still independent.
3. **Associative play** happens when the children adopt a loosely shared theme. They might decide at first that they are playing house. They might all pick roles. One child might be the big brother making dinner, another is the grandma going to a wedding, while a third is the mom going to work. They might interact by saying goodbye to each

FIGURE 2-3 This girl is involved in solitary play

other when people leave. The play of each child tends to move in its own direction, only loosely affected by the play of the others. The house play of Holly is associative play.

4. **Cooperative play** describes the play of children who are working jointly to develop a mutual story. Children take distinct roles. The game is based on children's interactions with each other. In playing house, it is now important for everyone to eat when it is mealtime. For children at this level, part of the excitement of the play is the way the different roles interact with each other, and the ability to create a joint story. The play of the first kindergarten group is cooperative play.

Parten discusses these as levels of development. Children engage in solitary play before parallel play, and parallel play before associative play, and associative play before cooperative play, but each new level does not replace the one before—a child who has learned to play associatively will also at times engage in both parallel and solitary play. As children get older, their solitary play can become complex and involved.

Single play episodes will often involve more than one of these levels of play. At other times, play may involve children who are interacting at different levels. In the play revolving around newspapers, Hannah and Willie are engaged in cooperative play, while Benje's play is at the associative level.

Since the play is so fluid, moving constantly between one level and another, it is often difficult to make exact distinctions. Instead teachers can look for trends in children's play. Which labels define much of the child's play? Does the child engage in the same types of play with different themes and/or with different children?

Teacher Support for Different Levels of Play

What does this mean for an adult supervising dramatic play?

Solitary Play

One might assume that solitary play need not be encouraged by teachers; yet often this play can be extremely meaningful. A child might reenact complex stories with a group of small people. This play may be more elaborate than that done with peers, since the child can devote total concentration to story creation without having to negotiate ideas with others. Teachers can support the child's right to play in this manner by expressing enjoyment of the child's play, by providing space where the child will not be interrupted, and by recognizing the validity of such play.

Parallel Play

A teacher of two-year-olds just beginning to develop parallel play should provide many duplicates of the same materials, because in parallel play the main form of interaction is doing the same thing next to a peer, it is essential to have multiples of objects so children can join in with each other.

Two-year-old Sean puts on a large floppy white hat, puts a pocketbook over his shoulder, and begins walking around the room. Heather, the teacher, comments to Siobhan, "Look, Sean has his hat on ready to go to work. There are some hats on the rack by the window if you want to go to work, too."

By remarking on a child's hat, and helping others to find hats, the teacher has set up a situation where two children can become involved in parallel play.

Some themes, such as doctor play, require the interactions of two roles: doctor and patient. One would not expect children at the parallel play level to be able to maintain the give and take that such play involves. Doctor themes can be played out using a doll, rather than another child, as the patient. Another alternative is for the adult to be the patient. Playing with the adult, who is skilled at interacting, will allow the child to play at a higher level.

Themes of this sort provide a good bridge to associative play. Children who are ready to interact with peers can do so on whatever level is comfortable. Some children will begin by interacting with dolls and adults, and as they build play patterns for this theme, move into playing with peers.

Associative Play

If children are involved mainly in associative play, then it is wise to select themes that allow for some interaction, but also allow for independent

FIGURE 2-4 Ready to go to work

FIGURE 2-5 The teacher promotes parallel play by helping others to also "go to work"

play. This will enable each child to find the proper balance. A good example is playing store. Paying for purchases requires some interaction. There is also much independent play as children select what they wish to purchase, and as the cashier explores the cash register between customers.

Teachers may help by encouraging interaction and by interpreting the children's needs to each other when necessary.

> *A grocery store is set up in a four-year-old classroom. Melissa is shopping. She fills her basket and starts to leave the store without paying Erica, who is sitting behind the cash register. The teacher reminds her, "Don't forget to pay Erica for your purchases."*
>
> *Melissa puts her basket on the counter next to Erica, saying, "Here." Erica is busy playing with the cash resister and does not notice.*
>
> *The teacher tells Erica, "Melissa is ready to pay for her groceries. How much do they cost?" Erica rings up the items, tells Melissa the cost, is paid, and returns change.*

As Erica and Melissa repeat these interactions, they will develop a pattern to use when playing shopper and cashier so they will no longer need the teacher's help. Another technique that the teacher might use to help the girls learn how to interact in a store is to take a role in the play, and model the appropriate behavior.

Teacher's questions or modeling might have helped the second group of garden store shoppers. For master players, like the first group in the garden store, these types of interchanges will come naturally. They will not need help from the teacher to initiate the play.

Cooperative Play

If children are involved mainly in cooperative play, adults will want to design the dramatic play to encourage children to take roles that depend upon each other. The teacher might set up an airplane where the pilots must talk to the air traffic controllers. A firestation could have a maproom where dispatchers direct drivers to fires. A beauty parlor could be set up with separate stations: a waiting area, a shampoo station, a cutting and setting station, and a manicure station. If needed, the adult can help children to explain their roles to each other, assist in negotiating the direction of play, and assist in resolving conflict.

Taking the Perspective of Others

Young children see the world from their own perspectives. Slowly they grow to recognize other perspectives as well. This growing ability to see beyond themselves and realize that other people exist in the environment,

FIGURE 2-6 Beauty parlor setup with roles that depend on each other

A STEP FURTHER *Playing Firestation with Dispatchers*

The four-year-old class is just down the street from the firestation. The children often hear the siren calling the volunteer firefighters to the station. Fire trucks often rush by the playground, causing all children to stop and watch. To build on this interest, a walk to firestation is planned.

The children are fascinated with a wall-sized map of the city and a radio in the dispatchers room. The dispatcher shows the children how to find their school on the map and how he would direct the trucks to that location.

When the children returned, they discussed playing firestation the next day. The teacher asked what would be needed. The maproom is in great demand, as is the truck. The children paint houses on large pieces of cardboard. The teacher makes a large map to use in the dispatcher's room, and numbers the buildings to coincide with the map. A long driving bench is used as a truck. The dispatcher on the radio can tell the driver of the fire truck the address of the fire, and direct the truck to the right house.

Here again children easily incorporate literacy into their pretend play. (See Chapter 4 for more about developing a partnership between dramatic play and literacy.

each with unique needs, is called **decentration** (Fenson, 1984, 1986; Piaget, 1962; Shantz, 1983).

Role Play and Perspective Taking

All pretend play requires some degree of perspective taking. When two-year-old Mary pretends to eat, she is thinking about what eating is like. She puts herself in the place of an eater. When she talks on the phone, she not only is creating her own conversation, but must imagine the conversation of the other person as well. When three-year-olds Holly and Mark are mommies, they must consider what it is like to be a mommy in order to take on that role. When five-year-old Nancy, the shopper in the garden store, interacts with the cashier and her fellow shopper, she must create her own role as well as respond to the role of the other players.

As children strengthen their skill at perspective taking, they can enact roles that are further from their own selves, and become involved in increasingly complex interactions with other players. Teachers who recognize children's level of skill in this area will be able to suggest appropriate roles, and know when they should encourage more interactive play and when they should expect more individual play.

Conflict and perspective Taking

If children cannot see other players' perspectives, they are likely to have more conflicts with other children, and to need help resolving the conflicts that arise. These conflicts can make dramatic play more difficult.

Two-year-old Lizzie is putting toy people into a dump truck. Amanda sees what she is doing, sits down on top of Lizzie, and begins putting more people into the truck. Amanda sees that to have fun with the people and the truck you sit where Lizzie is, so she does. The teacher, Janice, gently helps Amanda off Lizzie, walking her to a nearby shelf as she says, "Amanda, do you need some people and a truck? There are some over here for you. Lizzie is using those. Now you can both put people in a truck." She checks to see that Lizzie is all right and explains, "Amanda didn't see you. Now you each have a truck."

* * *

Three-year-old Justin enters the block area. He looks around for a dump truck. There is one parked next to Jill. He takes it. Jill screams, "It's mine."

Justin firmly replies, "But I need it."

Mr. Ortega tells Justin, "Jill is using that dump truck. You can ask her for a turn when she is done."

"But I need it!" Justin repeats.

"It sure is hard to wait, isn't it?" Mr. Ortega sympathizes. "Would you like some help asking for a turn when she is done?" After Justin asks her, Mr. Ortega helps him to speed the waiting process by involving him in building a house.

* * *

Four-year-olds Jameela and Lauren are playing with stuffed pets. Jameela is searching for the small brown kitten. She sees it in Lauren's pet bed. "I need that kitten," Jameela informs her friend. Lauren continues tucking in the kitten. She doesn't want to give it up.

Ms. Mooney tries to help. "Lauren is using that one right now. Here is a black kitten you can use."

"But I need that one," Jameela insists. "She's the one with the blue ribbon and blue is my favorite color."

"You could ask Lauren to let you know when she is done with the kitten," suggests Ms. Mooney.

Jameela bursts into sobs, proclaiming, "Then I can't play!" Lauren looks at the kitten, then at Jameela. She sighs, gives the kitten one last hug, then hands the kitten to Jameela. Now that she has the kitten, Jameela notices Lauren's sadness and says, "You can watch her when I go out shopping."

Ms. Mooney asks Lauren, "Do you still want that kitten? We can tell Jameela that you need it."

Lauren seems hesitant. She would like the kitten, but she doesn't want it enough to make Jameela cry again. "No, that's okay. She'll let me use it when she goes out."

The conflicts in all three situations arise from a child's personal needs predominating over his or her ability to see the other child's perspective. Amanda does not intentionally hurt Lizzie. She probably does not even think of her. Justin realized that Jill had the truck, but he feels that his strong needs should be so obvious to all that it justifies his possession of the truck. Jameela realizes that Lauren has the kitten and wants it too, but her vision of the game includes her as the owner of the brown kitten. This need is so great that she feels she cannot continue if she does not have it. Once she gets the kitten, Jameela is able to respond to Lauren's needs by offering to let Lauren watch it occasionally.

In each situation a teacher intervened. The techniques used varied in response to the different levels of the children. Janice helped Amanda to find her own toys, but she also pointed out the existence of Lizzie and her need for the toy. Janice made sure to check on Lizzie and to interpret Amanda's behavior to Lizzie. It is important for Lizzie to feel safe and protected at school.

Mr. Ortega offered Justin a different type of help. Justin was already aware that Jill was using the truck, but he felt his own need justified his ownership of the truck. Mr. Ortega made clear Jill's rights of ownership. He helped Justin find a way to get a turn. He also helped Justin to deal with the frustration of waiting, by offering sympathy and getting him involved so the wait would not seem so long.

Ms. Mooney's intervention is less successful. Jameela knows that Lauren is there and wants the kitten, but feels that her strong need for it should convince Lauren. Ms. Mooney's efforts to point out Lauren's needs and to redirect Jameela are ignored. Her efforts to help Lauren stand up for her rights are also unsuccessful. It is unlikely that any adult intervention would have helped at this point. Jameela needs time, and many more experiences like this one, to develop concern for others.

Ability to Enter Play

When looking at children's social skills, a wide variation in their ability to enter or initiate play with each other becomes obvious.

The Watcher

Some children are not sure how to enter new situations. They may see others playing pretend, but not know how they can be a part of the play. These children may just stand and watch.

> *A hospital is set up in the four-year-old class. The teacher, JoAnn, has recently had surgery and the class has been discussing many medical questions. Abby likes to play pretend, but often takes a while to enter new situations. She spends a long time watching the hospital play, but when a teacher invites her to join she says, "No." On the second day of hospital play she looks like she wants to play. JoAnn's inquiries about whether Abby needs an operation or would like to be a doctor, are both met with "No."*
>
> *JoAnn sees that Abby really wants to play. "I need an operation," JoAnn informs Abby. "Would you like to come and keep me company?" Abby agrees. The two of them lie down on the operating table together. Abby does not want the doctor to do anything to her, but keeps giggling and making suggestions about what the doctor should do to JoAnn. Dr. Michael listens to JoAnn's sore foot with his stethoscope. He then puts yards of masking tape on her shoe with Abby pointing out spots he has missed.*

The next day Abby takes the doctor role, and by the end of the week she even tries out the patient role and has her own solo operation. For some children, as for Abby, entering with the teacher is a comfortable, non-threatening way to start the play. Other watchers may be drawn in by mentioning a role that can be adopted—"I think the spaghetti needs stirring"; "This baby needs someone to feed it."

At times children do not enter the play because they do not know the story line of the current play, and do not know what roles may be available.

> *Lauren and Binta are playing house behind the hedge. Kyla is peering longingly through the bushes. She seems to want to play, but is unsure of what to do. Mr. Yang comes to help her. "Girls, what are you playing?"*
>
> *"House. This is my bedroom," Lauren explains, pointing to an indentation in the hedge.*

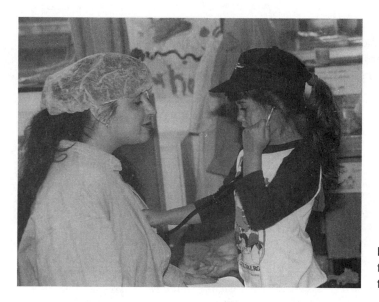

FIGURE 2-7 Playing with teacher is a comfortable, non-threatening way to start play

"Where is your room?" Mr. Yang asks Binta. She points to another inden-
tation. "And where can Kyla's room be?" Lauren points to a third indentation in
the hedge. Kyla ducks under the branches to join the girls in the house. They
spend a minute reallocating roles, then the house play continues.

Mr. Yang knew that the three girls often played together. He thought
it unlikely that Kyla was being excluded on purpose. His questions
helped Kyla to know what was happening in the play, and made Lauren
and Binta aware that Kyla wanted to join.

Being Aggressive

Often children who are unsure about how to participate in or enter the
play will use inappropriate interactions to get attention.

In a class of four-year-olds, Kyla is standing at the play stove stirring the contents
of a pot. She announces, "I am making cookies for Santa." Anthony approaches
with his hands up like claws. He is growling menacingly. She hugs her pot to her
asserting, "No, you can't have it." Anthony attempts to grab the pot.
*   The teacher, who is nearby, says to Anthony, "Did you want to play with*
Kyla? She is making cookies for Santa." Kyla resumes stirring, seemingly reas-
sured that there will not be a problem since the teacher is there. Anthony stands
for a minute and seems unsure. "Are you making lots of cookies for Santa?"
inquires the teacher. Kyla nods yes. "It will be good to have a helper," the teacher
comments. Kyla gives Anthony a bowl. He begins mixing, too. They discuss how
many cookies they will make for Santa.

Anthony first used aggression to enter Kyla's game. This was not successful. The teacher's help was subtle. She provided protection for Kyla and helped to define what was happening in the play. Kyla and Anthony were then able to create a joint script for pretending on their own.

Being Silly

Silliness is another ineffective means that children often use to enter play.

> A beauty parlor is set up in the pretend area. Micah and Ben want to play, but are not sure what to do. They hide under the cashier's table giggling. Miss Henderson is unsure what to do and ignores them. They sneak out and grab things the beauticians are using, stashing all their loot under the table. They seem to enjoy doing something with a buddy, but their play disrupts the play of the other children. When Miss Henderson tries to redirect them, the silliness has developed so far that the boys cannot take suggestions for other types of play. Finally another teacher comes over and tells them they need to find something else to do.
>
> The next day they crawl under the table again. Immediately Mr. Fahey comments, "People don't go under the table at the beauty parlor. We need cashiers who can collect money and make appointments." They now have something they can do together as buddies that is part of the play. The boys are cashiers for about ten minutes, then Ben goes to build in the blocks. Micah tries all the other roles in the beauty parlor—shampooer, hair stylist, manicurist, and even customer.

Silliness created a sense of camaraderie for the boys. They were not a part of the beauty parlor play, but they did create a satisfying social interaction. Unfortunately, their silliness interfered with the other children's play. Miss Henderson ignored the play, letting it escalate. Mr. Fahey's prompt intervention on the second day allowed the boys to play together as buddies within the dramatic play theme. Micah's exploration of the various roles might not have occurred if the under-the-table giggling had begun again.

Social Development and the Complexity of Dramatic Play

As you can see, the child's level of social development has a significant affect on the quality of the child's pretend play. It affects the length of play, the types of roles enacted, the degree of interaction with peers, the ability to resolve conflict, and the ability to understand and respond to action of others. Dramatic play also offers an opportunity to practice and hone these skills.

Observant adults will see which skills children have. They will see where their help will raise the play to a higher level, allowing children to practice new skills. They will see where lack of skill creates conflicts in the play and help children design the play so it can run smoothly given the current social development of the players. Close observation of social skills will help adults know when to step back and let the play unfold on its own.

FIGURE 2-8 Teacher helps children to negotiate conflicts so play can continue

Cognitive Development and Dramatic Play

Cognitive development also impacts the quality of children's dramatic play.

Symbolic Thought

Dramatic play requires **symbolic thought** (Bretherton, 1986; Fein, 1981; and Rogers & Sawyers, 1988). This increasing ability to symbolically represent objects and actions in their pretend play was termed *decontextualization* by Werner and Kaplan (1963). To enact the role of mother, a child must create a mental representation of "motherness," then use an action, a tone of voice, or a piece of clothing to help create a sense of "mother." Children who pretend to drink from toy glasses are using a prop to help represent the action of drinking.

More advanced children will be able to use cylindrical blocks as the glasses for their representation of drinking. The cylindrical block resembles a glass in shape, which makes this **symbolic transformation** easier for the child. Vygotsky (1967, 1978) called the block a *pivot*. It provides an anchor to help the child keep the mental image of the glass in mind. As a child gets better at this, the object used as a glass can be further removed from the actual glass. The child may use a rectangular block, which is not like a glass in either form or use. At a still more advanced level, children will drink from imaginary glasses, using just the action to represent the act of drinking. Symbolic thought is the beginning of the ability to engage in mental representation and abstract thought (Piaget, 1962).

FIGURE 2-9 Adults can model pretending

When children first begin pretending, they will engage in single acts of symbolic play, as in the case of a child pretending to drink from a toy glass. Often very young children will pretend with regard to action, without necessarily taking on another role. The child may care for the baby by rocking it, without pretending to be a mother or a father (Bretherton, 1986; Nicholich, 1977).

With experience, the child will then move to combining separate instances of pretending around a single theme. The child will put the milk bottle on the table, then put the dishes on the table, thus combining two actions or schema around the theme of setting the table. The child might feed the toy baby, pretending both that the doll is a baby, and that the action of putting a bottle to the doll's lips is "feeding the baby."

As children continue to develop, they will combine strings of sequential actions into episodes. Dinnertime might include cooking spaghetti, cooking peas, setting the table, and eating the food. These episodes will then be strung together to form more complex episodes. Playing family might include eating dinner, going to bed, and going to the grocery store (Nicholich, 1977). Fenson (1986) called this "increasing ability to combine individual actions into coordinated behavior sequences" "integration" (p. 58). Rogers and Sawyers (1988, p. 36–42) presented a good summary of Nicholich's stages.

Supporting Children's Play

Smilansky (1968) and others (Feitelson & Ross, 1973; Freyberg, 1973; Saltz & Saltz, 1986) found that tutoring from adults can increase the child's ability to play imaginatively. Smilansky described three types of pretending that occur in dramatic play: pretending with regard to role, pretending with regard to object, and pretending with regard to action. Adults can observe children's play for each of these components, and provide support in the areas where it is needed (Heidemann & Hewitt, 1992; and Smilansky & Shefatya, 1990).

Teachers can support and extend children's symbolic play by approving pretending in general, and each of these components of pretending in particular. If a child is pretending to cook, the adult can ask about what is cooking, showing that this act of pretending is valued. If a child needs help taking on or expanding a role, adults can model pretending. If an adult picks up a play phone and talks, often a child will then imitate by picking up the other phone and answering.

Children who are just learning to play pretend need more realistic props.

> Four-year-old Maddy is sitting passively in the house with a stuffed rabbit on her lap. The other children are all busy caring for their stuffed pets. Miss Clay picks up the dogfood can, "Maddy do you need some food for your rabbit?"
>
> "That's dogfood. This is a rabbit," Maddy explains.
>
> "We could pretend it is rabbit food," Miss Clay suggests.
>
> "But it's dogfood," Maddy replies showing Miss Clay the picture of the dog on the can.
>
> Miss Clay realizes that Maddy cannot imagine that the dogfood is rabbit food and tries another approach. "What does your rabbit like to eat?"
>
> "Carrots," is the prompt reply. Miss Clay picks up an orange knife and suggests using it as a carrot, but Maddy patiently explains to her, "That's a knife, not a carrot." Miss Clay looks for something that more closely resembles a carrot. She suggests making a carrot out of scrap paper. They get the scrap box and scissors and intently cut orange paper into pieces. But the bowl full of paper pieces is not carrot-like enough to allow Maddy to imagine that it was rabbit food. Just then another child discards a stuffed dog to play elsewhere. Maddy scoops it up and feeds it from the empty dogfood can.

Maddy requires props that closely resemble the needed object in order to use them in the context of her pretend play. Teachers need to supply more realistic props for children, who like Maddy, are just beginning to pretend with objects. More skilled players can use less representational props. There is some research that shows that less realistic props are preferable for older children, since the props do not put a limit on the direction of the play (McLoyd, 1986; Myhre, 1993; Pulaski, 1973). Although more open-ended props can be provided for older children, it is important to remember that more realistic props may be needed by the less skilled older players (Johnson, Christie, & Yawkey, 1987; Pulaski, 1973). Pulaski (1973) described the less skilled children as "having a low fantasy" level. The film *Dramatic Play: An Integrative Process,* illustrates well the effects of high and low fantasy level on children's pretend play.

Smilansky (1992) found that peers can serve as play tutors for other children as well. Children will stretch their pretending skills when playing with peers who are more skilled pretenders. If lack of pretending skills caused the problems experienced by the second group of garden store shoppers, then letting them join the game in action, rather than sending away all the current players, might have provided the appropriate play acting models which would lead them to successfully engage in pretend play.

Knowledge of the World

Because dramatic play involves symbolizing what the child knows about a role, action, or situation, the child's knowledge base will affect the pretend play. It is easier to create a mental image, and then a representation, for things which are better known.

Adults can easily "play house." They quickly come up with a list of family roles, a list of needed props, and some possible action. It is more difficult to come up with such a list for playing oceanographer. It is easier to pretend family, since this is something most people know well. It is harder to pretend oceanographer, because most people probably do not know what oceanographers do. Thus, a person's cognitive knowledge about the role is important—it is easier to create pretend stories when the theme is familiar.

Implications for Teachers

When planning for and facilitating dramatic play, adults must consider what themes and props are familiar to children. Teachers also consider what tools should be available to promote literacy through play. Early childhood programs can also provide experiences to help children expand their knowledge bases.

Themes Must Be Familiar

In order to facilitate rich play, adults should provide a play setting that facilitates the enactment of familiar themes. Such themes offer children a solid base for creating play. Younger children pretend themes such as home,

FIGURE 2-10 Familiar themes such as eating provide a solid base for pretending

babies, driving, or shopping. This does not mean that adults should not add new materials or ideas to the play. There are many ways to adjust even the familiar topic of family. Suggestions for expanding on the house theme are discussed in Chapter 3. For older children, who have had more experiences in the world, a wider range of themes is likely to be familiar. It is important to realize that even at an older age there will be a wide variation in experiences between the children. (See Chapter 3 for more about designing appropriate environments for dramatic play.)

Even with familiar themes, it may take children a while to become involved in the play. Children's imaginative play stories will grow from day to day. Once children have negotiated roles and decided on props, they will often use this as a basis for developing play again the next day. One of the problems experienced by the second group of garden store shoppers is that they had to begin the play again. If the teacher had been more flexible about the number of children in the area, letting the less skilled players join the play that was in progress, then the new players might have been able to find appropriate actions. It is easier to be a part of ongoing play than to figure out how to initiate the play.

Adults should watch carefully to see if the play is still unfolding or has become stagnant, so they know when to help children to expand their play.

*Delbert and Stevie ride their big wooden trucks around the central post divid-
ing the two parts of the classroom. They ride around, crash, fall off, and are
dead, then get back on and repeat these actions again, and again, and again. It
is clear that the camaraderie of doing this with each other is an important part
of the play. They continue this play for many days. They now appear bored.
They do not want to end the play, but they also do not know how to change it.
Reeva, the teacher, sees that they are stuck. The next time they crash, she asks
the "dead" drivers, "Do you need a doctor?" They like this idea, so Reeva
becomes the doctor, eventually giving the role to Carrie, who was intently
watching the play.*

*Delbert and Steve ride around, crash, fall off and are dead, are fixed by the
doctor, and get back on to repeat the sequence again. As the play continues to
develop over the next few weeks, Delbert and Stevie take turns being the doctor
when Carrie or another child is not interested. The play continues to expand
with the addition of an ambulance, a hospital, and a gas station to fuel and repair
the trucks.*

It only took a small amount of assistance from the teacher to enable Delbert and Steve to expand their play. The addition of props and an area to
play hospital will enhance the play which seems to have great meaning to
these boys.

Children Need to Become Familiar with Materials

Adults must consider the child's familiarity with the props as well as with
the theme. When children enter a pretend play area for the first time, they
begin by manipulating the props. They will explore how the materials
work before they begin to use the props as part of an imaginative story.
The need to explore may cause conflict when one child has completed
investigating and is now ready to use the cash register in pretend play,
while other children are still experimenting.

Some of this conflict can be avoided by placing favorite props on the
manipulative shelves for exploration, before they are added to the dramatic play area for use in imaginative play. Some cash registers can be
placed on a table where children can experiment with the keys and discover how they work. Stethoscopes can be placed near small clocks so
children can investigate how this tool transmits sound. Small medical
equipment—such as a reflex hammer, cotton swab, and a plastic thermometer—can be placed in a feely box to be felt, removed, and then
matched to outlines of their shapes.

Expand the Child's Knowledge Base

Teachers can provide a variety of experiences that will expand the child's
knowledge base, making a wider number of themes familiar. (See Chapter
3 for a discussion of how to do this.)

FIGURE 2-11 Experimenting with cash registers

Language Development and Dramatic Play

A third area of development impacting on children's dramatic play is language development. As children mature, their language develops in a number of ways: Pronunciation becomes clearer, sentence structure becomes more complex with longer utterances, more complex ideas can be communicated, and the contexts in which language is used are expanded (Bergen, 1988).

The Place of Language in Dramatic Play

Children use language when they enact the roles in their dramatic play, as when brother Willie asked Hannah, "Honey, do you want some tea?" Children also use language to set the context for the play, to establish roles, to negotiate the direction of the plot, and to indicate the pretend identity of various props. When Holly said, "I am the Mommy cause I have a hat," she not only claimed a role, but also provided justification for this claim. Often, before play starts, children will say something like this: "Let's play family. Willie, pretend it's nighttime." Language allows children to share their ideas for the plot with each other. Willie used words to change the identity of the newspaper when he explained, "This is a seat belt," as he folded the paper across his lap. The use of language to set the context for play will be discussed in more detail in Chapter 4.

Younger children will use language in more abbreviated ways. They may use simple language that belongs to the role or action they are enacting. As children's language develops, it will be relied on more heavily for defining the context of the play. Older children often spend a significant amount of time discussing and planning the directions of their pretend play.

It is important to realize that children with English as a second language may also use simpler language in play until they are able to find the English words needed to communicate their ideas. These children may use more body language. Unlike less mature children, children with a non-English first language "have considerable knowlege about language as a result of learning the one they speak at home" (Genishi, 1989). Dramatic play often provides a motive for them to expand their English (Gutierrez, 1993; Van Hoorn et al., 1993).

Implications for Teachers

For younger children, or other children with less developed language skills, adults can model appropriate language as they enact various roles. As she rocks the baby doll, the teacher may say, "Shh, it's okay, Mommy is here to take care of you." The teacher can also use language to describe what is happening in the play (Heim & Davidson, 1993): "Mark is cooking dinner in the big pot." This serves a number of functions. It shows the children that the teacher values their play. It provides verbal labels for what the children are doing, and it models the type of language that the children will later use for discussing their play actions with each other.

Children who are just beginning to develop conversational skills will find it easier to pretend roles in which talking is not required. Often in mixed aged groups the younger children pick such roles as baby or dog, where their part of the play is not language dependent.

For children who do not use much language in their play, familiar roles are important, since the shared meaning of the roles will make their actions understood by others without relying on language.

> Sachi is a bright four-year-old who only spoke Japanese when she began attending preschool. She often plays in the house area, cooking dinner and getting dressed. It is in the house that she first begins to interact with the other children. She scoops out pretend soup and offers Jenny a bowl. Even without words Jenny understands by Sachi's actions that she is being offered food.
>
> The dramatic play area is transformed into a museum. Sachi watches the others playing but does not join them. When the area becomes a store, Sachi again watches without playing. When the house is reestablished, Sachi happily rejoins the play.

The museum and store themes were less familiar to Sachi. Since she could not understand the language that children used to define the play, it was difficult for her to understand what was being done in these less familiar settings. These themes also required more verbal interactions in the context of play. Once the teachers realized what was happening, they made a permanent place for playing house.

Stretching Development to Enhance Dramatic Play

The complexity of children's dramatic play is affected by their physical, social, cognitive and language development. Linder (1990) described some of the ways in which physical disabilities (as well as other disabilities) can impact on children's play, and also presented ways to facilitate their play. Dramatic play provides a forum for practicing current skills. It also provides motivation for stretching development in each of these areas. A child who typically is involved in parallel play may stretch in pretend play by using another child to be the "Daddy" or some other needed role in their play. Children may stretch their ability to create symbols for actions and objects when they sit on chairs holding cardboards circle in front of them, pretending they are driving the car to the store. With the teacher's help Erica and Melissa talked to each other as cashier and customer in the grocery story, stretching their communicative abilities.

Stretching in this way requires a great deal of mental energy and concentration (Van Hoorn et al., 1993). It may be difficult to stretch in more than one area at the same time. Perhaps the second group of garden store shoppers were still developing the social interaction skills needed for cooperative play, had a low fantasy level, were unsure what happens in a garden store, and did not yet use language fluently for communicating the direction of their play. It may be that playing garden store required them to stretch their skills in so many areas simultaneously that they were overwhelmed, and thus their play was chaotic and disorganized. The same group might have been able to play constructively in a house setting, which would only require them to stretch socially. The comfort of a familiar theme with few language demands would have allowed them to concentrate their mental energies on negotiating social interactions.

Implications for Teachers

Teachers must keep in mind children's developmental levels and the need to balance the mental energies required by the emergence of new social, cognitive, and language skills. At the beginning of the year, when children are just getting to know each other and developing social interaction patterns, simple dramatic play themes will leave energy for these social negotiations. Although it is true that older children are able to use less realistic props in dramatic play, adults may want to provide more specific props when the theme is less familiar and requires a greater cognitive stretch.

FIGURE 2-12 Realistic props help children play with the unfamiliar theme of space shuttle

If a kindergarten class has been studying outer space and has read some books about the life on the space shuttle, the children may want to play act these roles. Because the children do not have much experience with these roles or actions, they will need to stretch their abilities to represent them in pretend play. The adult should provide realistic props, such as control panels, charts of the stars, magnifying glasses, air tanks, space rocks to collect, lab tools to study the rocks, and ropes for spacewalks. These props will offer familiar anchors for the space travel play. They will also serve as a springboard to suggest actions and directions for the play.

Observing the Differences in Children

In every group, children will vary widely in their pretend play skills. There will be some master players, some novices, and some children in between. Being able to observe and understand these differences is essential to enable teachers to facilitate the children's play. This chapter has presented some suggestions to adults for fostering dramatic play. Chapter 3 will examine more closely the adult's role in children's pretend play.

CHAPTER 3

What Do Teachers Do When Children Are Pretending?

What should early childhood professionals be doing while children are involved in pretend play? Should they join the play, observe it, or use this time to attend to other children? If they should join the play, how should they participate? This chapter will answer these questions. First, let's examine the "to enter or not to enter" debate.

To Enter or Not to Enter

Should adults intervene in children's play? There has been much debate over this question.

Intervention as Interference

Before the 1960s, most early childhood educators felt that teachers should observe but never intervene in children's pretend play (Johnson, Christie, & Yawkey 1987). They endorsed the **psychoanalytic theory** of play, seeing play as a forum for children to deal with life issues that concerned them, such as the birth of a sibling, the divorce of parents, or a trip to the doctor. Susan Isaacs (1930) described the teacher's role as setting the stage for children to play, then observing to discover what concerns the children have. Entering children's play would disrupt the play and prevent them from acting out, and thereby resolving, their problems and concerns.

Changing Views on Intervention

In the 1960s, early childhood educators began to alter their views about adult intervention in children's pretend play (Johnson et al., 1987). The cognitively based play theories of Piaget and Vygotsky supported the role of adults as facilitators of children's play. They believed that children developed an understanding of the world through play and that adults could support this development by appropriate intervention in that play (Monighan-Nourot, 1990).

Researchers began to investigate the effects of **play-training** on children's pretend play. Smilansky (1968) found that when early childhood professionals actively trained children to play by commenting on the play and modeling play behavior, the children's pretend play increased in both quantity and quality.

Although adult intervention in dramatic play was recognized as a way to extend children's development, it is important to remember that this must be used judiciously. Children's play can have great value without adult intervention as well.

Scaffolding Children's Learning

Early childhood professionals can provide **scaffolding** to allow children to stretch their cognitive, language, and social skills. Scaffolding children's play was first discussed by Ninio and Bruner (1978) to describe ways in which adults provided supports to stretch children's language skills. The term was later used to describe adult support for children's emergent literacy (Christie, 1994). Scaffolding is when the adult helps the child to function on a higher level than would be possible without the adult's intervention. Adult support will help children to eventually develop the skills to play at this level independently.

Stretching Knowledge of Roles and Materials

Adult intervention can help children gain knowledge of roles and materials.

> Three-year-olds Brooke and Marcus are in the doctors office. They are each holding a stethoscope, but do not appear to know what to do with them. Ms. Youngdeer puts on a stethoscope and listens to the doll's heart. "Dr. Brooke, could you listen to my patient's heart and see if it sounds allright to you?" As first Brooke, and then Marcus, put their stethoscopes against the doll, Ms. Youngdeer makes a "thump, thump" sound like a heart beating. They tell her the heart is beating and she asks if their babies' hearts are also beating. The children proceed to check all the dolls in the area. The stethoscope play continues after Ms. Youngdeer moves to another part of the classroom.

By modeling the appropriate use of the stethoscope, and by including the children in her play, the adult has helped the children to understand how to use the stethoscope, and helped them to find "doctor actions" to use as they play in the area. Once children have made these actions their own, they can easily continue the play after the adult leaves the area.

Stretching Language

Vocabulary and appropriate use of words and phrases can be modeled as the teacher plays with children (Linder, 1990).

> *Four-year-old Glenn is sitting at the receptionist's desk in the hair salon. Jeannine is sitting on one of the chairs in the waiting area. There has been no interaction between the two children. Mr. Fahey walks over to Glenn and asks, "Are there any appointments this afternoon?" Glenn looks on the calendar and nods his head. "Do you think I need a haircut, or should I just get a shampoo and blow dry?"*
>
> *Glenn looks at Mr. Fahey's hair and recommends, "A haircut and shampoo."*
>
> *"Please write me down in your appointment book for a haircut and shampoo." Glenn scribbles on one of the lines in the appointment book.*
>
> *"Jeannine, do you want an appointment, too?" She says yes. "Ask Glenn if he has any appointments left." She and Glenn then repeat the discussion about appointments and services needed, as they schedule an appointment for her.*

By enacting the customer role in the hair salon, Mr. Fahey models the type of conversation that occurs between customers and receptionists. He also provides words such as "blow dry" and "appointment." The children are able to imitate this model to continue the appointment-making dialogue.

FIGURE 3-1 Adult participation in play can provide a scaffold to raise it to a higher level

Stretching Social Interactions

The adult's participation in the play can provide a scaffold to raise children's social interaction to a higher level and extend the length of that interaction.

> *Three-year-old Allison puts on the pink negligee and the sparkly shoes. She tries on two different hats, examining each in the mirror. Meanwhile, Duncan is putting on his favorite blue blazer with the insignia on the pocket, big black shoes, and a grey hat. He selects a large white pocket book, with a long shoulder strap. Neither child seems aware that the other one is in the area. JoAnn, the teacher, comments, "Allison, you look so beautiful, are you going somewhere special today?"*
>
> *"I'm going to the ball," Allison replies.*
>
> *"A ball, what fun! How about you, Duncan, where are you going dressed up so handsomely? Are you going to the ball, too?" JoAnn asks. Duncan, who had not really considered where he was going, agrees that he is going to the ball, too. When they are dressed, Allison and Duncan take hands and walk around the room three times together. They return to the house, change their clothes, then "go to the ball" again. As they walk by, the teacher asks them how the ball was. Katie hears this, runs over to get a hat, then joins the going-to-the-ball walk around the room. Pretty soon the ball parade contains six children. Going to the ball continues to be a central part of the dramatic play with this group of children for the rest of the year.*

JoAnn's comments made each child aware of what the other was doing. Her excitement with the ball drew Duncan into Allison's play. Their play moved from isolated, individual play, to being an exciting social event. It also built a play pattern for these children that continued all year.

Celebrating Dramatic Play

Adult participation in the play communicates approval and support for pretend play. When Ms. Youngdeer enacted the doctor role with Marcus and Brooke, not only did she model what doctors do with stethoscopes, but she also demonstrated her enjoyment of pretending. JoAnn's excitement about Allison's ball drew Duncan, Katie, and others into the play. The teacher's excitement about the pretend play made it appealing to the other children. An adult who joins the pretend play is showing children that it is a fun and valuable activity.

Ignoring Children's Pretend Play

Unfortunately, in some early childhood settings adults only enter the dramatic play area when children are having trouble keeping their play going smoothly. Adult intervention in these settings tends to be negative. These teachers enter to tell children to play more quietly, that too many children are in the area, that they are not using the materials correctly, or

FIGURE 3-2 Teachers can show children that their pretend play is valued

to correct their behavior in some other way. If all adult interventions in the dramatic play area are negative, children may assume that adults do not like or approve of this type of play.

It is true that there are times when adults must redirect play that has gotten out of hand, but early childhood teachers should examine their interactions in the dramatic play area to make sure that they are sending predominantly positive messages about pretend play. At times adults should find unobtrusive ways to enter children's play for the sole purpose of showing children that the play is valued and appreciated.

Interfering with Children's Pretend Play

While it is true that adult intervention in children's play can serve to facilitate the play, inappropriate intervention can disrupt and interfere with children's play. In *The Play's the Thing*, Jones and Reynolds (1992) stressed the importance of children having the power to direct the play, or at least to share that power with the adults. Adults taking the power to direct the play often diminish the play for children. In Chapter 5, Jones and Reynolds provide an in-depth discussion of various ways in which teachers interfere in children's play.

There is an excellent example of a teacher interfering in children's dramatic play in the film *Dramatic Play: An Integrated Process for Learning* (1977):

> Two girls are sitting inside a U-shaped structure of hollow blocks. The one with the engineer's hat is driving the train with a plastic circle. A boy with a box of tools is fixing the broken motor in the front of the train by cutting a pipe cleaner. The children seem intently involved in their train play.

A teacher approaches and asks, "Can you tell me what you are doing? What are you building?"

"A train," the driver replies.

"What happened to your train? I saw you were fixing things. What was broken?" inquires the teacher.

"The engine," responds the driver.

"What kind of an engine is it?"

"A train engine," explains the girl.

"What kind of engine? A diesel engine? A steam engine?" asks the teacher.

"It's an engine that runs on the track," the girl replies.

"It runs on the track with what? Electricity? Coal?"

"Electricity. The wire broke the motor."

The teacher repeats then expands this idea, "The wire broke the motor. It burned out. It had an electric short."

The girl tries to explain, "Every time we get people on the train it is too heavy and we can't drive."

"You just have to tell the people you can't take so many. You don't need so many," directs the teacher as she moves away. When she leaves, the children resume their play as driver, repair worker, and passenger.

While this teacher was talking to the children, the play came to a complete stop. She asks strings of questions, without slowing down to give the children a chance to respond. She seems more interested in her own questions than in what the children are doing. She uses this as an opportunity to teach about types of engines, rather than listening to see

A STEP FURTHER   *What Else Could the Teacher Have Said?*

If the teacher in the above example wanted to discover what children knew about trains—without interfering with the play what might she have said? If the teacher does not know what the children have built she might marvel at the building and ask the children to tell her about it. "Wow! What an impressive building! I wonder what it is." On the other hand, if the teacher already knows what the building is, as did this teacher, then this introductory question can be skipped.

If the teacher does not know what the child with the wire is doing she might ask, "What are the wires for?" "Are you fixing something?" or "What is this part for?" These are all legitimate requests for information that ask the child to share what he knows.

If the child tells the teacher he is fixing the train, she can ask, "What is wrong with it?" "I wonder what you will have to do to fix it," or "Can I watch what you do to fix it?" These are asking the child to describe his actions rather then talk about parts of trains. It keeps the child in power by letting him be the one that shows or explains the process of fixing the train.

what is important in the children's play. In this case the play had enough significance to the children that they were able to return to it when the teacher left. Unfortunately, when this type of adult interference disrupts children's pretend play, children are often unable to resume the play.

Balanced Intervention

Although now most early childhood professionals will agree that teacher intervention can facilitate children's dramatic play, there is still debate about the degree to which adults should be involved. Too much intervention or the wrong type of intervention can dominate and interfere with play, rather than support and extend it. Establishing the boundary between supportive and intrusive intervention is not easy. How do early childhood professionals know what will support and extend the play, and what will stifle it? To answer this questions, let us examine more closely each of the ways adults can intervene in children's play.

Adult Roles in Children's Pretend Play

Adults can take six different roles in children's play: Observer, stage manager, player, mediator, interpreter, and social director. Many authors have defined the teacher's roles in children's play, but there is no agreement on the specific definitions. The first four of these roles are discussed in Jones and Reynolds (1992). Many of these roles are discussed in Griffing (1982), Johnson et al. (1987), and Van Hoorn, Nourot, Scales, and Alward (1993), although the authors often have their own terms for the roles. Each of these roles will be explored in more depth in the following section.

Observer

It is great fun to watch children's pretend play, but observing takes time (Bentzen, 1993; Schweinhart, 1993). Many early childhood teachers feel pressured by their large burden of responsibilities. They must facilitate the children's play, assess the children's progress, maintain order in the room, cover certain aspects of curriculum, help the children in areas of weakness, and attend to many crucial things simultaneously. Observing often seems to be a luxury they cannot afford, but observing is not a luxury.

Observing children's pretend play is one of the most important roles of the adult. Without observing, adults would not know how best to facilitate children's play. They would not know when their help is needed to mediate problems. They would not know what aspects of the curriculum intrigued children, and which aspects of the play should be extended. Observing children's pretend play also offers a wonderful window for assessing children's progress and needs. As Jones and Reynolds (1992) said,

FIGURE 3-3 The teacher watches the beauty parlor play while waiting for her "appointment"

Ongoing observations provide a much more adequate sample of behavior than any test for young children. They permit focus on children's abilities, not disabilities—what the child can and does do, rather than on what she has not yet mastered. (p. 70)

Learning to Observe

How do early childhood educators manage to observe children's play when they are so busy? First, adults must believe in the importance of **observation**. Committing themselves to this makes them more able to find time for it. Some teachers set aside short periods of time devoted to observing. Other adults do the observing more on the run, catching samples of the play between their many other tasks. Some teachers like to jot down notes as they observe; others prefer to use checklists for recording general observations; others prefer to make their recordings from memory at the end of the day; and others prefer some combination of these methods. Adults must each find the method that best suits their style. Heidemann and Hewitt (1992) provided a number of forms and checklists for observing pretend play.

What should early childhood educators be looking for when they' observe? The point of observing is to give adults a deeper knowledge of the children. Observation should help adults see children's strengths and interests. It should help them to understand where children are developmentally. Adults can observe children's development in all areas: social, emotional, cognitive, physical and language development. Keeping a record of children's play over time will show how children are developing. The specific areas where teachers observe will depend on what they want to know about the children and about the classroom.

It is important to remember that any new skill takes a while to develop. If observing children's play is new for adults, they may find it difficult at first. With practice they will see and remember more with less and less effort.

Why Observe?

Observing children's dramatic play aids the teacher in three main ways.

1. It gives adults a much richer understanding of the children and their play. This knowledge is necessary for the adult to facilitate dramatic play. The knowledge is needed to set the stage in ways that will extend the children's play, to provide background information to enhance the play, to mediate problems when they arise, to act as an interpreter between children when necessary, and to facilitate social interaction when needed.
2. It helps adults come to know each child better, seeing where the children are in all areas of development.
3. When adults observe children's play, it shows that adults find the pretend play interesting and important—it is something adults enjoy watching.

Stage Manager

Jones and Reynolds (1992) used the label **stage manager** to describe one of the roles teachers fulfill in facilitating children's dramatic play. In the theater, the stage manager establishes the setting for the play, ensuring that it is right for enacting the story, and that needed props are available. Between scenes, the stage manager removes props that are no longer needed, and moves small furniture to set the stage for the next part of the action.

An adult also sets the stage for the more informal drama that occurs in the early childhood setting. The adult prepares an environment in which children can pretend, provides props, arranges materials to best support the play, tidies and rearranges as the play unfolds, and also provides time for this type of play (Ford, 1993).

Setting the Stage for House Play

Each early childhood setting needs a permanent area where dramatic play can occur. House is a central theme in children's dramatic play, so I will begin by discussing setting up a house area. The arrangement of the area will vary depending on the size and shape of the room, as well as the age, interests, and needs of each class of children. Some guidelines should be considered when arranging the house area.

Allow Enough Space.   The dramatic play area should be large enough to allow children to move around easily. If the class includes children who use braces, wheelchairs, or other adaptive devices then it is important to leave larger spaces for entering and maneuvering within the house area.

If teachers are team teaching, where two classes are combined, teachers should provide two house areas to ensure that children have plenty of opportunity for dramatic play. Two separate areas are better than one large area, as this allows for two smaller play groups. The larger the group in the area is, the more difficult the negotiations over roles, props and the direction of the play become.

Clearly Define the Space.   The house furniture, and backs of shelves from adjacent areas, should be used to define and enclose the house area. A line of toy kitchen appliances along the wall does not communicate "house" in the same way that a cozily enclosed space does. Clearly defining the space also decreases disruptions from children not currently in the area. If possible, have the dramatic play area near the blocks, as children often use these two areas together.

Provide Dressup Clothing.   Dressing up is an integral part of playing pretend for most children. The house area should have a variety of clothing for both boys and girls. Ethnic and cultural clothing should be incorporated as appropriate. Thought should be given to how easily the clothes may be put on and taken off. Clothing with velcro fasteners or large buttons, pretied neck ties, and skirts with elastic waists will allow children to be more independent.

If clothing is too large, it may be hazardous or interfere with the child's ability to play. Adults can cut off long skirts and dresses, but even so, differences in children's heights may still leave some garments trailing on the floor. Colorful elastic sewn into a waist sized ring can be worn over the garment, allowing the top to blouse out over the belt, and thus shortening the length.

Men's suit coats are so large that they often drag on the floor, and are so heavy they are awkward for children to wear. Boys' coats in size 12 or

14 are big enough to give the feeling of grownup garb without being too heavy or awkward. Rummage sales and thrift shops are a good source for dress up clothing.

Provide a wardrobe or set of hooks for hanging clothing. A shelf or hat rack is useful for hats, purses, and briefcases. Do not use hangers for the dressup clothes as these are too frustrating for many children. Avoid storage boxes for dressup clothes as these tend to be a dumping ground for stray toys and props, making it difficult to find wanted clothing.

Provide Props.   Props often set the direction for the play. It is important to have enough of each so that children do not need to stop their play to wait for scarce props. On the other hand, too many props will result in dumping and clutter that will interfere with the play. For younger children, it is important to provide more realistic props and to provide many of the same type of material to allow for parallel play. For older children, less realistic props will allow for more creative use of the materials. Less duplication is needed, since children are likely to take more distinct roles. Even at the older ages, however, duplicates of the most popular materials will decrease ownership disputes.

Consider what props will support family play. Dolls, cooking utensils, jewelry, telephones, dishes, and plastic food are found in most dramatic play areas. The addition of other props will often add new direction

FIGURE 3-4 Dressing up is an integral part of playing pretend

to the play. Plastic tools will start a flurry of repair work. Stuffed animals and empty pet food cans will spur pet play. Baskets will encourage picnic activities. Other props that will add to house play are:

- Cameras (old models are often available for a minimal charge at thrift stores)
- Play dough to use as food
- Water in the sink for washing dishes
- Plastic flowers and plastic bowls each containing a styrofoam block for making arrangements
- Cleaning supplies such as brooms, mops, vacuums, sponges, and empty spray bottles
- Paper and pencils to make lists and take messages
- Baby toys
- Boxes or play crates to use as cars, with maps to plan trips
- Foam or cardboard birthday cakes with candles, and party hats for playing birthday party
- Suitcases for going visiting
- Lunchboxes for going to school or work
- Hair dryers, curlers, combs, and plastic razors for getting ready to go out
- Brushes to polish shoes
- Catalogues
- Flashlights to search for missing items
- Books to read at bedtime

    (Additional literacy props to add to the house area are discussed in Chapter 4.)

The list can be expanded by thinking of what you do in your house, or with your family, and adding props that will encourage these types of play.

These props should not all be put out at once. Gradually add a few to support the current play, or to offer a possible new direction to the play. Things that are no longer being used can be removed until they are needed again. Putting out too many things at once is often overwhelming. Children will try to use everything at once, and end up unable to use anything constructively. This gradual addition of props will keep the house area fresh and exciting (Myhre, 1993), while still providing the materials that children need for their ongoing plots.

Consider the Child's Home.   If the house area is to be a place that children can play out familiar themes of family, then it is important that the props suggest home to the children. Think about the child's cultural background and include the appropriate utensils such as woks, chopsticks, and tortilla presses. If families cook over an open fire, the dramatic play area should provide a play hearth to cook on. If families do not have running water, then constructing a play well outside the house area with buckets will allow children to play house in ways that fit their lifestyle.

Adults should also consider predominant occupations in the community and provide props which allow children to enact parental roles: In mining communities include helmets; if many parents are construction workers, include hardhats; if office work is common, include briefcases.

What Rooms Should You Have?   If space permits, have more than one room in the house. A kitchen area is important, as cooking is often a central part of house play. Sleeping is another common part of children's house play. A bedroom area is desirable, with beds large enough to hold the children, if possible.

The house could also include a living room or family room area, with such things as a couch, rocker, coffee table, and TV. A couch can be easily constructed by lining up three chairs, taping their legs together, taping a piece of cardboard across the three seats, then covering the whole thing with a colorful towel or piece of cloth. Other possible rooms are a study or office with a desk and typewriter or computer, a workshop with plastic tools and things to repair, a laundry room with a cardboard washer, drier, an iron and ironing board, and a bathroom with a shower made from an old refrigerator box, or a bathtub made from a box or a baby's bathinette.

No early childhood setting is large enough to include all of these rooms in the dramatic play area at the same time. Adults can vary what the house includes, being careful to consider the needs of the children. If children have been doing lots of cooking, add a table or some planks to lengthen the counter area, and include additional cooking and baking props. If infant care has been popular, adding a bathinette, some box cribs, and baby toys will offer ways to extend this play. If going to the ball is a common theme, adding a desk to write invitations will build on current interests.

Setting the Stage for Nonhouse Play

Environment communicates expectations of behavior. At the Boston Children's Museum, when children enter the grocery store area, they all play grocery. It does not matter how old they are, whether they share the same language, or whether they know each other. The shelves, cash register,

FIGURE 3-5 Writing invitations to the ball

food, sale advertisements, and baskets create a shared expectation of playing grocery store. If you walk next door to the garage, you will find that the children are all playing mechanic and driver. Upstairs in the old fashioned house, the children are all enacting family and house themes. The environment communicates certain social expectations to the participants. Goffman (1974) discussed how different community environments communicate different social expectations. People act differently in a library than in a gymnasium.

Adults can arrange the dramatic play area to encourage certain types of play, in the same way as at the Boston Children's Museum. Woodward (1984) and others (Kostelnik, Soderman, & Whiren, 1993; Shipley, 1993) suggested that the house area remains a house, utilizing another area of the room for enacting other themes. This has certain advantages. It allows children who still need the house area to continue the stories they have been enacting. For themes such as grocery store, it is important to have a house where groceries can be taken once they are purchased. It also provides more room for pretending, thus accommodating a larger number of children at a time.

Space restraints make it difficult for some early childhood settings to maintain both an ongoing housekeeping area and a special theme area for dramatic play. Other parts of the room can be employed for dramatic play when needed. (See Chapter 7 for an indepth discussion of other places for dramatic play.) Children will often build things with the unit blocks or with hollow blocks to support their pretend play. Shipley (1993) suggested having an **active role play center** next to the house that combines large muscle equipment with pretend play. (For a fuller discussion see Shipley, Chapter 11, pp. 171–187.)

Some adults find that if the theme area is exciting, the house area will remain empty. When this happens, replacing the house area with a larger theme area will better meet the children's needs. Each adult must consider the needs and interest of the children when deciding how to allocate space for pretend play. (Chapter 6 will discuss a variety of themes and supporting props.)

When designing a theme area, it is important to give thought to the arrangement of furniture and props. A poorly designed environment will not set the stage well for the children's play.

Ms. Ginsburg's class is talking about plants. They have been exploring the many parts of plants and how you can eat various parts: seeds such as peas, roots such as carrots, leaves such as lettuce, stems such as celery, flowers such as broccoli, and fruit such as apples. She decides to set up a plant cafe that serves various parts of plants. She lines the kitchen appliances along one wall, places a long table coming out from the back of the block shelves that mark the other boundary of the area; and tapes together a stack of hollow blocks to hold a cash register at the opening to the area. The refrigerator contains various plastic fruits and vegetables; the cupboard houses dishes, pots, and small plastic baskets with handles. A menu listing items by parts of the plant is on the table.

The children are excited about the new area and eagerly enter to begin their play. Amanda and TJ began piling all the food into the baskets. When the baskets are full they take their "groceries" to the cash register. Meanwhile, Kyla is sitting at the table looking at the menu. Jameela is cooking in the kitchen. She discovers that only a few pieces of food are left. "I need that food." She demands of the shoppers. They ignore her. "It's not fair!" She proclaims loudly. "They have all the food." Susan, the teacher who is supervising the area, spends the day arbitrating this and similar disputes.

FIGURE 3-6 The teacher spends time arbitrating disputes at the poorly designed Plant Cafe

The area that Ms. Ginsburg has designed for pretend play does not create a shared social expectation. To Amanda and TJ, the area is a grocery store and elicits shopping behavior. To Jameela and Kyla, the area is a restaurant and elicits cook and customer behavior. There are not enough props, or enough room in the area, to support both types of play. The result is conflict.

Continuing Play from Day to Day

Teachers need to constantly review the dramatic play area to see if any minor changes will better support the play. At the end of the day, Ms. Ginsburg analyzes what happened in the restaurant. She saw that the area she created did not encourage constructive play. She also saw a need for grocery play. To accommodate the "shoppers" she takes two large garbage bags of food containers and some baskets outside to use with the hollow blocks. She also redesigns the restaurant area. She takes out the long table and adds two small tables with colorful table cloths and floral center pieces. The cashier's table is moved to the side to create extra room for eating tables. The baskets are removed. Small clipboards with checkoff order pads to match the menus are added. An additional stove is included to accommodate more cooks. With this new arrangement, the children easily take on roles of customers, cooks, waiters and waitresses, and cashier.

On the Spot Scene Changes

Not only do teachers evaluate and adjust their dramatic play area from day to day, they also watch to see when additional props will expedite the current play. Griffing (1982) and Van Hoorn et al. (1993) called this role of the teacher "artist apprentice," because the teacher is providing needed materials for the children—the artists—to create their story.

It is now the third day of Ms. Ginsburg's restaurant. Play has been going smoothly for the last few days, since the area was modified. Anthony, who often has trouble sustaining dramatic play, has been a customer. He now is wandering aimlessly around the area knocking things to the ground. TJ is following Anthony's lead. Both become wolves stealing food, but the other children object. They are robbers, but that too meets with objections. Anthony lifts the dishpan out of the wooden sink saying, "It's broken."

He is about to drop the contents of the sink onto the floor when JoAnn, the teacher, says, "Are you here to fix our sink? I am so glad; it has been giving us lots of trouble." Anthony, who was expecting to be corrected, looks surprised. JoAnn opens the doors of the sink saying, "The pipes are back in there. They are sort of hard to see. They are way in the back."

Anthony kneels down and puts his head and shoulder in the cupboard. "I can see it. There is a big hole."

"Oh, dear," says JoAnn in a worried tone. "Do you think you can fix it?"

"Yup!" says Anthony with confidence.

FIGURE 3-7 Tools draw these boys into constructive play

"Do you need some tools? We could go get the box of plastic tools." Anthony, TJ, and JoAnn go out to the storage closet to get plastic tools. They get a few extras in case any other workers come to help with the repairs. Anthony and TJ repair the sink, stove, refrigerator, and spend the last fifteen minutes working on a particularly hard-to-repair table. Duncan joins the repair work. Without the constant interruption of robbers and wolves, the restaurant play continues to unfold.

The suggestion of a new role from the teacher and the timely addition of tools drew Anthony and TJ into constructive play and provided protection for those children who wanted to continue the restaurant play.

Props for Nonhouse Play

Props help the area to communicate certain roles and themes to children. Stethoscopes will elicit doctor play, while a row of firehats will spark raging infernos to be doused. Many people suggest that for older children it is better to have less realistic props to allow children scope for their imagination, and to allow them room to create their own stories and roles (McLoyd, 1986). Although less structured props are good for familiar play, when less familiar themes are being enacted, realistic props will act as a prompt to help children know what types of actions may be done in this environment.

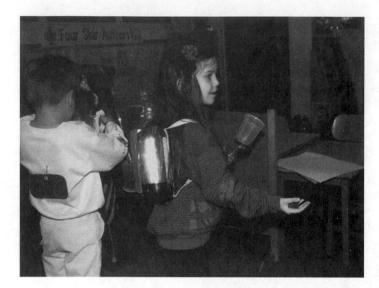

FIGURE 3-8 Props like air tanks can help children play less familiar themes

The children in this kindergarten have been discussing the space shuttle. Many children have been using the climber outside to "blast off" to various outer space destinations. The teacher thinks a spaceship in the dramatic play area will provide a way to extend their current play. Because the children do not have much knowledge of what happens on a spaceship, she provides more realistic props: a control panel with buttons for the pilot to press, a lab table with microscopes for the astronauts to examine their finds, brightly painted "moon rocks" to find on the various planets they explore, and air packs so the astronauts can breathe when they walk in space to fix their rocket. Some of the children rely on the teacher-made props, while other more skilled players easily use unit blocks to create supplemental props as needed.

When a theme is less familiar, children need to stretch cognitively to develop the play. More realistic props can act as a scaffold for the play. It is important to have a balance between such adult-designed areas and more open-ended areas that allow children to design their own play. If elaborate adult-made props are provided all the time, it establishes an expectation that adults, not children, are responsible for creating props and deciding the themes that should be played.

Keep the Area Uncluttered

In their role as stage manager, adults arrange the dramatic area to be warm and inviting when children enter at the beginning of the day. Clothes are hung so they are easy to find and props are displayed to make the choices clear (Jones & Reynolds, 1992). As children play, the area becomes chaotic, sometimes making it difficult for other children to see the options. Adults can support children's play by picking up dropped clothes, restoring unused props to their original spots, and removing other clutter. According to Jones and Reynolds,

> What [the] teacher does is to keep reestablishing clear figure-ground relationships, spontaneously creating order out of disorder to make the possibilities clear to children. If they "mess up" (use and change) what she has provided, she knows she's succeeded in supporting their play. Their order is always different from hers. And the classroom is theirs, not hers; she sets it up so they can re-create it (pp. 18–19).

Some might say cleaning up should be the children's job. There are times when adults can ask children to put things away as they play. There are other times when having the children clean will disrupt the play.

Adults can encourage hanging up dressup clothing, if it is done in the context of the play. As Chunga takes off her dress and is about to drop it on the floor before climbing in bed, the adult says, "Here is a hook just waiting for your dress." Chunga can place the dress on the hook as easily as drop it on the floor. Hanging it up does not interfere with the bedtime enactment. There are other times when asking children to put things away WILL interrupt the play. If Chunga is already sleeping in bed, then asking her to get up and hang up her dress will interfere with her play.

If children are playing hurricane and the dishes are being blown off the shelves, the clutter is a necessary part of the play. To insist the dishes be picked up is likely to stop the play. On the other hand, if a child is wandering aimlessly through the area knocking other children's dishes and pots onto the floor, then it is appropriate to ask the disrupter to pick up the dishes so the other children can continue their game.

Provide Time

It is important to allow long, uninterrupted blocks of time in which children can play pretend. Johnson et al. (1987) suggested that blocks of time at least 30 to 50 minutes long are necessary to allow dramatic play to unfold. It takes a while for children to choose roles, collect needed props, negotiate the story line, play out their stories, and modify and expand on the original stories. Extended time allows children to build a block structure, then create a pretend story to enact with the structure as a base. Extended time allows children to experiment with new materials, then when comfortable, use them for pretending. Extended time allows more cautious children time to watch, then gradually join the play.

If the time allocated is too short, children will not be able to fully develop their play. Christie and Wardle (1992) described the problem of short play periods.

Shorter periods, on the other hand, reduced both the amount and the maturity of the children's play. During short periods, children tended to wander around more and not get involved in play at all. When they did play, children settled for simple play forms, such as functional (motor) play and parallel-dramatic play, which do not require much time to play and execute.

Extra play time did not result in children getting bored and having nothing to do; rather, it prompted them to engage in more complex, productive play activities (p. 30).

In a half-day program, at least one large block of inside time and one large block of outside time should be allocated for children to select activities, with dramatic play being one of the possible options. In a full-day program, dramatic play should be an option for a much longer length of time.

Some adults say they have too many things to teach the children, they do not have large blocks of time that can be open for dramatic play. But as Kostelnik, Soderman, and Whiren (1993) rightly asserted

Preschool teachers and kindergarten teachers should plan for pretend play first and for other activities thereafter . . . For these youngest children, the development of play skills is critical for the emergence of abstract thinking and problem solving abilities. Therefore, pretend play should be a priority. Teachers should ensure that all children in the earliest years have opportunities for extended time for pretend (p. 225).

Provide Background Experiences

Many times books, trips, films, group discussions, classroom visitors, or other shared experiences serve as a prompt for dramatic play. Teachers can plan activities that will stretch children's knowledge about themes of joint interest. The activities can become the basis for dramatic play, and the dramatic play will serve to enrich the original experience.

Trips. Trips are an excellent way to offer children knowledge that can be used in pretend play. Play acting a farm theme will have more meaning after the children have visited a farm, fed a calf, milked a cow, and seen the eggs being collected. As children milk the cardboard cow, they will envision the size, smell, and sounds of a real cow. Set up the dramatic play area to let children enact what they actually saw on that trip. One year the highlight of the trip to the firestation was watching the hoses being put through the hose washer. After the trip, an astute student teacher added a hose washer to the dramatic play firestation.

Stories and Discussions. Stories and discussion can also provide shared knowledge that will serve as the basis for pretend play. A class of four-year-olds began the year by investigating insects. One week was devoted to learning about bees. An aquarium with some live bees to observe was added to the classroom. Books about bees were read to the whole class, read in small groups, and explored by children on their own. Stories, discussions and games at group times explored such things as how bees collect nectar to make honey, how bees cool their hives by fanning their wings, and how bees dance to tell other bees where the good nectar flowers are located.

A beehive in the dramatic play area allowed the children to act out these ideas, and thus come to understand them better. Of course, children play acted the theme in the context they understood. They used what they knew about bees to play family. There were many mommy and daddy bees each taking care of their own larva babies. When a bee did a dance to show where the pollen was, the other bees left their larvae with bee babysitters before going off to get the pollen. The discussions and stories provided a basis for the dramatic play, which in turn helped the children to come to a better understanding of that information.

Stage Managing Is Not Simple

As stage manager, the teacher has many jobs: setting the stage, knowing what themes to offer, selecting and arranging appropriate props, keeping the area neat, ensuring that there is time and space for play, providing background experiences, and creating an environment where children are free to enact their stories. To do this adults must be tuned into the needs and interests of the children in the class. This brings us to the third important role of adults in facilitating children play—the role of player.

Player

Adults can be players, or participants, in the children's dramatic play. How active a role the adult takes will depend, in part, on the children's level of skill at dramatic play. If children are having trouble starting or maintaining the play, then the adult may need to take a more active role—modeling, or suggesting ideas—until the play is moving along smoothly. With more skilled pretenders, adult players should take a smaller role in the children's stories. With these master players, adults need not be a leader, or director, of the play. Johnson et al. (1987) and Wood, McMahon, and Cranston (1980) described two less intrusive ways for adults to be players when children are pretending: The adult can be a parallel player or a coplayer.

Parallel Player

As **parallel player**, the teacher plays along in a parallel fashion to the child.

Three-year-old Katie is filling a bucket with sand. The teacher, Christine, is sitting at the other side of the sandbox, also filling a bucket with sand. "I'm going

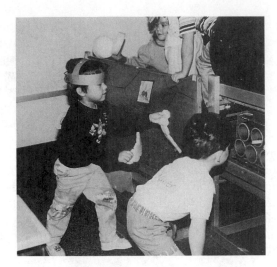

FIGURE 3-9 Bees checking on their larvae

to make a cake," Christine comments to herself. "First I need flour, then I need some milk." Christine continues making her cake and commenting on the process. Katie begins to pretend that she is also making a cake. When the bucket is filled, Katie sticks some small twigs into the top as candles.

By playing along next to Katie, Christine has modeled how to pretend that sand is ingredients for a cake. Once Katie has started pretending, she adds her own idea—placing candles on the cake. As parallel player, the adult can model behavior, language, and pretending with props, roles, and situations. Children can pick up on the adult's behavior or ignore it.

Coplayer

As **coplayer**, the teacher takes a role in the children's pretend stories, as one of the players, but not a leading or directive role.

The teacher, Stacey, walks over to see what is happening in the hair salon. Colleen is at the reception desk. She asks if Stacey wants an appointment. The teacher says, "Yes, I am going to a party tonight."

Colleen directs the teacher, "Write your name here for a turn." The teacher writes her name on the appointment pad, then sits in the waiting area.

Orion, the stylist, comes to get the teacher. "Are you next?" he inquires.

"Yes, I am getting my hair done for the ball tonight," Stacey tells him, as she goes to sit in his chair. He drapes a towel over her. The two of them then discuss what should be done to Stacey's hair. When she is done Stacey pays Colleen. In the next half hour, Stacey returns three or four times to get her hair done at the request of various hair stylists.

Stacey joins the play at the request of the children. She takes a minor role. She does not change the play in any way, but her presence is enjoyed by the children. They like time with the teacher. When she joins their play, it is clear that she likes what they are doing. Adults may also use coplaying to model pretend play, language, or social interactions.

In a More Active Role

With less skilled players, adults may take a more assertive role in the play. In the example on (page 27), Abby was hesitant to enter the hospital play on her own. When JoAnn took a more active role in the play, Abby was willing to tag along. Abby first entered the play by making suggestions for how JoAnn should play the role. After being JoAnn's shadow in the play, Abby was then able to enter the play on her own.

Johnson et al. (1987) called this more active role **play tutoring** and suggest that there are three times when this play tutoring is appropriate:

1. When children do not engage in make-believe play on their own
2. When children have difficulty playing with other children
3. When children engage in make-believe play, but the play becomes repetitious or appears ready to break down (p. 41)

These are indeed times when adults may want to enter children's play, but tutoring can also be provided in each of these situations through the less intrusive role of coplayer or parallel player. When Katie was filling her bucket without engaging in make-believe, the teacher's parallel playing modeled using sand as pretend cake ingredients. This unobtrusive modeling was all that was needed to encourage Katie to pretend. At other times, like with Abby, a more directive type of playing may be needed. It may be that Johnson and Associates used play tutoring in a narrow sense. Many of the research studies that involved play tutoring have teachers take a more directive role in the play. They do, however, point out that Smilansky (1968) talked about two types of play tutoring: tutoring from the outside and tutoring from the inside. Tutoring from the outside occurs when the teacher helps expand children's play by asking pertinent questions from outside the play, "Are you the cook? What are you making for dinner?" Tutoring from the inside is when the teacher takes a role in the play, and helps expand children's play by modeling and asking questions as one of the players.

Leading Master Players. Johnson et al. (1987) limited the more active role of the teacher to helping less skilled players. However, there are also times when it is appropriate for adults to play a more active role with master players. Even with skilled players, adults can help the children to stretch their play to a higher level.

A new building is being constructed next to the school. The kindergarten class has been watching the construction process with great interest. They watch the construction from the play yard, and take walks to the site for a closer view. Blueprints of the new building are posted on a classroom bulletin board and often compared with the current progress of the building.

In response to this interest, the teacher, Mr. Johns, has arranged the dramatic play area as a construction site. There is a desk with paper and pencils for drawing blueprints, and a row of hard hats for the workers. Saw horses fence off the construction area with signs saying HARD HAT AREA. Wheelbarrows are in the block area to carry the "bricks" to the construction site.

Some of the children begin by drawing blueprints, others haul bricks in preparation for the building that will begin soon. The blueprints are posted near the construction site. The architects discuss the plans with the workers, as bricklayers begin arranging the blocks. The blocks are laid and pretend mortar is spread. Finally, the block shelves are empty, and the building is finished. Delbert suggests knocking the building down and starting again. As the children are about to converge on the building, Mr. Johns asks, "Do you need to demolish that building to make way for a new one? What do construction workers use when they want to knock down a building?"

Cathy says, "They use a big ball."

Mr. Johns gets out a book on construction, and turns to the page with a wrecking ball. "Like this?" he asks. The children agree. "What will we need to make a wrecking ball?" After some discussion, Mr. Johns gets out a rope and ties a block to the end. (The ball that was originally suggested would not stay on the end of the rope.) Cathy notices the barricades in the book where the spectators stand to watch the demolition. It is decided to move the saw horses back. Mr. Johns is the foreman and escorts everyone but the wrecking ball holder behind the barricade.

The children soon discover that the wrecking ball only knocks off a few blocks at a time. After a conference Peter suggests putting the block behind the building and pulling. Again, only a few fall. With Mr. Johns acting as foreman,

FIGURE 3-10 Preparing to pull the rope on the wrecking ball

the children take turns trying out their hunches on how to get the building to fall down. As each new wrecker is about to pull the rope, Mr. Johns calls for all spectators to get behind the barricade. Finally, the building falls. The rubble is hauled away, new plans are drawn, and the new building is begun.

These children are obviously master players. Their dramatic play is rich and involved. They easily use props and their imaginations to make needed materials such as mortar. They play cooperatively, working together in their selected roles towards a joint goal.

The foreman role that Mr. Johns adopted allowed the construction work to incorporate demolition play as well. He took a lead in assigning jobs, and keeping the spectators involved as they watched each attempt. His presence kept the game moving, as children deliberated the problem of how to knock down the building, yet he also insured that children had an active role in the process as well. In this case, the teacher was an active player in the children's story, in order to advance the play of master players to a still higher level.

Avoid Overusing This Role. Teachers must be judicious in their use of the active player role. They must be careful not to interfere with children's play and to avoid overusing this role (Van Hoorn et al., 1993). When JoAnn took an active role to lead Abby into hospital play, it was to help Abby to do something she appeared to want to do. The teacher's lead met the child's needs, and did not interfere with her play. It is easy to interfere without intending to as Miss Henderson did in this same hospital play.

> *Jenna is at the reception desk of the hospital. She is answering the phone and scribbling messages on the calendar. Michael is the doctor. Miss Henderson has been the nurse assisting Michael with his operations. No more patients are coming. Michael seems at loose ends without someone to operate on. Miss Henderson goes over to Jenna. "Dear me, you look like you have a sore leg. Dr. Michael has room for you in his operating schedule."*
>
> *"I have to answer the phone," explains Jenna.*
>
> *"I can answer the phone for you. Dr. Michael is all ready for you." Reluctantly, Jenna leaves the reception desk and goes to the operating table.*

Jenna did not really want to be the patient. She was busy as the receptionist. She changed her play under pressure from Miss Henderson. Miss Henderson mistakenly felt that Jenna should be involved with her peers and she was looking for a patient for Michael. Miss Henderson could have become a patient herself, checking in with Jenna, then being operated on by Dr. Michael. (Jones and Reynolds (1922) presented an excellent discussion on how to avoid interfering with children's play in Chapter 5 of *The Play's the Thing*.)

If the adult is an active player in the children's play too frequently, or maintains this role for too long, then the dramatic play becomes the adult's play, rather than the children's play. Overusing this role is particularly problematic with less skilled players. It is easy for these children to defer to the adult, even if this is not what they had originally intended. Teachers must find the delicate balance that allows them to facilitate children's play without dominating it.

Mediator

When children play together, especially when they are involved in something as personal and changing as dramatic play, conflict is sure to arise. At times children can resolve the conflict on their own; at other times they will need the adult's help.

The term **mediator** is used rather than disciplinarian, because the teacher's role is to help children learn to deal with conflict by acting as a mediator when conflict arises. It takes skill to learn how to arbitrate conflicts in ways that involve children in the process, and in ways that allow the play to continue.

Sending children to **time-out** for misbehaving will stop the conflict, but it will not help the children to develop skills for resolving their own conflict, and it stops the play. Instead, the adult should listen for what the children need, and then help them find appropriate ways to meet these needs.

The dramatic play area has been busy. A group of girls are preparing for a picnic in one corner. Syou Syou is putting her baby to sleep in the bed. TJ and Anthony, who have been wandering the room as dogs, come into the house. Duncan comes over and joins the dog play.

TJ tells Duncan, "No, you have to be the owner." Duncan does not appear to hear TJ and continues being a dog. TJ tackles Duncan and they begin rolling on the floor. Duncan stands up looking baffled. TJ kicks at Duncan's legs.

JoAnn, the teacher, comes over and says, "It looks like there is a problem here."

"Yeah! He won't be the owner," TJ says accusingly. "I told him, but he didn't listen."

"Maybe Duncan didn't hear you," JoAnn replies. "Duncan, TJ wants to know if you will be the owner."

"No, I'm a dog," declares Duncan.

"TJ, it sounds like Duncan wants to be a dog too," JoAnn explains. "Perhaps, you can find another owner. Maybe you can ask one of the girls to be your owner. You could ask Syou Syou."

Anthony, who was eager for the play to continue, asks Syou Syou, "Will you be our owner? We're dogs." Syou Syou agrees. She puts down plates of pretend food and water for her new pets. Soon others become pets as well. At JoAnn's suggestion the dogs move into the block area to build dog beds for themselves. Syou Syou feeds all the pets, and invites other children to come to her "dog day care." This dog play, with block beds and owners to care of them, became a favorite dramatic play theme in this classroom.

FIGURE 3-11 Owners check on their charges at the dog day care

The teacher avoided commenting about TJ's aggressive behavior. She did not tell him "That's not nice," or "Fighting is not allowed in school." Instead, her comment—"It looks like there is a problem"—recognizes that a problem existed without making a value judgement about the behavior. She then helped the children to communicate their needs to each other (Wittmer & Honig, 1994).

When it was clear that TJ and Duncan had opposing desires, the teacher suggested an alternative which satisfied both boy's needs. Once the alternative, asking someone else to be the owner, was suggested, the teacher stood back to see if the children could implement the solution on their own. If the children had been unable or unwilling to ask Syou Syou, then JoAnn could have asked her for them. The amount of help, and the type of help, that adults provide when mediating problems will depend on the ages and social skills of the children involved.

Even if the teacher is a skilled mediator, there will be some problems that cannot be amicably resolved. There are not always solutions that will make everyone happy. It takes much practice to learn to key into the child's true intent, and to develop ways to lead children to resolve their own conflicts.

Interpreter

According to Piaget (1974), young children are **egocentric**. They assume that others know what they know. If they want something, everyone must also know this. They do not realize that things can be viewed from more than one perspective. Misunderstanding the comments or needs of other children can at times make it difficult for children to enter or maintain the dramatic play with others. Adults can act as **interpreter**, helping children to understand other children's points of view.

The dispute between TJ and Duncan resulted from a number of misunderstandings. TJ assumed Duncan had heard and was ignoring the request that Duncan be the owner. Duncan wanted to be a dog and thought that desire should be clear to TJ. In mediating the conflict, JoAnn interpreted the boys' needs to each other, allowing them to accept an alternative solution.

Adults can interpret, or describe, children's actions to make them aware of other children. When two-year-old Mary was making dinner (page 15) teacher Christine commented, "Mary's making us dinner." Kathy looked up, noticed Mary, and went to sit at the table. With two-year-olds, narrating children's actions is an effective technique for helping children to become aware of their peers.

This same technique can also be used with older children, as when the teacher points out to Melissa the shopper that Erica is the cashier (page 23). At times adults can use questions to help children to interpret their actions to each other. When Lauren and Binta were playing house behind the hedge (page 27), Mr. Yang's questions prompted them to interpret their game to Kyla.

Adults can also use questions to help children to clarify their own play to themselves. When Robbie was building a jail with blocks (page 13 and 14), he had not really thought about what would happen to the prisoners once they were in jail. When the teacher asks how they will get food, Robbie has to clarify the details of the game to himself in order to answer. The question pushed him to interpret his game more clearly to himself.

Jones and Reynolds (1992) suggested that the teacher can take written notes of the children's play to read back later. This is a more formal way to act as an interpreter. They call this **teacher as scribe**. They suggest that being a scribe has many benefits. It communicates that teachers value play. It creates meaningful written language and it stimulates children's writing. These written accounts of children's play can also be used to interpret children's play to parents. (A full discussion of how and why teachers fulfill the role of scribe is found in Chapter 6 of *The Play's the Thing* by Jones and Reynolds [1992]).

Social Director

At times children are unsure how to enter play, what role they can take, or how to find someone to fill an important role in their play. As **social director**, the teacher helps them to enter, assists them in finding a role, and draws other children into the play when needed. Van Hoorn et al. (1993) used two separate labels for this role. Their "guardian of the gate" helps children to enter play. Their "matchmaker" helps children to find peers for needed roles (pp. 66-68). When TJ and Duncan needed an owner, JoAnn thought about who to suggest. There was a group of girls preparing for a picnic, two of whom could easily take the leader role in play. Syou Syou was also in the dramatic play area. She has tended to play by herself, but lately has been reaching out to join others in their pretend play. JoAnn's suggestion of Syou Syou provided a catalyst to draw the girl into more social play. After this, the class dogs often sought out Syou Syou as their owner.

The role of social director does not always go so smoothly. Syou Syou could have declined the offer to be owner, then JoAnn would have needed to help the boys find another owner. Obviously the children's current level of social skills will influence the type of social directing that adults do. If most of the children's play is parallel play, the adult will not direct them towards large cooperative ventures.

The teacher's intervention in the play of the less skilled kindergarten shoppers (page 19 and 20) assumed that the children could organize their play on their own. Had the teacher been a more assertive social director, giving them each a role and a direction to move with that role, the children might have been able to develop more constructive play.

Which Role When?

Many times a single action by an adult can fulfill more then one role. When JoAnn helped TJ and Duncan to solve their problem by inviting Syou Syou to participate, she was acting as a mediator, an interpreter, and a social director. Look at your own interaction with children during their dramatic play. Which of these roles do you use? Some of the roles will be much easier than others. How can you stretch yourself to new roles you have not yet tried?

How Do You Get Started?

As a novice teacher, or one who has not given much thought to dramatic play, how do you get started being a play facilitator? Here are five suggestions:

1. Observe children involved in dramatic play, and adults who are master players and master play facilitators.
2. Play along with children who are master players.
3. Plan for themes that are familiar.
4. Allow enough time.
5. Don't expect to become a master player or play facilitator immediately.

We will explore each one of these suggestions in more detail.

Observe Children and Adults at Play

Observing children involved in rich dramatic play is an excellent way to begin. This can be done in a number of ways. Observing the classroom of a teacher who is a master player will provide a vivid picture of constructive dramatic play. If a visit to another classroom is not possible, consider inviting a teacher who is a master player to spend some time in the dramatic play area of your early childhood setting. This will serve two purposes: It will give you a chance to observe the way adults facilitate dramatic play, and it will allow your children to expand their play skills.

You can also observe the children in your care. Where, and in what ways, do they pretend? Even if you do not yet have a dramatic play area, children will find places to pretend. They will often engage in pretend play outside, while building in the blocks, when using manipulatives, or even as they look through a pretzel at snack, pretending it is a pair of glasses. In a Montessori classroom I once visited, there were neither blocks nor a dramatic play area. The children still found ways to play pretend. They built forts with the sorting rods, and used the graduated cylinders as a family. Even after the teacher calmly explained to the children that this was not how the toys were to be used, the toys kept turning back into blocks and families.

Learning to see how and where the children in your class pretend has two advantages. First, it will help you to understand the nature of children's pretend play. Second, it will let you know about the favorite themes, strengths, and weaknesses of this particular group of children. This knowledge will help you know what themes, props, and support will be needed when designing a dramatic play area for your group of children.

Playing along with Master Players

One of the best way to get the feeling for rich dramatic play is to take a minor role when it is occurring. When you observe the play of the children in your care, identify who are the most skilled players, then join them when their play is in progress. Be sure that you take a minor role, following the children's lead as to what actions are appropriate.

Many adults do not enter children's play unless there is a problem. These are the times when intervention is the most difficult, requiring the most skill from the teacher. If you are a beginning player, intervention at times of conflict can be frustrating and make you doubt that dramatic play is worth the trouble. Make a point of joining play often when it is going well. This will give you an understanding of how good play feels. This knowledge will make it easier to facilitate the play of less skilled players, and to mediate when conflict arises.

FIGURE 3-12 Teachers can become better players by joining children who are master players

Pick Familiar Themes

Children who are beginning players find it easier to pretend around familiar themes. The same is true for adults who are beginning players. When playing a familiar theme, such as house, it is easy to generate roles that newcomers can take, to suggest alternative scenarios if conflict arises, and to follow the direction of the play easily. As you and the children get more skilled, you can expand to more exotic themes.

Allow Enough Time for Dramatic Play

Many times, when we are nervous about something, we try to sample it a small amount at a time. It may be tempting for teachers who are just beginning to support dramatic play to allow it for short periods at first. Resist this urge. It takes a while for dramatic play to get going. Leaving only a short time will not enable children to develop their play. Johnson et al. (1987) described the problem.

> If play periods are too short, children will have barely finished preparing for their play when it is time to stop and clean up. After many such experiences, children may simply give up trying to engage in dramatic play (p. 27).

Therefore, if you are attempting to introduce dramatic play into your early childhood setting, long periods of time are a necessity. If you want to start gradually, it would be much better to have time for dramatic play two days a week, but leave a long time on these two days rather than have a short time each day. As you get more comfortable with dramatic play, it is important to expand the days allotted, until dramatic play is a regular part of every day.

Don't Expect to Become a Master Player Immediately

It takes children time to develop into master players; it will take adults time to develop these skills as well. After you have spent time observing and playing with master players, take some time to observe yourself. Which of the roles for facilitating dramatic play do you fulfill? Which ones seem easier or harder? Pick one role that you currently do not do, or that is difficult, and work to become more proficient in this one role. Remember that progress does not come without many mistakes. Reevaluate periodically so you can see where you have grown as a play facilitator.

Common Questions Adults Ask

When facilitating children's dramatic play, adults will occasionally come across situations in which they are unsure what to do. Here are some commonly asked questions and some possible answers.

Why Won't They Play What I've Planned?

"I set up a wonderful post office, but some of the children kept crawling under the table being dogs," bemoans a student teacher after her first day in charge. There are a number of reasons why this may have happened.

1. The dog theme may have been one the children had been exploring. They might have needed more time to play this theme before moving on to other things.
2. If only a few children needed the dog theme, and they were interfering with the others who were trying to play post office, the teacher might have been the postmaster, posting signs saying "No dogs allowed in the post office." Then a separate dog area could be set up in another part of the room. Perhaps they could build dog houses with blocks.
3. The theme might not be one that was familiar to the children.
4. The post office area might not have been set up to create an expectation of the behavior that belongs in the post office. If the paper, pencils, markers, and envelopes are all behind the counter the play may revolve around buying and selling writing supplies, rather than writing and mailing letters.

What Do I Do if There Are Too Many Children in the Area?

It is difficult to play if there are too many children in the dramatic play area. Conflicts over materials, roles, and storyline are more likely to occur when the area is overcrowded. Some adults solve this by designating a maximum number of players for the area. This solution has a number of problems.

1. How crowded an area feels is as much a function of the particular combination of children who are there as a function of the overall number of children in the area.
2. Often the children who need to watch a while before joining the dramatic play will find that the area is full when they are finally ready to enter.
3. If a group of children has a game that they want to continue from day to day, they may find that there is not enough room left in the area for all the children in the continuing saga.
4. Adults are more likely to notice that too many children are in the area when the louder, more disruptive children are there. These children tend to get sent away from the dramatic play area for exceeding the number limit more often than other children.

So what can the adult do to prevent overcrowding in the dramatic play area?

1. The design of the area can communicate how many children will fit comfortably. A grocery store with 3 carts and 2 cash registers is likely to get 3 shoppers and 2 cashiers. Other children are likely to wait until they can get the props they need to play.
2. If overcrowding continues to be a problem, adults may want to consider setting up a second dramatic play area, and/or looking for other ways to explore the same themes in other parts of the room.
3. Overcrowding may also indicate that the dramatic play area is not available often enough. In a halfday program it should be open at least 45 to 60 minutes a day. In a full-day program, it should be open for long periods of time, both morning and afternoon. When it is open infrequently, children will rush there to ensure they get a turn.

How Do I Avoid Overcrowding on the First Day of a New Dramatic Play Arrangement?

A teacher who usually did not have trouble with overcrowding in her dramatic play area describes what happens when she set up a new area. "I set up a firestation for the children. When playtime started, almost the whole class ran to the area. They fought over the materials. It was so crowded that no one could play. Some children got silly. Many children left in frustration." If you do not set a number limit, how can this be avoided?

Discuss with the children what will happen if everyone goes to the firestation at the same time. Will there be enough toys? Will there be room to play? Suggest to the children that if it is crowded when they go over, they might want to come back later.

Make sure there is an adult in the area to help children decide if there is room for more players, and to ensure that excluded children get a chance to play when the current players leave.

Adding some equally attractive new activities in other parts of the room will also reduce the crowds in a new dramatic play area.

What Do I Do about the Child Who Spends the Whole Day in the Dramatic Play Area?

Dramatic play takes a long time to plan and carry out. Children will often repeat favorite themes for many days in a row. Therefore, it is to be expected that some children will spend long periods of time in the dramatic play area. However, if a child never tries other things, the teacher might try some of the following techniques.

1. Do not change the arrangement of the dramatic play area too frequently. If the child needs a long time to initiate new dramatic play, each new change will require a long period in that area. Also, knowing that the same dramatic play materials will be available for many days makes it easier for the children to venture forth to other areas.

2. What does the child play in the dramatic play area? Can these things be offered in other parts of the room? If the child cares for the baby doll when in the house area, you could invite the "parent" to show the baby the art activity, or how to do a puzzle. The water table can be setup for washing baby dolls. Family figures can be added to the blocks to allow for parent and baby play. Family figures can be placed on the felt board, or included with the manipulatives. Once these children have moved to other parts of the room, they will often discover the joy of activities and materials they had not tried before.

3. Engaging these children in some other activity at the beginning of the day is often successful. They may enjoy other activities, but find it hard to leave a dramatic play episode when it is in progress.

4. Asking the child "What else are you going to play today?" is often an effective way to communicate the expectation that children will play in more than one area. After asking, the adult should allow time for the child to conclude the current play, and offer assistance in finding something else of interest.

What Do I Do if No One Wants to Play?

Lack of players can be caused by a number of factors.

1. Children are busy elsewher
   everything in the room to b
2. Sometimes if the area is em
   Inviting some children ovei
   get play going.
3. It may be that the area was
   ests the children? One they
   mote play?

What Do I Do if the Child

Silliness is a common social tech
puts a pot on his head and gigg
and giggles. They have establisl
ness in itself is not a problem. It becomes a problem, however, when it
interferes with the play of others in the area, and when it escalates until
the children are out of control. A good technique is for the adult to join the
silliness when it first begins. The adult might also put a pot on her head
and giggle, or just comment on what strange hats the children have. This
gives the silliness legitimacy. It is no longer "naughty" behavior.

The teacher can then help the children to find a direction for their
play. The hard hats could turn them into construction workers, Johnny
Appleseed, or Kings and Queens of the kitchen. By using the children's
silliness as the basis for the play, the teacher shows them how to progress
beyond their silly beginnings to social interactions—a model they can follow in the future.

If the adult does not notice the silliness until it has escalated to an
uncontrollable high giddiness, it is unlikely that redirection will work at
this point. An example of this is Micah's and Ben's under-the-table silliness in the hair salon (page 29). When the silliness has gotten out of control, the adult will need to stop the play and help the children to find other
calmer activities.

What Do I Do if the Children Keep Playing Robbers, Superheroes, Power Rangers, and Other Aggressive Themes?

Robbers, superheroes, and Power Rangers are all powerful. Young children have little power. Playing these powerful roles allows children to
transform themselves into people of power. This play has great meaning
for children. It also brings disruptions that adults would prefer to avoid.
The play tends to be loud, fast-moving, and aggressive. When those in
roles of power exercise their power against other groups of players, it
interferes with the play of others. The play is often shallow and repetitive:

ers take things from others, Superheroes capture bad guys, Ninja Turtles eat pizza and fight. These actions are repeated over and over again. The play fighting often accidentally escalates into real fighting.

Some adults ban superhero, Power Ranger, and gun play. Even when banned, this type of play will surface in illicit ways. Guns will be made from manipulatives, sticks, or even fingers. Children become sneaky, calling the gun an airplane, or some other acceptable object when the adult is watching, but turning it back into a gun when the adult leaves.

Other adults, realizing the importance of such play to children, will allow it but not actively participate. This permits the play, but does not condone it with adult participation. This laissez-faire approach allows children to fulfill their need to play powerful roles, but it does not deal with any of the negative results of such play.

Carlsson-Paige and Levin (1987, 1990) present a more indepth discussion of this issue and recommended that adults take a more active role. Since this play has great value to children, they believe it should not be banned. Since it often becomes disruptive, children need help channeling it into more constructive directions. Some suggestions are:

1. Adults can help children to expand the characters beyond the narrow stereotypes. Where do they live? Where are their families? Where do they go on vacation? Once children realize they do not need to stick to the limited information they know about the characters, then they can the be powerful figures who play stories as wide as their imaginations.
2. By accepting this play, adults will be able to enter and redirect it as needed. This will allow adults to help children to expand their play before it gets out of hand.
3. Think about what the children are trying to accomplish and help them reach these goals in ways that you find acceptable. If a child is shooting a stick gun at someone, stating the no-guns-in-school rule will make the child defensive. The following approach will be more effective.

> Adult: Why do you need to shoot him?
> Child: He stole all our money.
> Adult: That is terrible! We can't let him do that! But if we shoot him his children will be very sad. What if we use our sticky glue guns and stick him to the ground?

This offers the child the opportunity to still be the good guy, to still be powerful, to still own a powerful tool, and to still win against the bad guy. It also often leads to an imaginative exploration of alternatives to killing people.

Adults will need to decide how they feel about aggressive play and develop their own methods for responding to it.

FIGURE 3-13 Dramatic play may involve many small individual stories

What Do I Do if the Children Won't Play Together?

If a group of adults were playing house together in the dramatic play area, they would divide up roles to create a scenario involving all the players. Adults often feel they should foster this same group cooperative play among the children in their care. But are the children in the class developmentally ready for such advanced social play? It may be that the children won't play together because they are not developmentally ready for cooperative play. Instead, the adult may want to work to foster a series of pretend play episodes each involving pairs of children, or even individual players.

Listening to the Children

It is interesting that the answers to all of these questions involve listening carefully to the children's needs, and helping them find more acceptable ways to reach these needs. Chapters 2 and 3 have explored how dramatic play develops. With this knowledge, adults can listen more closely to children's play. These chapters have also illustrated how adults can use their observations of children as the basis for helping children develop rich, constructive dramatic play.

In the last three chapters there have been many examples of how children have used written language in their pretend play. Chapter 4 will explore how children develop knowledge about written language and how dramatic play can provide a forum for this development. With this information, adults will be able to listen more closely to children's exploration of written language. Techniques for facilitating this development will be presented.

CHAPTER 4

Emergent Literacy: Children Construct Understandings of Written Language

Although young children do not read and write in conventional ways, they are beginning to construct knowledge about reading and writing, as can be seen in the following examples.

> *Eighteen-month-old Michael loves having books read to him. He is beginning to look at the print as much as the pictures. On a family trip to the Boston Children's Museum he is fascinated with the large sign out front. He points at the writing on the sign saying "L-M-N-O-P." He continues around the museum pointing out writing and labeling it with his new word, "L-M-N-O-P."*

Michael has discovered that letters are different from other marks, and has created his own word for writing "L-M-N-O-P."

> *Four-year-old Ashanti is filling up her paper with strings of letters. She shows it to Ms. Mooney. "I am writing a story. I am going to fill the whole page."*
> *"Will you read it to me?" Ms. Mooney asks.*
> *"You have to read it to me." Ashanti replies. "I don't know how to read."*

Ashanti knows that stories can be written down and read. She does not yet realize that the writer must know what is being written, and must put the letters in a specific order.

Jeremy, who is three, is making a picture for his mother. He scribbles with blue marker, then with red, then with blue again. When he shows it to his teacher Tanya, she reminds him to put his name on the paper.

He picks up a purple marker and scribbles with a flourish in an empty space as he quickly recites the letters of his name "J-E-R-E-M-Y."

Jeremy knows the names for the letters that make up his name. He knows that marks on paper are writing, but he does not know that these letter names go with specific letters, and that these specific letters are needed to write his name conventionally.

Five-year-old Christin is writing her name,—K-H-R-I-S-T-I-N. "I decided to use the K 'cause it makes the same sound as the C."

Christin is learning to match speech sounds with letters. She likes playing with these sounds and making them do what she wants them to do.

What Is Emergent Literacy?

These children all know some things about written language, although they also have much to learn. This developing knowledge about literacy has been called "emergent literacy." Teale (1987) described why this term is so appropriate. "Emergent" describes something in the process of becoming—young children are in the process of becoming literate. "Emergent" suggests that children's developing literacy is continually growing and continually changing. According to Teale (1987),

> "emergent" suggests that growth in this period of development occurs without the necessity for an overriding emphasis on formal teaching. Instead, the young child develops literacy in the everyday context of home and community" (p. 47).

The term "literacy" is also well chosen because it encompasses both reading and writing. Young children build understandings of reading and writing concurrently, with knowledge about one adding to the knowledge about the other. Sulzby (1989, 1991) defined emergent literacy as "the reading and writing behaviors that precede and develop into conventional literacy" (1991, p. 273).

This chapter will explore the emergence of literacy, beginning with oral language development, then looking at **written language** development. A discussion of how this knowledge should influence teaching practice will conclude the chapter.

Oral Language: The Beginning of Emergent Literacy

The children at the beginning of the chapter are all using **oral language** as they explore written language. This is not surprising, since oral language is developed first, and is often used to explain and give meaning to early written language (Dyson, 1993). Jeremy's scribbles would not mean anything to the casual observer, but accompanied by his verbal description, it becomes clear that he is writing his name. At this point it is the child's oral language that mediates the meaning rather than the written marks. As children develop more knowledge of written language and more skill in manipulating it, the writing itself will be the medium of communication. Since oral language is the basis for later written language, an exploration of how oral language develops is a good place to start.

Learning to Talk

It is amazing that children can master the complex task of learning to talk in such a short time, and without any formal instruction. By the time most children are two years old, they can communicate in some fashion with their family (Kostelnik, Soderman, & Whiren, 1993). By the age of five, the structure of children's language is similar to adult language (Glazer, 1989; Morrow, 1993), although they will continue to expand their vocabulary, the complexity of sentence structure, and their uses for language throughout their lives.

First Words

Infants begin by playing with sounds for the physical pleasure they receive as air moves through their mouths in different ways, and from the enjoyment of the different sounds they create. As they make sounds, people in the world around them react. Sound making may be followed by a sound from an adult, the approach of another person, the appearance of an object, or caring physical contact. Children become aware that the people in their environment also create strings of sounds. Often these sounds accompany actions or mark the appearance of objects.

In a similar process to Michael, discovering that there is such a thing as written language, these children are discovering the existence of oral language. They are beginning to realize, although subconsciously, that sounds can communicate. Making sounds has an effect on what happens in the world around them.

At about one year of age, children begin to connect a specific group of sounds to specific actions or objects. In the following example, Lily is using her first word.

> Lily is almost one year old. She pulls on her mom's skirt, saying "nana, nana, nananana" in an insistent voice.
>
> "Would you like some banana?" her mom asks as she cuts some small pieces for Lily to eat.
>
> After eating, Lily again says "nana," and points to a jar of applesauce that is sitting on the counter.

"Would you like some applesauce too?" her mother asks.
Lily says "nana" again in an insistent voice pointing to the applesauce.

Lily has learned to use a specific group of sounds "nana," or at times a longer string of the same sounds, to mean food. She has often heard the people around her use these sounds as they give her banana, her favorite food, to eat. She has overgeneralized the meaning for this word, using it to mean all food, not just banana. In a few weeks she begins to add other food words to her oral vocabulary. Slowly "nana" comes to be used just to request that specific food.

The first fifty words may come quickly or take several months, but from ages two to six vocabulary increases at a rapid pace. It has been estimated that children learn as many as two to six new words a day during this period (Snow & Tabors, 1993).

Combining Words

Between one and two-and-a-half years of age, children begin to put words together into phrases, such as "more milk," "doggie gone," and "Mommy up" (Caplan & Caplan, 1977). Children omit smaller, less important words, but still transmit the gist of the message. As adults we can listen to these phrases and add the missing words—"I want more milk," "The doggie is gone," and "Mommy pick me up." This compressed speech is often called "telegraphic speech." It is interesting that although many words are missing from these utterances, the children do use the existing words—mainly nouns and verbs—in the correct order.

With experience children will expand the number of words they put together in a sentence. Between three and four years old, children's utterances expand to complex sentences. Their oral vocabularies expand to include pronouns, adjectives, adverbs, possessives, and plurals (Glazer, 1989).

The Uses of Oral Language

As children expand their skills with the mechanics of language, they also expand their uses for language. Beginning talkers use language to express needs, to ask questions, to express feelings, or to share information. By four years old, children are using language for these purposes, but also in more complex ways—they are telling stories, creating make-believe, stating and defending opinions, describing events in their lives, and more. The children are able to speak from different perspectives.

Putting It All Together

As this description illustrates, learning language is more than just making the right sounds or knowing the meaning of words. Children are learning a set of complex systems, each with its own rules. Children are mastering the **phonologic system** as they learn to make sounds and combine them into words. They are learning the **semantic system** as they learn words and expand the meanings they have for the words they know.

As children combine words into phrases, sentences, and paragraphs, they are learning the rules of **syntax,** or grammar. They are learning the rules of the **pragmatic system** as they use their language in many different situations for many different functions.

These systems are not developed sequentially or in isolation. Children learn about sounds, word meaning, sentence structure, and language function simultaneously, with growth in knowledge about each system contributing to growth in knowledge of all the systems. The next section will explore how children learn the rules of these language systems.

Constructing Knowledge about Oral Language

Children construct their knowledge about language through being active participants in a language-rich environment. In a review of research on children's language learning Genishi (1988) described how children develop language to represent things they have experienced and to interact with others. In the earlier example, Lily had created a mental image of being fed, an activity she experiences repeatedly. She then used the word "nana" to represent the event of being fed.

According to Genishi (1988), "The child's language learning proceeds from action or experience, to concept, to word, and not from word, to concept, to experience" (p. 18). Children first experience an action or object,

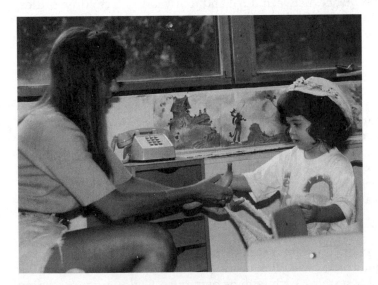

FIGURE 4-1 Children develop language to represent things they have experienced and to interact with others

and then create a concept to capture what they have experienced. Only then do they attach a verbal label. Children learn language best when it is imbedded in meaningful contexts, not when it is taught in isolated lessons (Nelson, 1985). As children experiment with sounds, words, sentences, and conversations, they begin to build a subconscious understanding of the rules that govern these aspects of language.

Constructing Rules about Sounds

When infants experiment with sounds, they begin by exploring a large range of sounds, but gradually their babble will be narrowed to contain a larger percentage of the sounds that are used by the language speakers around them. Children of English speakers will play more with the sounds of English, while children of Chinese speakers will play more with the sounds of Chinese. The infants begin to conform to the phonetic rules that govern their native language.

As children are playing with sounds, they also begin to establish interaction patterns with the people around them in the environment. They will make sounds in response to the conversation they hear. They are able to use these sounds to do such things as call for attention, express joy, and protest.

Constructing Rules about Words

Learning about words is more than just learning the meaning of individual words. Children also must know the shades of meaning, and the ways in which these words are used with other words. As can be seen in the example of Lily and "nana," children will often overgeneralize the meaning of words, then gradually refine their definitions with more experience.

Children wish to communicate, and in the process of communicating their meaning they must often stretch to find words that mean what they intend to say. This causes children to use words in ways that adults would not.

> Michael at three visited the Sleeping Bear Sand dunes on Lake Michigan. He was impressed by the height of the sand hills, and their rolling, seemingly unending quality. A week later he passed rolling grassy hills. "Look," he exclaimed excitedly, "grass dunes."

Michael is looking for a word to describe the rolling quality of the hills. Currently his only use for "rolling" is to describe what a ball does, so he uses the word "dune," which describes a land configuration similar to the one he is viewing. With more experience he will learn the wider meanings of "rolling," and that "dune" is used more narrowly to describe only mounded sand.

The specific words that children learn and the meanings that they construct for these words will depend on their experiences, interests, and the language that surrounds them. According to Nelson (1973), children's first words reflect their individuality and interests. Some children begin by labeling things (learning many nouns); others use words that prompt social interactions (greetings, or words that influence the behavior of others). Children continue to learn new words and expand the meanings of known words throughout their childhood and their later lives.

Constructing Rules about Grammar

According to behaviorists, children learn language through imitation of an adult model (Skinner, 1957; Morrow, 1993). Although children certainly do imitate the sounds, the intonations, the vocabulary, and even the sentence structure of those around them, they also actively construct their knowledge about language. This is particularly clear as children learn the rules of syntax.

If children were merely imitating adults, one would never hear such child-like phrases as "I runned faster than you," "I made two snowmans," or "mines is blue." These phrases indicate that the speakers are beginning to apply the rules for past tense (adding -ed), for making plurals (adding -s), and for making possessives (adding -'s). These speakers have not yet realized that many words are exceptions to these patterns. Children learn syntactical rules "by interacting with mature language users who provide many utterances from which abstract rules can be inferred" (Schickendanz, York, Stewart, & White, 1990, p. 181).

If one tries to correct a child's incorrect speech, it becomes clear that the process of constructing syntactical rules is not a conscious one. Cazden (1981) described how "impervious to external alterations the child's rule system may be" (p. 4). She cites an example that McNeill (1966) used of a parent trying ineffectually to correct her daughter's immature use of negatives.

C. "Nobody don't like me."
M. "No, say `Nobody likes me.'"
C. "Nobody don't like me." (eight repetitions of this dialogue)
M. "No. Now listen carefully; say `Nobody likes me.'"
C. "Oh! Nobody don't likes me" (McNeill, 1966, p. 69).

Though the child tries to speak as her mother requests, she continues to use the incorrect form. When she listens to the mother's corrections, the child attends to the content of what is being said, and does not realize that she and her mother are using a different form to state the same content. With repeated experience, this child will learn the correct rules for the use of negatives.

A STEP FURTHER   *When to Teach and When to Listen*

This example points out the importance of really listening to children. It is not just the child who is unable to hear the sentence correctly. The mother in this example also does not hear well what is being said. She is listening to the form of her daughter's language, but does not tune into the content—that her child is upset because she believes that she is not liked. A discussion about what has happened to cause this statement, about hurt feelings, about the wonderful qualities of her daughter, or about ways of getting together with other children, would all be appropriate responses to this child's statement about being disliked.

Adults should always attend to children's social and emotional needs first, before considering using a situation to "teach" children something.

Constructing Rules about What Language to Use When

As children use language in different contexts, they must change the way they talk to fit the situation. Parents know their children's language well. Often at home children are understood even when scanty information is given in their utterances. When children are at school, they may need to add more details in order to be understood. In telling a story about what happened at home last night, the child will need to include more detail to communicate to a teacher who was not there than to a sibling who was present when the event occurred.

Children also begin to understand what types of language fit which situations. Calling a doll "pooh pooh head" may be met with shrieks of laughter from classmates, but is likely to cause disapproval if used with a adult.

Children Build an Awareness of Their Own Language Learning

Children master the rules of each of these language systems unconsciously in the process of hearing and using language. Snow and Tabors (1993) suggested that at some point these rule systems "emerge into consciousness and become a topic of conversation for children or a topic for play" (p. 2). When children start making rhymes for their name—"Sue, boo, goo, moo"—they are consciously playing with the sounds of language. When children use words in silly ways—"He has gooey hair,"—they are consciously playing with the meaning of words. When children play with a sentence by substituting words ("as small as a mouse, as small as a house, as small as the world"), they are consciously playing with syntax. When children change their way of talking to fit the situation, they are

FIGURE 4-2 Children adjust the way they talk to fit the context of the situation

consciously playing with semantics or content—"Sh!! Talk quiet, so the wolf won't find us." This explicit talk about language use is called **metalinguistic awareness**.

Language as a Social Symbol System

Children learn language in a social setting (Morrow, 1993; Gibson, 1989). They cannot learn language unless they are in an environment where language is used, since words have no meaning outside of the culture that uses them. Words are arbitrary symbols that a culture attaches as a label to represent objects, actions, and concepts (Schickendanz et al., 1990). The word "chair" represents a four-legged object with a seat and a back that people sit on, because as an English-speaking society we have given this meaning to that word.

For children who are learning English as a second language, the social nature of language is particularly important. Gutierrez (1993) said that "Language acquisition is more than learning to speak; it is a process through which a child becomes a competent member of the community by acquiring both the linguistic and the sociocultural knowledge needed to learn how to use language in that particular community" (p. 95).

Learning oral language involves creating mental images of objects and actions, then attaching verbal symbols (or words) to these images. Written language is an even more abstract set of symbols. The written word "chair" represents the oral word chair, which in turn represents the mental image, which represents the actual object. Let's look now at how children learn about this written symbol system.

The Development of Written Language

Children's development of written language follows a similar pattern to their development of oral language (Gibson, 1989; Teale, 1986; Temple, Nathan, Temple, & Burris, 1993). Both emerge as children explore and interact with language users around them in the community. In developing oral language, children first randomly explore sounds. They develop a holistic understanding that sounds can communicate. Then, through interactions with oral language users, and by experimenting with their own uses of oral language, children gradually construct and revise the rules for oral language. Let us look at the ways in which written language development parallels oral language development.

The Emergence of Written Language

In developing written language, children first randomly explore written marks. They play with cursive and print-like marks in imitation of the writing that is in their environment, and they explore print. They carry, look at, and manipulate books in imitation of those around them.

Children develop a holistic understanding that writing can communicate long before they can connect specific words with specific groupings of letters. Children's awareness of written language as a form of communication can be seen in many ways: when they ask someone what a sign says; when they know that a specific book always contains the same story; or when they make random marks and discuss what they are writing.

Children gradually construct knowledge of the rules governing written language. They learn that words are made up of sounds and that specific groups of letters are needed to make specific words. They learn that spaces are needed to separate words, and that written language moves from left to right and top to bottom. Eventually they will be able to read and write in conventional ways. They construct this knowledge through being immersed in an environment full of written language, and by observing adults modeling the uses of written language. According to Gutierrez (1993) and Nathenson-Mejia (1989), children with English as a

FIGURE 4-3 Children carry, look at, and manipulate books in imitation of those around them

second language will experiment naturally with writing English in the way native speakers do.

Constructing Knowledge about Written Language

Oral and written language are alike in many ways. While they use the same words and grammar, and both are used to communicate, written language is more than just oral language written down. According to Snow and Tabors (1993), written language is a system in its own right. "Many aspects of literacy build on, but also go beyond, what children know about oral language use" (p. 6).

Like oral language, written language is based on a complex combination of rule systems. The systems are the same for both written and oral language, but the rules are different. Snow and Tabors suggested, "many of the difficulties children can have in acquiring literacy skills derive from these areas of difference between oral and literate usage" (p. 7). The next section will explore how children learn the rules of written language.

Constructing Rules about Sounds in Written Language

Children play with marks on paper long before they have any idea that letters are tied to speech sounds. Exploring and putting sounds together orally is usually the first step to the development of oral language. On the other hand, exploring letter-sound connections, or even realizing that there is a connection, comes much later in the development of written language awareness.

Connecting Letters and Sounds

The letter-sound connection is hard for children to develop because each letter makes an abstract segment of the word, rather than a syllable (Snow & Tabors, 1993). We say that the letter "T" makes the tee sound, but if it actually made that sound, the word "toy" would be pronounced "teeoy." In fact, once children discover that written marks stand for sounds in words, they will often use a letter, or some other mark, for each syllable they hear in the word, so the word "chicken" would be made with two marks (Teale, 1987).

Before they can connect sounds with letters, children must first realize that words are made up of collections of minute sounds. Playing with rhyming words is a good way for children to begin isolating sounds. The words "ball," "call," "tall" are composed of the sound produced by the initial letter plus "all." In this context it is easier to explore the letter-sound relationships.

Which Letters Do Children Use?

When children do begin to connect marks to specific sounds in words, they will write only the most noticeable sounds. In writing the sign in the accompanying photo, Nicholas used "BK" to say be careful. He wrote two of the most prominent sounds in the words (see Figure 4-4). When children begin connecting sounds to letters they will often use the letter name rather than the letter sounds.

> Ashanti, who is almost five, has recently become aware that specific groups of letters can say specific things. She is using letter cookie cutters to make letter marks in the sand table. She puts out AXT. "What does it say?" she asks Tanya, the teacher.
>
> Tanya explains, "When the letters are arranged like that they do not make a word I know. It makes a funny word, 'axt.' If I move them I can make them into a real word. Should I move them?" Ashanti agrees. Tanya moves the letters to say TAX. "Now it says tax.'"
>
> Ashanti picks up the letter C and adds it to the end of the word. "Now it says 'taxi,' " she proclaims proudly.

Ashanti used the letter name "Cee" to make the final sound at the end of "taxi." Temple et al. (1993) give many examples of this "letter-name spelling." This reference also has an excellent, in-depth discussion of the development of spelling that is invaluable for classroom teachers. It

FIGURE 4-4 A sign warning people to BK (be careful)

allows teachers to more clearly understand what is happening in children's writing, to be more successful in reading invented spelling, as well to provide suggestions for how to support children who are at the different levels of developing knowledge about spelling.

Children will gradually come to learn the sounds that letters make, separate from the letter names. Phonetic spelling—spelling based on the sounds in the words—will gradually become more complete. Children will add more consonants, and the long vowels. They will begin to learn how to create blends and to spell words containing short vowels.

When children move from phonetic spelling to transitional spelling (Temple et al., 1993), where many of the smaller words are spelled correctly, irregular words are still usually misspelled. Children at this stage are usually readers. Their spelling will become more correct with more reading, more writing, and more attention to the way words are put together (Temple et al., 1993).

Constructing Knowledge about Words in Written Language

Children come to know words in their oral vocabulary through hearing them used often in relation to an object or action. Lily, in the example at the beginning of the chapter, had heard the word "banana" when bananas were being bought, pictured in books, cut up, and eaten. From these repeated experiences she came to connect the word "banana" with the object banana.

Reading Environmental Print

Children also come to connect written logos with meaningful objects. Children as young as two or three will connect the McDonald's logo with a Happy Meal, the Oshkosh label with their favorite pair of overalls, and the Sesame Street logo with a much-read book about Bert and Ernie. There have been numerous studies about children's recognition of **environmental print**. (See Teale [1987] for a review of the research on reading environmental print).

Clay observed children's early writing and came up with a list of "concepts and principles" that children discover as they try to make sense of writing. (Temple et al. [1993] provide an excellent discussion of these principles, along with a discussion of how adults can help facilitate development of these principles.) The children who recognize logos have come to understand Clay's (1975) "sign concept," the idea that "a sign carries a message" (p. 65). The McDonald's logo carries the message that a McDonald's is near. It is important to realize that children are getting meaning from the design of the logo as well as the letters (Mason, 1980). Masonheimer, Drum, and Ehri, (1984) found that children who could read "McDonald's" in the logo were often not able to read it written in conventional print. Children also failed to notice when letters were changed within the logo (OcDonald's instead of McDonald's). The children are reading the print embedded in the environment, but not the print in isolation (Teale, 1987).

Early Attempts to Make Sense of Print

Although the children may not be getting meaning from the print of the logo, environmental print reading shows that children realize that non-pictorial symbols (the McDonald's logo) can represent something else (the restaurant). To make the step from reading logos to reading conventional print, children have many things to discover.

Written Words Do Not Physically Resemble the Object

In trying to make sense out of written language, many young children will seek to find a connection between the physical appearance of the writing and the object it is meant to represent. Schickedanz (1990) described how her two-year-old son Adam labeled three vertical lines as his name. He proclaimed, "These are three two's for Adam"(p. 7). When Mom seemed surprised and said she thought this was his name, showing him his name written in standard form, Adam replied, "That has four; I two" (p. 7).

Ferreiro and Teberosky (1982) wrote of a girl who felt her name should be longer on her birthday, because now she was older. Here again the child related the way her name was written to her age. They also described a boy who felt the word for bear should be longer than the word for duck because bears are bigger than ducks. This child felt that the size of the word should be related to the size of the object it labels.

One boy wrote "cat" "oia," and then wrote kittens "oiaoiaoia." This child seemed to feel that things that look the same should be written the same, even if they do not sound the same, and that more characters are needed to write about more of the same objects (Temple et al., 1993).

Creating Strings of Letters

Once children realize that the physical appearance of written words is not related to the physical properties of the object, they must begin to construct concepts about how to combine letters to make writing. As children write and talk about their writing, we can see these concepts developing. Clay (1975) and Temple et al. (1993) described some of the concepts that children develop about writing.

When children first began to produce writing that is differentiated from their drawing, they will often make long lines of repeated marks as can be seen in the pseudo cursive writing in Figure 4-5 and the repetitive "+o" used in Figure 4-6. Clay called this the **recurring principle**. These children have concluded that "writing consists of the same moves repeated over and over again" (Temple et al., 1993, p. 24).

FIGURE 4-5 Psuedo cursive writing

Writing Must Have Variety

Children begin to realize that the writing is not the same mark over and over again, but a variety of different letters. Clay called this the **generative principle**. With just a few symbols arranged in different ways, children can generate a limitless amount of writing. In Figure 4-7, Amanda uses the letters in her name in different combinations to write about her picture. Although Amanda is only using a few letters for her writing, the principle of using a few letters in different order to write anything describes well how we use the twenty-six letters of our alphabet to produce written language.

Is This a Letter?

Children begin writing with a limited number of letters. They usually start by using the letters in their name. Amanda's writing uses a combination of letters from her name: A, M, D, and N.

English letters are made of a combination of lines, loops, circles, and dots. Some combinations of these elements are letters, others are not. Children will experiment with various combinations. At times they will use the letters they know, turning them upside down or adding extra lines. Children are excited when they discover that they have created another letter. One day Patrick discovered that when he wrote his "P" upside down he made a "d." What a remarkable discovery! (For a full account of this story see A Step Further on page 95.

FIGURE 4-6 The recurring principle: Here the writing consists of a repeated "+o" pattern

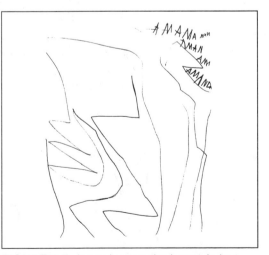

FIGURE 4-7 Amanda uses the letters in her name in different order

Children also have to discover that each letter can be written in a variety of ways. All letters can be written in both upper and lower case. Sometimes the visual difference between these two forms of the letter can be quite pronounced.

> *It is Mary's day to visit her new classroom before school begins. Mary makes a picture and proudly writes her name on it all in caps. Mary and her teacher, Tanya, go to find Mary's cubby so she can put her picture in it. "Can you find the one with your name?" Tanya asks. Mary looks at the cubby with her name on it, but moves on. After she looks for a while, Tanya points to the name Mary, written in lower case, as in Figure 4-8A. Tanya points at the name, "Look, it says 'Mary' on this cubby. It must be yours."*
>
> *"No," says Mary, "My name doesn't have a 'P.' " Tanya is puzzled at first, then notices that she has made the "a" carelessly and the line is hanging down. Mary must think the "a" is a "p." "I didn't write carefully. I will make a new label so it looks more like your name." She rewrites it as shown in Figure 4-8B.*
>
> *"That's not my name. My name doesn't have a 'p,' " Mary explains as she points to the carefully written "a."*

Mary only knows the capital "A"—the lower case "a" does look more like a "p" than like the capital "A." Until Mary realizes that the letter "a" has two quite different forms she will not be able to accept the cubby sign as her name. Tanya later took care of the problem by explaining that there are two ways to write Mary's name, with upper case letters and with lower case letters, she put both versions on the cubby. To confuse children still further, the print version of letters "a" and "g" used in books often look different from the way that people print these letters. For that matter, each writer makes the letters slightly differently.

 Children discover that,

> by varying letter forms that we know, we can produce letters that we didn't know how to make. But we must be careful, because not all the letter forms we produce in this way are acceptable as signs [letters]" (Temple et al., 1993, p. 29).

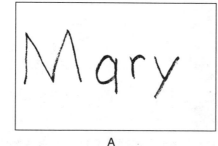   

A   B

FIGURE 4-8 First (A) and second (B) versions of Mary's cubby label

Clay called this the **flexibility principle**. Temple et al. suggested that playing with letters in this way allows children to "gain active control over the features or principles of print" (1993, p. 29). Children also need to build concepts about how words fit together in written language. The next section will discuss this learning.

A STEP FURTHER   *Patrick Discovers He Can Write the Whole Alphabet*

Patrick, who has just turned five, is writing his name and mistakenly makes a "d." He is about to cross it out when the Tanya, the teacher, exclaimed, "Look you made a 'd.'"

"No," says Patrick, writing an upper case D, "This is a 'D.'" Tanya explains that letters can be written two ways, in upper and lower case. Together they look at the alphabet strip on the wall that shows both forms of the letter. Patrick writes a lower case d next to his upper case D and reads "D, d." He takes a new piece of paper and copies Aa and reads "A, a." Patrick spends the rest of play time, 45 minutes, copying the letters of the alphabet. When he is done, Tanya suggests stapling the pages together to make an alphabet book. He proudly shows and reads his book to the other children in the class.

This activity had a great deal of meaning to Patrick. It allowed him to use his newly discovered knowledge about upper and lower case letters in a task that was important to him. The value of this activity lies in the fact that the child selected it to explore an idea he had just discovered. This activity would not have the same meaning if the teacher had assigned a class project of making an alphabet book. This example illustrates well how teachers can use "teachable moments" to help children explore and expand their current concepts about writing.

Constructing Knowledge about Strings of Written Words

To an experienced English reader it is obvious that we read from left to right, top to bottom, and that, when writing, a space is needed to mark the beginning of each new word. This information about how strings of words are created and read is not as obvious to children. Most things in our environment remain the same no matter which direction we view them from. A car is still a car if you view it from front to back, back to front, top to bottom, or even if you climb under it and look at the underside. Writing, however, is not the same when it is viewed or written in different directions.

Learning to put spaces between words is a particularly difficult concept for children to grasp since it involves omitting something, rather than doing something.

Christina, at four and one-half, began writing sentences using invented spelling. She felt the need to separate the words she had written in some way. She used vertical slash lines. These slashes looked like I's, so she began to use dashes. She was frustrated when she came to the end of the paper and she still had not finished a word, so she used an arrow to take the reader to the next line where the word continued.

When playing on the word processor, Christina was thrilled to discover that the word would automatically move to the next line if there was not enough room. She also learned that the space bar would make a separation between words. She made spaces between words on the computer; however, she still used dashes to separate words when she was writing by hand.

The computer offered Christina an action, hitting the space bar, that could be used to create the division between words. When writing, she still used the dash, because this too provided a direct action that recognized that words should be separate. Leaving a space appeared to be too abstract, too much of a non-action to satisfy her need to consciously register the spaces between words. Clay (1975) referred to the knowledge described here as the directional prinicples, the space concepts, and concepts of page and book arrangement.

Putting words together into strings also requires understanding the rules of grammar and syntax. The rules of grammar used in oral and written language are the same, though as Snow and Tabors (1993) pointed out, written language tends to use more varied, and more complex, sentence forms.

Constructing Knowledge about Uses of Written Language

Children's knowledge of written language usually begins with discoveries of its function. They observe adults reading newspapers and books, making lists, checking the TV listings, reading recipes, checking the ingredients on the side of the box before purchasing something at the supermarket, writing checks, reading or writing letters, and checking the sports scores in the paper.

Children also participate in literate activities with adults. Children listen to stories being read. They are helped to write their names on pictures they have made. They are helped to follow picture directions of a recipe. Adults will take dictation from children, writing down their words about a picture, or in a thank-you note to grandma. Reading and writing are an integral part of daily life (Teale & Sulzby, 1989). Many researchers have found that young children tend to experience literacy as a part of other activities. The literacy is directed to another goal—it is not an end in itself. Observation by a number of researchers has supported this statement (Heath, 1983; Taylor, 1983; Taylor & Dorsey-Gaines, 1988; and Teale, 1986).

FIGURE 4-9 Enjoying a book with a teacher

Clay (1975) found that next to writing their names, lists of the words and/or letters they can write are children's most common early writing. It is like the young talker trying out the sounds and words they know. Young writers also engage in this type of self-motivated practice behavior.

As children grow, they build clearer understandings about when and how to use written language. Unconsciously, they begin to differentiate the type of language that is used to tell stories in a book from conversational language. Sulzby (1988) found that in retelling storybooks, children moved from labeling pictures to creating a story with the phrasing and wording of written language. (See Chapter 8 for a more detailed discussion of the research on storybook reading.)

Snow and Tabors (1993) suggested that the uses, and therefore the pragmatic rules, affecting written language often differ from those affecting oral language. They suggest two main dimensions in which these forms of speech differ. First, oral language tends to involve active participation of the listener. Oral statements will be met with agreement or disagreement, questions, requests for clarification, or additional information from the listeners. Written language must communicate without any assistance from the reading audience.

A second dimension in which the pragmatics of these forms of speech tend to differ is how much shared knowledge the speaker/writer can assume he or she holds with the audience (Snow & Tabors, 1993). When speaking to someone about a shared event, the context is understood. Many fewer details are needed. In written language often the audience is unknown. Care must be taken to create the context and provide all pertinent details.

There are times in which oral language also demands that the speaker talk without collaboration from the audience, such as when telling stories. Describing an object to someone on the phone, or to a friend who cannot see it, will require elaborated detail in the way that written language does.

Snow and Tabors (1993) suggested that "young children can best be exposed first in oral contexts to the pragmatic considerations that govern sophisticated literate use of language." Giving children opportunities to talk in more formal ways, such as telling stories, describing things, describing dramatic play events, and giving directions, will help build the language skills needed later for reading and writing.

Supporting Children's Emerging Literacy

According to Snow and Tabors (1993), many of the difficulties that children encounter in developing knowledge about written language may come from the differences between written and oral language uses. They suggest that children who have developed some conscious awareness of language (metalinguistic awareness), will find it easier to understand the relation and differences between oral and written language. Therefore, opportunities for children to explore and talk about both oral and written language should be a natural part of any early childhood program.

Does the Reading Readiness Model Match the Way Children Learn about Literacy?

The **reading readiness model** used in many schools and supported by many textbook companies is incompatible with what is known about how literacy develops (Teale & Sulzby, 1986). The term itself implies that children have to be "ready" before they learn to read. This approach assumes that children must master a set of skills before they can begin learning to read, while it is now clear that children gradually emerge as readers and writers. We know that children do not acquire literacy knowledge skill by skill, but rather they develop holistic understandings that then become refined. They learn about literacy through seeing it used around them (Goodman, 1986).

The reading readiness model teaches reading before writing. It assumes that children must learn to read before they can write, while it is now clear that children develop their knowledge about literacy through engaging in both reading and writing activities. Reading readiness instruction focuses on skills, ignoring the functional uses of reading, while it is now clear that children learn literacy skills through using reading and writing in functional ways. (Teale & Sulzby, 1986; Spodek & Saracho, 1993).

The reading readiness model assumes that the learning that children bring to school is not important as long as they are given enough instruction and practice in school. This approach sees children as passive in the learning process—if the teacher tells the children something, they learn it. It sees each child as an isolated learner, while it is now clear that learning about literacy is an active process (Spodek & Saracho, 1993). Children construct knowledge about literacy through interacting with readers and writers at home, in the community, and at school. This process of constructing begins at home and continues at school when it is encouraged and supported (Daiute, 1993; Gibson, 1989).

An Appropriate Model for Supporting Children's Emerging Literacy

If one discards the workbooks and skills drills of the reading readiness model, how will literacy be taught? Literacy should not be thought of as an isolated skill to be taught, but rather as an integral part of all aspects of the early childhood program (Teale & Sulzby, 1989). Children construct knowledge about literacy by being immersed in an environment where they can observe, practice, experiment with, and explore literacy.

What does such an environment look like?

1. It contains adults who model the functions of literacy by writing lists, making reminders, labeling things, writing letters, and reading recipes, books, notes, and directions. These adults see *children* as readers and writers. They communicate the expectation that children will use their emerging literacy skills. The environment invites children to use and expand upon their current literacy knowledge. Adults provide support for children to explore new skills or stretch

FIGURE 4-10 Adults model literacy

their current ones when this fits the child's current needs and interests. All levels of reading and writing development are accepted, encouraged, and celebrated by the adults.

2. Children are surrounded by print, such as labels, books, posters, signs, directions, messages, and lists. The print around them is incorporated into ongoing activities. They follow picture/word recipes when cooking, read books to the babies in the house, check the calendar to find when their birthdays are, look in a reference book to identify an insect that is crawling by, use signs to mark their buildings in the blocks, and check the message board to see if any are for them.

3. An assortment of writing materials are available, and writing becomes an integral part of children's activities. Children create signs for blocks or the play yard, place names on artwork, compose notes to friends or parents, contribute to newsletters, make shopping lists, and write things such as phone messages, letters, and instructions to sitters as a natural part of pretend play.

Although it is the atmosphere of the room that assures the best support to emergent literacy, rather than the specific activities, some broad general areas of activity are part of this environment: storybook reading, interaction with a variety of print, writing, and dramatic play. (Chapter 8 looks in more detail at the way storybook reading supports both literacy and dramatic play. Chapter 9 explores the diverse ways that early childhood settings offer experiences with reading and writing outside of the dramatic play area.) It is clear that activities related to reading and writing will support the development of emergent literacy, but why dramatic play?

FIGURE 4-11 Writing materials are available to make signs for the yard

Dramatic Play and Emergent Literacy: Natural Partners

Dramatic play and literacy are natural partners. To illustrate why, an example of some children engaged in dramatic play follows.

> *Play time has just begun in the four-year-old class. Carlos lies in the bed and begins to make fussing noises. Ashlinn claims the mother role and begins filling sheets of paper with strings of letters. Shakera tells Angel, "I'm the little sister and you're the big sister, all right?" She agrees and they both start getting dressed.*
>
> *Shakera goes over to the crying baby. "Quiet! Go to sleep!" Carlos continues crying. "Mom, the baby's crying."*
>
> *"Don't bother me, I'm working," responds Mom Ashlinn.*
>
> *"Here, I'll do it," says Angel pushing Shakera aside. "You make the dinner."*
>
> *Shakera protests, "I can't make the dinner! I am the little sister."*
>
> *"I know," Angel offers, "let's pretend we are twin big sisters. I'll take care of the baby and you make the dinner, okay?" Shakera agrees. Angel pats Carlos's back and says in baby talk, "What's the matter, baby? If I read you a story, will you go to sleep?" Carlos nods. Angel takes a book from the table by the bed and begins to tell the story, "Once upon a time . . . "*
>
> *Shakera takes two cans from the cupboard. One has beans on it the other has soup. "Do you want beans or soup?:" she asks the mom.*
>
> *"Soup," Mom answers. "Shh! I'm working."*
>
> *Shakera looks at the printing on the side of the soup can. "How do you make this?" she asks herself. She runs her finger along the print. "Here it is. Cook 2 hours." She pretends to empty the can into a pot and begins stirring.*

Dramatic Play Provides Real Life Reasons to Use Literacy

As can be seen in this example, dramatic play allows children to use their emergent literacy for meaningful real-life purposes as a means of accomplishing tasks (Hall, 1991). They are writing as a part of work, and reading to quiet the baby and to prepare dinner.

Dramatic Play Encourages Oral Language Development

According to Glazer (1989), dramatic play "is a powerful vehicle for guiding the growth of oral language" (p. 20). Oral language flourishes when children are in contexts where they desire to talk. Dramatic play provides children with such a context. The children playing house talk to each other as the characters within the story: "Don't bother me, I'm working." Children talk to themselves as the character in the pretend story: "How do you make this?" Talk is used in dramatic play to establish the roles and direction of the game: "Let's pretend we are twin big sisters. I'll take care of the baby and you make the dinner, okay?"

Playing different roles lets children experiment with the different types of language that fit the different roles. Babies speak baby talk, people calming the baby speak differently than an overworked mother demanding quiet.

Dramatic Play Involves Metacommunication

In order to pretend children must use **metacommunication**—"communication about communication" (Fein & Schwartz, 1986, p. 101) to establish that they are pretending—"let's pretend we are twin big sisters." Language is used explicitly to define objects, as when a child sits in a chair and says, "Let's pretend this is the car." It is also used explicitly to assign roles—"I'll be the mother"—and to define the action—"let's pretend it is dinner."

Giffin (1984) suggested that children use a variety of techniques to communicate to each other about the play. They move back and forth between speaking inside the play (as the actors in the story) and outside the play (as the children planning the story). Children prefer, when possible, to communicate within the play context. Ashlinn establishes the mother's activity without stepping outside the pretend story. She makes a statement as the mother: "Don't bother me, I'm working." Angel steps outside of her role as sister to make adjustments to the play—making Shakera an older sister, and assigning jobs. This moving from inside to outside the play takes linguistic skill. With more practice Angel will be able to communicate these guidelines without leaving her role (Fein & Schwartz, 1986). She might say, "Hi, big sister. Remember, it is my turn to take care of the baby and your turn to make the dinner."

Snow and Tabors (1993) suggested that

> children who have developed considerable metalinguistic skill in each of the language areas many be in a better position to analyze and learn about the oral/literate differences than children who have not (p. 7).

Dramatic play provides an opportunity to develop metalinguistic skills.

Dramatic Play Provides Practice in Constructing Narrative

Much written language involves **narrative**. Dramatic play involves creating stories, thus giving children practice composing narratives. In fact, Temple et al. (1993), who describe how children create written compositions, have referred to dramatic play as a form of composition that children can do even before they can write.

The talking about what is happening, or metalanguage, that occurs in dramatic play makes play language more like the language of books. Pellegrini (1986) suggests that

> the house keeping or dress-up areas encourage children to practice forms of language they will be expected to produce (in talking with teachers and in writing) and comprehend (in reading) throughout their school careers (p. 86).

In other words, dramatic play provides children with the opportunity to use oral language in ways that simulate written language, something that Snow and Tabors (1993) have said expedites emerging literacy.

Dramatic Play Supports the Wide Variations in Children's Emergent Literacy

When children are pretending, they can participate in literacy related activities in whichever ways are most comfortable for them. Ashlinn is a working mom making rows of scribble. Other children might write strings of letters, actually sound out some words, list words they know, write conventionally, or like Shakera not write, but be a part of pretend play where writing does occur. Angel can read to the baby by telling any kind of story, by telling a story that coincides with the pictures, by retelling the story that is in the book, or by actually reading the story. All children are able to participate comfortably at their own level of literacy.

Children Employ Symbols in Dramatic Play

Oral language is a system of symbols; written language is a more complex system of symbols. Dramatic play also is a system of symbols. Children use actions, props, and words to create symbols for the things they are imagining. Carlos's fussing communicates to the other children that he is the baby. He creates a symbol of baby to use in the play. Literacy develops from many experiences with symbolic activities. Saracho and Spodek (1993) suggested that the intellectual skills needed in literacy "result from a broad range of experiences with language and with other symbolic activity, including discourse with others, play and the arts" (p. xi). Vygotsky (1978)

FIGURE 4-12 Children discuss what should happen next in their pretend play story

saw symbolic activity and writing "as different moments in an essentially unified process of development of written language" (p. 116).

Putting the Partnership to Work

This chapter has explored the development of oral and written language and looked at the theoretical connections between literacy and dramatic play. The next step is to put this into practice. Chapter 5 will focus on how adults can design the early childhood center to make the most out of the partnership between literacy and dramatic play.

From All-Encompassing to Incidental: Different Modes for Integrating Literacy into Dramatic Play

Four-year-old Mark's doll is crying. He pretends to change its diaper. "You sit here, I'll get your breakfast" Mark assures the doll as he settles it in the high chair. Mark takes a can out of the refrigerator. He carefully checks the ingredients on the side of the can to be sure the food is good for babies before emptying it into the baby's bowl.

* * *

Avril, five years old, is striding around the room with a notebook and pencil in hand. The badge taped to her baseball hat proclaims that she is a REPORTER. She quickly scribbles down letter approximations as she watches the bustle of building in the block corner. She rushes back to the newsroom in the dramatic play area. She goes to the composing table and begins to carefully transcribe her notes in a more readable form to be the basis for her news flash on the block construction work she observed. When the story is done she goes to the set-up room to tape it onto the mock-up of the paper.

Both Mark and Avril are integrating literacy into their play, yet there is a significant difference in the importance that literacy plays in these two incidents. For Mark, the game revolves around baby and Dad. The glance at the ingredients was just a small piece of the play. In Avril's newspaper play, writing is definitely a central part of the activity.

Assessing the Literacy in This Dramatic Play

If observers were evaluating the literacy programs in Avril's and Mark's classrooms, how might they assess these two events? Clearly, Avril devotes most of her pretending time to writing. She goes through the steps of a writer, taking notes, looking at the notes, writing a draft, and revising the draft. Avril is using her writing in a context that is meaningful to her. She is using what she knows about letters to sound out the words that she writes. Working in the newspaper office appears to be a literacy activity that has intrinsic motivation for Avril.

The analysis of Mark's play is likely to vary in accordance with the astuteness of the observer. All observers will see Mark's involvement with the role of the caring daddy. But, because the literacy element of Mark's play is brief, it might easily be overlooked. If the label-reading incident is noticed by an observer, it might be viewed as too brief to have any value in Mark's development as a reading/writing person. A more discerning observer might realize that, for Mark, print is a part of many small tasks. Mark knows that checking ingredients is part of preparing food for babies. For Mark, reading is an integral part of the role of caring dad.

How Should Literacy Be Integrated into Dramatic Play?

When designing the dramatic play area to enhance literacy, what should teachers strive for? Is the newspaper play, where literacy is central, more valuable than Mark's incidental use of literacy? Is the incidental use of literacy just a chance occurrence, or is this something that adults can enhance and even plan for? How does a teacher know when the dramatic play is providing a rich, literate environment for play? This chapter will examine different ways in which literacy can be integrated into dramatic play, develop a framework for defining different modes of integration, discuss the relative merits of each mode, and explore the adult's role in supporting literacy.

Different Modes for Integrating Literacy into Dramatic Play

The vignettes at the beginning of the chapter illustrate two very different modes of integrating literacy into dramatic play. In the first example,

Mark spontaneously included literacy in his play. In contrast, Avril was participating in a adult-planned dramatic play activity where literacy was a central component. The differences between the two can be defined by three characteristics.

1. *The importance of literacy to the overall play:* in Mark's play literacy is incidental; in Avril's play it is central.
2. *Whether the use of literacy is child- or adult-initiated:* Mark initiates the use of literacy in his play, while Avril is involved in a writing activity introduced by the adult.
3. *Whether the use of literacy was planned or happened spontaneously:* Mark's reading of the label was spontaneous, while Avril worked at a newspaper office that had been preplanned.

Using these three factors to examine the use of literacy in dramatic play, four general modes of integration emerge.

1. *All-encompassing integration of literacy into dramatic play.* **All-encompassing integration** occurs when literacy is the focus of the dramatic play theme. The newspaper play is a good example of this mode of integration. The adult has planned and initiated a dramatic play that revolves around a theme dependent on written language.
2. *Enrichment integration of literacy into dramatic play.* **Enrichment integration** occurs when the adult adds written language to enrich a dramatic play theme that does not center around literacy. A good example of this is a restaurant dramatic play where the teacher adds menus and notepads to the play. Restaurant play could occur without these props, but the literacy activities enrich the play. The adult plans this dramatic play and initiates the literacy activities, but literacy is NOT central to the play theme.
3. *Incidental integration of literacy into dramatic play.* **Incidental integration** occurs when the teacher initiates literacy activities as a spontaneous response to the unfolding play. As a child is trying to settle down a doll at bedtime, the adult might suggest getting a book from the library corner to read to the baby. This type of integration is not preplanned. The adult initiates a literacy activity that might add to the evolving play. This type of integration is not central to the activity.
4. *Child-initiated integration of literacy into dramatic play.* **Child-initiated integration** occurs when children spontaneously incorporate literacy into their play without adult intervention. Mark's reading the can label is a good example of this. The use of literacy is unplanned, child-initiated, and not central to the play theme.

Table 5-1 illustrates the differences between the four modes of integrating literacy into dramatic play. Now let's take a detailed look at each.

TABLE 5-1 Four Modes of Integrating Literacy into Dramatic Play

MODE	IS IT PREPLANNED?	WHO INITIATES USE OF LITERACY?	IS LITERACY CENTRAL TO THEME OF PLAY?
All-Encompassing	Yes	Adult	Yes
Enrichment	Yes	Adult	No
Incidental	No, spontaneous use of literacy	Adult in response to children's play	No
Child-Initiated	No, spontaneous use of literacy	Child	No

All-Encompassing Integration of Literacy into Dramatic Play

All-encompassing integration of literacy into dramatic play occurs when teachers plan dramatic play themes such as the newsroom described at the beginning of the chapter. In these themes, writing is the central focus. To be part of a newspaper staff, for example, children must write stories and take notes on what people tell them.

Newspaper Play

Let's take a closer look at the newspaper office. It is set up in a kindergarten classroom. To start things off, the teacher brings a newspaper to group time. This begins a discussion about what is in a newspaper. The children all know what a paper is and each knows slightly different things about its content. This information is pooled. The teacher describes the reporting process. She tells the children that the reporter looks around for interesting events, observes the events, interviews people, and writes down what is heard and seen. Many children have seen people being interviewed on TV, where the information does not need to be written, since the interview will be recorded on tape. Because a newspaper must be read, the interview is different. The reporter must make notes, then use these notes to write a story for the paper.

Once children begin playing newspaper, it is interesting to observe them interviewing people. The children seem to realize that it is important to write fast to get down all that is being said. Michael and Andy can sound out words and arrive at a phonetic approximation. For kindergartners they are capable writers, but writing this way is a slow process. Because interviewers must record information quickly, Michael's and Andy's interview notes are hurriedly scribbled using random letters and marks rather than stopping to slowly sound out

FIGURE 5-1 A reporter searching for news

A STEP FURTHER   *Comparing Written and Oral Language*

The last chapter discussed the importance of encouraging children to talk about their language knowledge. A class discussion of the differences between a TV story and a newspaper story provides an excellent forum for children to think consciously about the different demands of oral and written language. To make this less abstract, the class could plan to report on class events for a parent meeting. They could talk about what parents might want to know about their class. They could make a video story about some events, and a written story about other events. This could lead to a discussion about what elements are required for each of the stories.

words. Writing slowly and accurately at this point would interrupt the flow of the pretending.

When Michael and Andy arrive back at the newspaper office, they begin writing the final draft of the story. Here their writing is slower and more precise. Other children, who have not yet mastered phonetic spelling, use random letters, letter-like marks, and pictures to record their stories. They also tend to do quick recording during the interview and more careful "writing" when back in the press room. This change in writing styles to fit the situation has been documented in the research of Sulzby and others. They found that children used less mature forms of writing to accomplish more mature compositional tasks, although the rereading of this writing was more mature (Sulzby, Barnhart, & Hieshima, 1989; Sulzby & Teale, 1985).

The children become involved in the newspaper play, but need a good deal of help from the teacher to understand what types of actions are expected of a newspaper employee. The teacher interviews the people playing in the blocks area to model interviewing. She helps some children by being a co-reporter. They talk about who they want to interview and what they want to know. By providing this type of scaffolding for children's play, the teacher enables the children to become involved and maintain play, which they might not have been able to do on their own. At times the teacher takes the role of interviewee or of editor. Once the children are involved in the play and have created roles that feel comfortable, the teacher steps back, leaving the children more in charge of the play. Some children need a good deal of support to get involved in the play; some children need only a little.

As stories are written, the teacher reads and discusses them with the author and with other interested children. The teacher's obvious interest in and pleasure with the stories give authorship a special honor. Children who have not yet been involved want to produce stories and be part of the exciting event of producing the class paper.

This all-encompassing mode of integrating literacy into dramatic play definitely does generate involvement with written language in this kindergarten. It also clearly requires a major time commitment from teachers.

Other Literacy Center Themes

Many of the other dramatic play themes that lend themselves to all-encompassing integration of literacy, such as "office" and "publishing house," are also distant from children's experiences, thus requiring some introduction. It is not really surprising that literacy themes tend to be unfamiliar to children. By their nature, activities that center around reading and writing are not likely to be ones that have involved nonreaders and nonwriters.

There are, however, two literacy-dominated themes that are likely to have been a part of a young child's life: going to the library and going to the post office. Although children are likely to have been to both places, they know them from an extremely narrow perspective.

Children know the library as a place to get books. They may realize that books have to be checked out before they can be taken home, but they are unlikely to know much about the librarian's role other than as someone who puts date cards in the books, and perhaps someone who reads stories. They are unlikely to know that books are sorted by types, that librarians sort the books and reshelve them, or the function of the card catalog. These are all things that children could learn about, but are not likely to have noticed. So like the newspaper play, library play may also need some initial introduction from the adult as well as some adult modeling of roles.

Post office play is another theme with which children will have a passing familiarity. Children will know a bit about the letter-mailing process, but may need some information and modeling from the adult to play post office in a more realistic way.

FIGURE 5-2 Mailing a
package is a familiar activity

Advantages of All-Encompassing Integration of Literacy

As compared to other modes of integration, all-encompassing integration definitely offers certain advantages.

Drawing Children into Literacy Activities.   This type of dramatic play draws children into literacy. It would be impossible to play in the library without using books. It would be impossible to be in the newspaper office without creating written text, or at least moving around other people's written language. For children who like to pretend, but who do not spontaneously choose literacy activities, this mode might offer them an entrance to the world of readers and writers. It might help them feel like insiders in the reading/writing process.

Dramatic play that focuses on literacy themes requires children to use written language in simulated real-life settings. They use written language in functional ways: to record a story, to find a library book, or to send a message through the mail. In the process of pretending they use the tools of literacy.

Making Adults Comfortable with Dramatic Play and Literacy.   The second advantage offered by dramatic play with all-encompassing integration of literacy is best illustrated by a story about a colleague.

> *When Patti first became the kindergarten teacher at a university lab school she did not realize the value of dramatic play. She had been trained in elementary education, which usually does not include dramatic play in the curriculum. Like*

many teachers, Patti did have a "house area" in her classroom where children could play pretend. It was stuck in a spare corner of her room, but she did not really know what to do with it.

In talking with the director one day, Patti asked, "Can I get rid of the dramatic play corner? It seems like a waste of space."

The response was, "In your classroom it is a waste." Patti grumbled about this conversation to me. She said she wanted extra space for language arts in her classroom. I suggested she could improve both her language arts and her dramatic play by centering the pretend play around some language arts theme: post office, library, newspaper, etc.

Patti designed a library for her room. It was exciting. She could see the importance of dramatic play, and also discovered the power of integrating literacy into this part of the classroom. Patti now has incredibly rich exciting dramatic play in her classroom. Often literacy is an important part of this play, but at other times the dramatic play is designed to support other aspects of the curriculum. She now sees the validity of simple house play.

For teachers like Patti, who are themselves not comfortable with dramatic play, all-encompassing integration of literacy is a good way to ease into using dramatic play in their childcare setting.

Converting Parents and Early Childhood Professionals Who View Dramatic Play as "Just Play."   Like Patti when she began at the lab school, many parents and administrators see dramatic play as "just play." When they see children playing house, the educational benefits are not apparent to them, but the literacy benefits of newspaper office, play are easily evident even to those who tend to doubt the value of more traditional dramatic play. When children are observed actively writing and editing in the newspa-

FIGURE 5-3 Library play involves children with literacy while they play pretend

per office, it is clear that they are "learning" not "just playing." Hopefully, seeing the educational value of newspaper play will lead these doubters to accept the validity of other pretend play as well.

Possible Problems Created by All-Encompassing Integration of Literacy

All things have two sides. While it is true that all-encompassing integration of literacy into dramatic play has many benefits, there are also three possible problems when adults choose this type of integration.

Heavy Demands on Adult Time.   As can be seen from the newspaper example, this type of integration can be extremely demanding of adult time. The teachers must provide background so that children know the kind of things that happen in a newspaper office. This can be done with stories, discussions, videotapes, or field trips.

Sometimes adults will have to do some homework to learn the background information they wish to provide to the children. The adult must design the dramatic play area so that the setting and props encourage newspaper play. The adult must also devote time to facilitating the play through modeling, asking questions, and celebrating the many interesting things that result. The teacher's involvement and excitement with play tells the children that this play is something the adult values, thus investing the play with a special status that encourages the children's participation.

Some argue that this amount of adult time is not necessary. They say that background information need not be supplied. If the props are provided children will use them in ways that are meaningful to them. If the resultant play isn't like an authentic paper, it really does not matter. It is true that authenticity is not important for all dramatic play. But it IS essential that children are acquainted with newspaper office procedures in order for this play to provide the benefits that we have discussed.

If the reason to use dramatic play to support emergent literacy is that such settings allow children to use reading and writing in functional ways and in real life settings, then it is important that children be comfortable enough and knowledgeable enough about the setting to make their play simulate the real-life situation. Thus, the adult time devoted to introducing, setting up, and facilitating the play is essential.

Teachers have many goals to accomplish and must apportion their time wisely. Dramatic play such as newspaper office or other themes in which all-encompassing literacy integration occurs can be offered occasionally, but not constantly. It is important to allow adults time to devote attention to other areas of the room and curriculum.

Accommodating Different Levels of Pretend Play.   Children vary in their ability to enter and maintain pretend play. For children who are just beginning to play pretend, it is important to have themes that are familiar and comfortable, themes centered around home activities such as cooking, eating, sleeping, childcare, and driving the car.

Children who are still involved in this beginning level of dramatic play may find it difficult to develop pretend play around the unfamiliar themes of newspaper or publishing house. If the theme is unfamiliar, the children may merely explore the materials and never move beyond this to use the materials in the context of their pretend play.

This does not mean that dramatic play with all-encompassing integration of literacy should be eliminated, but it does mean that teachers need to be aware that these children will need significantly more adult help. It is also important to balance this type of dramatic play with significant opportunities for simpler themes that better meet the needs of the novice pretenders.

Be Prepared for Less Mature Forms of Writing.   When using writing in pretend play, children often seem to regress to less mature forms of writing. In the newspaper office, Michael and Andy both used scribble writing to record their interviews, although both were able to sound out words and write them phonetically. If the boys had stopped to do their "best writing," they would not have been able to maintain the momentum of the pretend play.

It is important to assess the boys' writing experience not just from the product that results, but from the overall situation. Their verbal rereading of the notes was a detailed, accurate retelling of what they had observed. For them the writing was a prop in the process, rather than the medium that communicates their ideas (Dyson, 1993). Children who can write conventionally when involved in short projects will often use less mature writing when the task is above their current writing skills (Sulzby, Barnhart & Hieshima, 1989; Sulzby & Teale, 1985).

Adults who stress the importance of "good" writing are likely to turn the newspaper play into a formal writing activity rather than a context for pretending. Writing correctly is not the most important literacy experience that children get from this activity. Being part of the literate culture, and trying on pieces of this culture—such as taking notes quickly—is more important than writing correctly.

Enrichment Integration of Literacy into Dramatic Play

Julia, who has just turned four, is playing house. She has gotten her baby out of bed and is getting ready to feed it. She is about to open the refrigerator when she notices a pad of paper and pencil taped to the door. "What's this for?" she asks the teacher. Mr. Sanchez tells her it is a shopping list—if she needs anything at the store she can write it on the list. Julia glances inside the refrigerator and says, "We need milk. How do you write milk?"

FIGURE 5-4 Julia's writing of "milk" is second on the list

Mr. Sanchez says, "What do you think?" He sees she looks puzzled. He goes through the processes of sounding it out. Very slowly he says, "milk: m-m-m-m-m What do you think makes that sound? m-m-m-m."

"D", Julia says with great assurance as she writes that down on the paper. They continue sounding the word together. When done, Julia has written milk, "DLR". She rips the list off the refrigerator pad and finishes feeding her baby before going to the store (see Figure 5-4).

* * *

A doctor's office is set up in a four-year-old class. Kevin, the receptionist, sits at the small table in front of the examining room. He scribbles marks on his calendar as he discusses appointment times with a patient on the phone. In the waiting room Sachi reads a magazine to her baby while waiting for the doctor. The examining room has a scale, an eye chart, an examining table, and a supply shelf. The supply closet offers a wide variety of doctor's tools: stethoscopes, bandages, swabs, cotton balls, reflex hammers, prescription pads, and a clipboard with a place to record the patient's name, a picture of a scale to record the weight, a thermometer to mark the temperature and a place for recording symptoms. Each shelf of the closet has a sign proclaiming the contents of the shelf with both word and picture labels.

Ms. Chang, the teacher, is stretched out on the table. Doctor Patrick administers numerous shots. Doctor Helen wraps a long cloth bandage strip around Ms. Chang's legs. Doctor Paul is asking Ms. Chang questions about how she feels. He scribbles cursive-like marks onto his clipboard chart as she describes her symptoms. When the exam is done; Doctor Patrick writes some numbers on a small pad, and he gives her the "prescription" to take to the drugstore.

What Is Enrichment Integration of Literacy?

These are both examples of the second mode: enrichment integration of literacy into dramatic play. Unlike the newspaper office or library play, neither of these themes requires literacy. House play and doctor's office play can both be carried out without any reading or writing activities. Yet in each of these cases, the teacher has added props which will encourage children to use written language as part of their pretend play.

Dramatic play with enrichment integration of literacy can be as simple as a pad of paper taped to the refrigerator in the first example, or as elaborate as the three-room doctor's office in the second example. Even with the same theme, the level of integration can vary significantly. A doctor's office can have a few scraps of paper by the phone, or it can have calendars for appointments, charts for keeping patient's records, and pads for writing prescriptions. The writing can be a major part of the activity or a minor one. The choice between these will depend on the needs and interests of each particular class of children.

Adding Literacy to Doctor Play

The children in the doctor's office described above were immersed in their role playing. This was the third day that this office had been in the classroom.

The First Day of Doctor Play.   The doctor play looked quite different the first day. On that day the children were excited about the doctor's office. Everyone wanted to be there at once. Ms. Chang suggested that if everyone came at once it would be too crowded. She encouraged some children to come back later when there was more room. Even so, the area was crowded with the children who just could not wait.

FIGURE 5-5 For these doctors, writing prescriptions is an important task

Children did not do much pretending. They were too interested in examining and experimenting with all the wonderful tools. The doctors were in need of patients, but no one was willing to give up the tools to be a patient. Ms. Chang became the patient, as did the baby dolls.

Adult Support of Doctor Play.   As the newness of the setting wore off, Ms. Chang began asking questions to encourage dialogue between patients and doctors. "Doctor, do you think my stomach will feel better soon?" "Is there anything I should not eat?" "When would you like me to come back for another checkup?" She also facilitated discussion between children. "Doctor Helen, it looks like Marcus has hurt his arm. Did you ask him how he hurt it?"

At another point, Ms. Chang became the nurse who cared for the tools. She recruited Patrick's help to reorganize the supply closet so the doctors could find their tools. She handed Patrick the tools from the floor and the examining table. He had to find where they belonged, which made the previously ignored signs an important point of reference for him.

Doctor Chang elicited much language from her patients as she examined them. She recorded their symptoms and wrote out prescriptions for medicine. Soon other doctors were also taking notes and writing prescriptions. The teacher wisely gave the children some time to experiment with the materials, then helped them to expand their role play.

Some children moved easily from experimenting with props to pretending, whereas other children needed a bit of help from teachers to become comfortable in their pretend roles. As Ms. Chang found, children who are less skilled at dramatic play may need the teacher's help for a longer period of time. At some point, though, the perceptive teacher gradually pulls back from the play as children are able to continue independently.

The Literacy Options in Doctor Play.   In watching the doctor play in the example above, it is obvious that some children are intently involved with written language. For Kevin the receptionist, Sachi the reading mother, and Patrick the note-taking doctor, reading and writing are an integral part of the play. Other children spend their time giving shots, listening to hearts, and applying bandages, ignoring the available literacy materials.

Doctor play need not be as elaborate as the above example, nor must the play include as many different forms of written language. Here is a simpler, but no less captivating, example of doctor play from another four-year-old classroom.

> *A cot is placed near the house area. Near it is a table with two pretend syringes, two stethoscopes, an empty bandaid box, and a pad and paper. The children come over from the house to be examined by the doctor. Some doctors make a point of writing out prescriptions on the pad, but others do not.*

FIGURE 5-6 The cookbook prompted children to read the recipes and to cook

Although this arrangement is simpler, it too offers the children the opportunity to try on the roles of doctor and patient, to use verbal language appropriate to these roles, and to integrate writing in a functional way into their pretend play.

If the doctor play is done with three-year-olds, the writing would play an even smaller part. The adult would strive to encourage verbal language between the doctors and patients. Verbal language used in play will become the basis for later integration of written language into the play. The adult, as the doctor, may pretend to write out a prescription for the patient to take to the pharmacist. Even if the children do not choose to write themselves, they see written language as part of going to the doctor.

Adding Literacy to Other Themes

Enrichment integration of literacy can be added to any dramatic play theme. Some themes, like house play, lend themselves easily to the inclusion of literacy activities. Written language is a natural part of most homes: Writing letters, making lists, reading, checking the calendar, following recipes, and making notes while on the phone are all common household activities. Menus are a natural part of restaurants, just as shopping lists and signs belong in the grocery store.

Other themes do not seem to lend themselves as readily to the inclusion of print, or at least not at first glance. Boat play is a theme that seems to require action, not reading and writing. People must pilot the boat, and there may be fishing, swimming off the side, or the household chores of eating and cleaning, as well as sleeping.

With a bit of practice adults can easily see the literacy potential in these less likely themes. Maps and charts can be studied to set the course.

A control panel with labeled dials will encourage sailors to check the boat's speed, direction, and other important factors. The addition of a radio to contact the shore will lead to message taking. If the boat has berths for sleeping, books can be nearby for the sailor's bedtime reading. With a bit of thought, and with practice, it becomes easy to see the literacy possibilities in even the most unlikely theme.

Advantages of Enrichment Integration of Literacy

Like all-encompassing integration, enrichment integration has both advantages and possible problems. When analyzing what enrichment mode integration of literacy offers, it is important to remember how varied dramatic play of this type can be.

A Gradual Entrance into Using Written Language. For children who do not yet see themselves as insiders in the reading/writing process, enrichment mode integration allows them to gradually move into these roles. As Siobhan is playing waitress at the restaurant, she may began to write on the pad because this is what she sees her classmates doing. For some children the addition of the pad on the refrigerator may be enough to generate writing. Being in an environment where others are involved with reading and writing, and where many literacy props are available, will offer children many opportunities and enticements to become involved as well.

A Wide Range of Developmental Levels Are Accommodated. Children vary in both their interest and skill at using written language. In dramatic play

FIGURE 5-7 One child integrates literacy in his house play; his friend does not

FIGURE 5-8 This child writes a pizza order for the cooks in the pizza parlor

with enrichment integration of literacy, children are free to respond at a wide variety of levels. In doctor play, for example, written language can be a major part of the child's play; it can be a cursory part; or the child can play doctor without any direct involvement with written language. Yet even for children who do not choose to incorporate written language into their role play, they are still part of an environment where these materials are being used.

Children also vary in their skills at pretending. Enrichment integration can be added to simple family-related themes so that those children who still need many chances to play out familiar roles can have that opportunity. Other children stretch their role play by incorporating written language, or more complex plots, into these simple themes.

The Demands on Adult Time Need Not Be Great.   This type of integration need not require great expenditures of adult time. Unlike some of the all-encompassing literacy themes, many of the enrichment themes are familiar, and thus do not require the adult to provide as much background information. Because children know the theme better, they will not need as much assistance from the adult to enter or maintain this play. We all recognize that teacher's time is limited. Planning a time-intensive activity in the dramatic play area will reduce the amount of time adults can devote to other things, so it is important to balance the amount of time such preparation requires.

Some enrichment themes may be less familiar—few children have been in a castle, but it is a setting that, with some introduction, offers great potential for play. Some enrichment themes use written materials that may be new to children, such as navigation charts on a boat. Teachers can choose less time-intensive dramatic play when they have more demands in other areas of the room. When other demands are not as great, more elaborate dramatic play can be prepared, if this is indicated by children's needs and interests.

Using Written Language in Real-Life Settings.   Emergent literacy experts stress the importance of having children interact with written language in real-life settings where writing and reading are used for functional purposes (Teale & Sulzby, 1986; Harste & Woodward, 1989). Children see written language used in many settings: In restaurants they see menus and order pads; at the grocery story they see signs, labels, shopping lists, and receipts; and at home they see books, letters, lists, and TV guides. Dramatic play of house, store, and restaurant themes can recreate the common ways that children meet literacy in their environment. These play settings offer children the opportunities to use written language in functional ways in simulated real-life settings.

Often the addition of written language brings the children's pretend play closer to reality. Including menus and order pads adds a reality to a restaurant dramatic play that is missing when the written language is omitted. By including written language in familiar everyday themes, print becomes an integral part of everyday life both for the user of print and for the child who is playing in an area in which it is used.

Introducing Adults to the Joy of Using Literacy in Pretend Play. Early childhood educators have long resisted the inappropriate pushes from parents and elementary school teachers to include more "academic" learning in the preschool. Young children learn best through play and hands-on experiences, not through formal instruction in reading and writing. Teachers who have come to equate written language instruction with developmentally inappropriate teaching methods may feel uncomfortable planning ways to involve children in written language.

Adding small amounts of print to dramatic play—a shopping list on the refrigerator, a pad by the receptionist's phone, or books by the bedside—will allow these adults to see the great power and excitement that using written language can have for young children. Even Julia, who had not a clue about how to write real words, was proud of her ability to make a shopping list for "milk." As adults begin to see written language as an integral part of play, they will expand the ways in which they enrich dramatic play with print.

Possible Problems of Enrichment Integration of Written Language into Dramatic Play

Although enrichment integration of written language into dramatic play offers many advantages, this type of integration also sets a few traps which adults must be careful to avoid.

Beware of Overusing Certain Props or Forms of Writing. Do not allow yourself to get complacent about the way that written activities are integrated. It is easy to find a favorite way to add print to dramatic play, then unthinkingly use this technique for every type of dramatic play. If children were excited by the clipboards used for recording the patient's symptoms in the doctor's office, it is easy to use the clipboard again and again as the means of writing—a clipboard for shopping lists, for waiters and waitresses, for taking notes in a science lab—until this means of using print becomes stale.

Add variety by having receipt books for the restaurant, pads of stapled-together scrap paper for taking notes in the entomology lab, little books for recording discoveries at the archeological dig, and perhaps tape and large sheets of paper to add advertisements to the grocery store. These small variations help to keep the dramatic play fresh and exciting. The old props—clipboards, extra pads, extra books, and so on—can be recycled into the writing center to be available for more spontaneous literacy events.

Beware of Making Writing a Mandated Task. It is important to always remember that the written language is added to enrich, not dominate, the play. The value of this type of integration is that children can use writing in a natural, comfortable way. It should not be a required part of the activity.

It is great to have a place to make a shopping list before going to the grocery store. If children do not seem to notice this option, the adult might elicit interest by modeling list writing. "Let's see, I'd better make a shopping list before I go to the store. Yi Bai, can you check the refrigerator and see what we need at the grocery store?" When at the store, the adult might enlist the grocer's assistance to find various things she has on the list. These methods may draw Yi Bai into list making, but they may not.

If Yi Bai does not make lists (or engage in other literacy activities) even after adult modeling, there may be several possible reasons: She is too interested in actually shopping and in using the cash register to stop to make a list, the plot of her pretend story may not require writing, or list making may not be a form of writing that carries meaning for her at this time. If adults force children to write, explaining that today in order to go to the grocery store, you must first write a list, then the writing no longer becomes a joyous, meaningful activity. Even though she is not directly using written language, Yi Bai is a part of a play environment where print is used in a functional way.

Remember, the writing in dramatic play should be something that children feel is an integral part of their play and their lives, not something that the adult artificially imposes on that play. When the writing is integrated in a meaningful way, it will develop naturally.

FIGURE 5-9 Making his own membership card for the health center is necessary if he wants to exercise

Incidental Integration of Literacy into Dramatic Play

Incidental integration occurs when the teacher initiates literacy activities as a response to the children's unfolding play. This type of integration is not preplanned. Sometimes this mode of integrating literacy is as simple as suggesting, "Would you like to add a sign to your building so everyone will know it is an apartment building?" or encouraging a child to read to the baby that is crying at bedtime. What seems a small addition to the play can sometimes have a major impact on the direction of the play, as can be seen in the following incident.

Cheng-Ming is a quiet, slow moving four-year-old, who tends to look for adult interaction rather than initiate play with other children. Today he comes to the adult and says, "Miss Mommaday, Patrick is a policeman." Patrick is wearing a blue blazer with a crest on the pocket, a tie, and a captain's hat bearing an anchor insignia over the brim. It is clear from the tone of Cheng-Ming's voice and the longing in his eyes that he wishes to be a police officer with Patrick.

Police officer play is not something that Miss Mommaday usually encourages in her classroom as it tends to lead to aggression, wildness, and general nonconstructive behavior, yet it is obvious that a police outfit would allow Cheng-Ming to enter play with a classmate. Miss Mommaday finds a baseball hat, and prints POLICE on some scrap paper that Cheng-Ming tapes to the brim. Cheng-Ming cannot read, but the writing does give the hat an air of importance. In the wardrobe she finds another coat and tie. Of course, Miss Mommaday is then approached by many more aspiring police officers. She searches for extra coats and ties.

A few minutes later the police officers are shooting finger guns. "Wait!" says Miss Mommaday. "Police officers don't hurt people. They are good."

"We're shooting the bad guys," the children reply.

Miss Mommaday asks, "What did these people do wrong?"

They robbed some things," proclaim the officers.

Miss Mommaday explains, "Yes, that is very bad, but we don't need to kill them. We should give the bad guys tickets so they know they are not allowed to steal things." Miss Mommaday gets a pile of paper from the scrap box, which she staples together into ticket books. Soon the police officers are busily writing out their tickets. Some children use strings of letters, some use letter-like marks, others use wavy, script-like lines, and still others use pictures.

Matthew does not write. He just stares at the ticket pad in puzzlement saying, "It's supposed to be rectangles. How can I rip it?" Miss Mommaday is confused for a moment, then realizes that Matthew is thinking of theater or amusement park tickets that come in a long roll and are ripped off one at a time. She gets him some long thin strips of paper from the scrap box so he can rip the little rectangles that he needs.

Matthew tells Miss Mommaday, "You have to do the writing." When Miss Mommaday asserts that it is Matthew's job to do the writing, he says in amazement, "Are you crazy? I don't know how to write." Miss Mommaday's suggestion that he can "just pretend" receives a blank stare.

"Deja is just pretending. Maybe he can show you how to do pretend writing." Matthew looks at Deja's line of stick people and begins making circles and lines on his little rectangles.

With some help from the adult, Matthew begins to see himself as someone who can create pretend writing.

Not only did a few bits of stapled paper and a comment from the adult divert the children from gun play, but it also generated tremendous interest in writing. Each child wrote at his or her own developmental level. The adult's faith and encouragement helped those who were unsure to feel confident in their ability to be writers. These children were part of the reading/writing culture.

As with the other two modes of integration, incidental integration has both pros and cons. Since many of the same virtues and problems apply to the child-initiated integration, the relative merits of both will be discussed after the section on child-initiated integration.

Spontaneously thinking of meaningful ways to add literacy to children's play is not easy at first. But the more adults push themselves to integrate literacy into play, the easier it becomes to see the unlimited possibilities for doing so.

Child-Initiated Integration of Literacy into Dramatic Play

In this mode of literacy integration, the child is the one to initiate the use of written language. The description of Mark's reading the baby food label at the beginning of the chapter is a typical example of child-initiated integration of literacy into dramatic play. Often children will spontaneously reuse written language in ways that adults have introduced earlier in the year. Children who have recorded symptoms on the clipboards in the doctors office may look for these writing props months later when a sick baby in the house play requires a visit from the doctor. Having a place where children can go to get favorite writing props will allow children to continue play themes which have personal meaning (Chapter 9 discusses how to arrange the environment to support this type of child-initiated writing).

Sometimes children will create their own literacy props for their play.

Frank, a teacher in a mixed age class with two-and-one-half to five-year-olds, adds many travel props to dramatic play this week. He knows many families are planning trips. A row of child-sized cardboard boxes with cardboard steering wheels serve as cars, trains, planes, or other desired modes of transportation. Suitcases are waiting to be packed, maps are taped to the wall and folded by the suitcases to allow children to plot their courses of travel. Some children incorporate maps into their play, others do not.

The maps make a strong impression on three-year-old Brian. He is going on a trip to Grandma's next month and many maps have been examined at home. Brian puts a pile of clothes in a purse and stuffs it under the chair he is using as

FIGURE 5-10 This child's self-initiated writing has great personal meaning

a car. Before he begins his trip he gets some paper and markers from the writing shelf. He scribbles some lines and a series of letters on a piece of paper. Now that he has his own map he can start the trip.

Frank can see that Brian is deeply involved in his own play. Adult intervention at this point would be distracting. Later he will stop by to exclaim over the marvelous map.

Often, as in Brian's case, home experiences prompt children to integrate written language into their pretend play.

Gabriella's parents are both professors. She has often seen them preparing lectures at home. One day four-year-old Gabriella dresses up to go to work. She leaves her baby doll with Kevin who is babysitting for many busy mothers. She goes to the writing area and begins typing a page full of random letters. Miss Kelly, childcare provider, stops to observe Gabriella's work. "Are you typing something special?"

"Yes," Gabriella tells her. "I am typing my lecture." The provider asks what the lecture is about. She is told, "It is a lecture on how to be smart." Miss Kelly asks some further questions about the lecture.

It is clear that Gabriella does not realize that lectures are about something, though she knows clearly that her parents write lectures to make their students smarter. Although Gabriella's understanding of "lectures" is incomplete, she does perceive "writing lectures" as an important activity in the adult world that she knows.

The teacher wisely does not try to instruct Gabriella about lectures, because it is clear that such knowledge is unneeded. Playing an adult who can type lectures that make people smart already has great personal meaning for Gabriella.

Often literacy events seem to derive jointly from both the teacher and the child. The child may make a comment about the need for a sign, a map, or some other form of written language. The teacher then expands on the child's comment to create a rich literacy experience. This is clearly illustrated by an incident that occurred in a four-year-old class.

> *Tanya, the teacher, reads* Christina Katerina and the Box *(Gauch, 1971) to the class. It is about a girl who turns a big box into a club house, a boat, a castle, and many other pretend things. The next day the children paint their own special pretending boxes. Like the box in the story, their boxes go through many changes of identity.*
>
> *During free play Julia turns her box into a house. She uses markers to add windows and furniture to the inside of the box. As she examines the outside she says, "My house needs a mailbox."*
>
> *Tanya exclaims loudly, "A mailbox! What a wonderful idea, then I can send you letters." Other children hear this exchange and also want mailboxes for their boxes, which have suddenly become houses. Tanya and the many box dwellers staple paper into pocket-like mailboxes, which are proudly taped to the outside of the each box.*
>
> *The children begin busily writing letters and delivering them to each other's houses. Kathy decides she needs numbers on her mailbox just like the numbers on her mailbox at home. "What a great idea!" says Tanya, "then the letter carrier will know your address and be able to deliver your letters." Other children also add numbers to their mailboxes. Kathy is so pleased with her idea that she copies Julia's "address" onto the letter that she is about to deliver to Julia's mailbox. The letter play continues for the next few days. Some children spend a great deal of time writing and reading letters. Others deliver a few then move on to other things.*

Each of these settings provides an environment that encourages the use of written language. Supplies for writing are readily available, as are props that children can use to enact play themes that are personally meaningful. Teachers are available to celebrate and encourage children's written language, but also know the importance of not interfering too much.

The Value of Incidental and Child-Initiated Integration of Literacy into Dramatic Play

Both the incidental and the child-initiated modes of integrating literacy into dramatic play provide real-life opportunities to use written language in meaningful ways. The teacher who uses tickets to redirect unconstructive play and the child who types a lecture because that is what Mommy does at work are both using written language in order to accomplish something.

Children can see when and where adults turn to written language. They see how naturally written language fits into the everyday events. The models provided by adults encourage children to integrate written language into their own play. Children gain experience as people who turn to written language to enrich every day activities.

Cautions about Incidental and Child-Initiated Integration of Literacy into Dramatic Play

Early childhood educators must work to avoid some faulty assumptions about both these modes of literacy integration.

Faulty Assumption #1: Incidental Integration Does Not Take Any Forethought from the Adult. One could easily assume that incidental integration of literacy is something that "just happens." However, if teachers are not used to integrating literacy into dramatic play, they will not spontaneously come up with ideas that combine pretending and literacy.

At first adults will need to think about and consciously work on finding ways to add written language to the children's unfolding play. They may need to review the type of play that happened that day and think of how they can "spontaneously" integrate literacy if the same type of play occurs the next day. With experience they will become better able to come up with appropriate literacy ideas in response to children's play.

Faulty Assumption #2: Child-Initiated Integration Occurs Spontaneously without Need of Adult Encouragement. As with incidental integration, one must not assume that child-initiated integration of literacy is something that "just happens." When it is not happening in the early childhood environment, the adult could erroneously blame it on the children. "They don't have books at home." "These children are just not ready yet." If children are not using print in their pretend play, it is because the adult has not created an environment that values and encourages this use. Adults must model the use of print in play. They must provide children with needed tools and props, along with many opportunities to become people who see themselves as readers and writers. When this is done and children are given time to develop these skills, then children WILL spontaneously integrate literacy into their pretend play in developmentally appropriate ways.

Faulty Assumption #3: The Same Prompts from Adults Will Always Result in the Same Type of Literacy Experiences for Children. It is easy to assume that if one class was excited about tickets or mailboxes, then other classes will share this same excitement. Adults must remember that each class is unique. Some children will find the suggestion of mailboxes captivating; others won't. Adults must tune in to the children to know which suggestions to pursue and which to let go.

Faulty Assumption #4:   Literacy Ideas Are the Most Important Direction That Adults Can Add to the Child's Play. This book describes how to add written language experiences to children's pretend play. This can provide a wonderful rich way to make children part of the reading/writing culture, but it is wrong to assume that this is always the "best" way adults can facilitate children's play. Adults need to sensitively observe children's dramatic play before stepping in with additional modeling, props, or ideas.

If the children in the doctor's office are enacting shot giving in order to cope with fears they have about the doctor, then prescription pads may not be the scaffolding that is most needed. Instead, the adult should facilitate discussion about shots, and other worrisome procedures that may occur at a doctor's office. Enacting the role of doctor, and being in control of the syringe that inflicts the pain, may make the fear more manageable.

Which Is the Best Mode of Integrating Literacy into Dramatic Play?

The glamour of the newspaper office and the elaborateness of the doctor's play are impressive, but the simple writing of shopping lists and reading to a baby doll are equally valuable experiences with written language. It is not the case that if a little literacy in dramatic play is good a lot must be better. Each mode of integrating literacy into dramatic play offers unique opportunities to children. Adults must insure that a balance between all modes of integration is provided.

How is this balance created? As an early childhood professional, where should you begin? You should start where you feel most comfortable. If you are uncomfortable with writing, think of dramatic play as the focus and integrate small amounts of enrichment-mode integration. Let the dramatic play gradually show you the excitement of using written language in pretend play. If you are uncomfortable with dramatic play, then begin with all-encompassing integration. Let the writing experience introduce you to the value of pretend play. Wherever you start, practice will make you better able to see the wonderful possibilities and opportunities offered to children when dramatic play and literacy are combined.

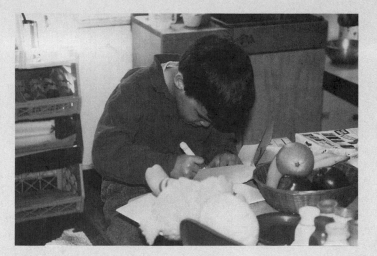

CHAPTER 6

Variations on Dramatic Play Themes: Many Faces of Restaurant Play and Other Themes

How do early childhood professionals know the best way to set up for a specific dramatic play theme? Is there a best way? How can literacy materials and activities be integrated into different dramatic play themes to enrich the play? In order to answer these questions, this chapter will explore variations on restaurant play, then look at variations on other themes.

Let's visit three early childhood settings where different types of restaurant play are occurring.

Matt, the headwaiter and cashier at the Kindergarten Cafe, sits at a small table with a big reservations book, a phone, and a cash register. Beside him is a chalkboard where he scribbles strings of cursive-like writing to tell customers about today's l.

Ashanti and Belinda are at one of the two tables inside the restaurant. They are looking at menus that have foods listed by picture and name. Jeremy is waiting for their order. He has a clipboard with an order pad and pencil attached.

The second table is piled high with food and dishes left by the last customers. It is Lesley's job to bus the table. She is wearing a long white apron and carrying a large plastic bin. She piles the mess from the table into her bin and takes it to the kitchen. Pergi, the teacher, helps her sort the food into the food tray and the dishes into a large cardboard box labeled, DISHWASHER. Lesley pushes one of the buttons on the front of the box, makes a humming noise, then unloads the dishes onto the shelf and the silverware into her bin. She carries this back to the table and sets the table by matching the silverware to the outlines on the place mats.

Jeremy finishes writing down the order and takes it back to the kitchen. Angel, the cook, is wearing a tall paper chef's hat. "One hamburger, one spaghetti," he tells her. She sorts through the tray of cardboard food pictures that match the ones on the menu. She puts a hamburger and some spaghetti in a large pot, stirs for a few minutes with her spoon, then puts each picture on a plate and hands it to Jeremy, who delivers it to the customers.

* * *

Three-year-old Masoud and Jacalyn are putting on dressup coats, hats, and shoes. "Boy, you're all dressed up. Where are you going?" asks Ms. Cerasi.

"I'm going to Friendly's for dinner," Jacalyn answers. After the children are dressed they walk around the room two or three times and come back and sit down at the table in the dramatic play area. "Let's pretend you're the waiter," Jacalyn suggests to Masoud.

"I want to eat too!" he insists.

"Do you need someone to take your order?" Ms. Cerasi asks.

Four-year-old Wendy, who had been dressing a doll, proclaims, "I'll be the waitress." She hands each of the children a book saying, "Pretend these are menus. What will you have?" As the children order, Wendy pretends to write down what they say on her hand. She puts some plastic vegetables into a pot, and plunks it on the table. "Here." They pretend to eat, then go to the wardrobe to change clothes. They repeat the walk around the room to the table. This time Francie is the waitress.

* * *

Mr. Adams, the teacher in a four-year-old class, works at a pizza restaurant several evenings a week. The pizzas are made assembly-line fashion, then placed on a conveyer belt that carries the pizza through the oven and drops it out the other end when it is finished cooking. He thinks the children will be fascinated with the oven. Unfortunately, the restaurant is too far away for a field trip, so he takes some photographs of the restaurant, which he mounts in a book, telling the story of how pizzas are ordered, made, and eaten at his restaurant.

After hearing the book, the children then play in a pizza restaurant that is like the one where Mr. Adams works. The dramatic play area is divided in half with a long counter. On one side of the counter are two small tables. Each has a table cloth and a vase of flowers. Mr. Adams and Francie are sitting at one of the tables eating their pizzas.

On the counter are pencils and order sheets with a place to check the desired size of pizza and the ingredients. A line at the bottom is for the customer's name. Charlie stands behind the counter taking orders. "Do you want a large pizza?" he asks Abby. When she responds in the affirmative, he puts a mark in the box next to the big circle. He then asks her about each topping in turn and checks the appropriate boxes. "It will be ready in 2 hours," he tells her. She goes to wait at the table.

Charlie takes the slip to the long table in the center of the kitchen. In front of him is a box divided into segments for holding the different ingredients. On one side of the table are a pile of small red cardboard circles, and a pile of large ones. Charlie looks at the order sheet, picks out a large circle and piles on paper mushrooms and pepperoni. As he is doing this, Mr. Adams and Abby bring back the pizzas they have finished eating and sort the toppings into the appropriate bins.

Once the pizza is ready, Charlie takes it to the pizza oven, which is on a table against the wall. The oven is made out of a long thin box with a stiff cardboard tube running from front to back at either end. A heavy stretchy material has been sewn into a cylinder and stretched over the tubes to make the conveyer belt. When the tubes are turned, the cloth moves. Large holes are cut in the sides of the box so the pizza can be placed on the conveyer belt at one side and removed at the other side (see Figure 6-1).

After sending the pizza through the oven, Paul delivers it to the counter. Charlie calls Abby, "Your pizza is ready. That will be thirty twodee dollars." She pretends to pay him and takes the pizza to the table to eat it.

These visits show three distinctly different ways of playing restaurant. The Kindergarten Cafe has specific roles for the workers and elaborate props. Friendly's is played spontaneously with the children creating props as they are needed. The pizza restaurant has a specific process for the cook to follow. Which way is best? Should you try to do them all? Let's look more carefully at what types of learning are occurring in each of these examples.

Objectives for Restaurant Play

What objectives might the adults have set for each of these restaurant episodes?

FIGURE 6-1 Watching as the pizza moves through the oven

Learning in the Kindergarten Cafe

The teacher who designed the Kindergarten Cafe might have been thinking of the following objectives:

1. Children will engage in cooperative play, with each child playing a distinct role.
2. Children will build an awareness of the social roles and interactions that occur in a restaurant.
3. Children will work out solutions to social problems when they arise. Although it was not shown in the small sample of play described, the children did need to negotiate who played what roles. They needed to negotiate the direction the play would take when one child wanted to close the restaurant for cleaning, while the other children still wanted to come to eat.
4. Children will practice language fluency through giving and taking orders, taking reservations, conversing at the restaurant, and discussing what will be played and how.
5. Children will use written language in functional ways when reading menus, taking orders, taking phone messages, marking down reservations, and writing down the specials.
6. Children will use matching and classification skills when sorting food and dishes, selecting foods, and setting the table.
7. Children will exercise motor skills in writing, setting and clearing the table, cooking, and dressing up to go to the restaurant.

Learning at Friendly's

While the children are playing Friendly's, these objectives may be met:

1. Children will increase their ability to make believe with regard to objects. They imagine a book is a menu, and pretend the existence of a pencil and order pad.
2. Children will use written language in a functional context when reading the menu and taking orders.
3. Children will construct and implement their own play.
4. Children will increase their language fluency through conversing within the dramatic play, and through planning the play. Ordering requires more language here than in either of the other restaurants. In the other restaurants, children can point to pictures on the menu or order sheet; here they must rely totally on verbal language.
5. Children will work to resolve problems that arise in play with minimal help. The children needed a little adult help to mediate a dispute over roles, then they were able to divide the roles on their own.

Learning at the Pizza Parlor

The children at the pizza parlor were also learning in many ways. Mr. Adams might have had these objectives in mind as he planned and guided this activity:

1. Children will use written language in a functional way in taking orders and using order sheets to select ingredients for the pizza.
2. Children will practice skills in picture reading.
3. Children will practice writing their own names and perhaps the names of classmates.
4. Children will match ingredients to the order sheet and to the correct container when putting them away.
5. Children will correctly follow a sequence of events for pizza preparation.
6. Children will expand their understanding by exploring the workings of the pizza oven.

Selecting the Best Form of Restaurant Play

Now that we have seen the variety of objectives, let's return to our earlier question. Which way of playing restaurant is best? All three ways of playing restaurant foster many important areas of learning. Perhaps the answer is to combine the best points of each in order to achieve all the objectives at once. Although this may be appealing to the adult, it would actually not be possible. If combined into one play setting, some of the objectives would work against each other. At the Friendly's, children design and implement their own play, while the sequence following of the pizza parlor requires adult-made materials and an adult-organized manner of playing.

Often, trying to accomplish too much can make the play situation overwhelming and dilute the activity's effectiveness. Mr. Adams could have added a cash register and money to his pizza parlor, so children could use money and math in a functional manner. He could have added drinks and salads to the menu to provide more jobs and to introduce other foods. However, either of these additions would have interfered with the simplicity of the setup, a simplicity that made clear the sequence of actions that children were to follow.

Rather than trying to accomplish everything with a particular episode of the restaurant play, adults should pick a focus or organizing goal for the play. In selecting a focus, think about the children's interests, the skills that children are working on, available resources, and the amount of time available for preparing the area.

Most important, teachers should consider the developmental level of the children when planning dramatic play. If children do not yet play cooperatively, then a restaurant modeled after the Kindergarten Cafe would not be appropriate, since it requires children to be able to sustain cooperative play. For these children, it would be more appropriate to design a more free-flowing restaurant, where children may move comfortably between roles, perhaps ordering, cooking, and serving their own food.

If a number of options seem appropriate, remember that the restaurant theme can be repeated a number of times over the year, employing a different focus and arrangement if desired. Including the children in the planning process insures that the resulting restaurant incorporates those things most important to them.

And Still More Restaurants

The three examples at the beginning of the chapter were just a few of the many ways for implementing restaurant play. If none of these options fits the needs of a specific group of children, here are a number of other possibilities. No matter how many options are described, it is unlikely that the perfect focus for each unique group will be listed; however, seeing many options will provide a wide array of ideas to use as a springboard for designing the type of restaurant play to best meet the interests and needs of your children.

Color Restaurant

The color food restaurant encourages color matching, use of color words, and expansion of food word vocabulary. Foods are separated on the menu by color. A green page has such things as beans, broccoli, peas, salad, and spinach pasta. In the kitchen the food is stored by color. Children can order a surprise meal by asking for two red foods, and one green food. The order sheet has boxes that the children fill in with the color(s) they wish to eat. The cook matches up the food by color to the order pad. Children can help to make the menus by cutting out foods from magazines and gluing them on the appropriate pages.

Healthy Food Restaurant

A healthy food restaurant is set up to support a class unit on nutrition and healthy foods. The menu is divided into food groups. Children are encouraged to order one thing from each food group. Of course, some children order in silly ways. Joe doesn't like vegetables so he orders a hot dog for his vegetable course and giggles. In order to be silly, purposefully getting it wrong, Joe must know which foods belong in the vegetable group. For an older class, the menu could be divided into three sections—breakfast, lunch, and dinner—with each meal having subsections for each food group.

Children have a chance to use what they know about foods in a functional way. Their knowledge of food groups and nutrition is expanded. Children may also learn about new foods and have an opportunity to hear and use a large food vocabulary.

Plant Parts Restaurant

During a unit on plants, one class explores the many different types of plants that people eat. They also learn about the different parts of plants, and then look at the different parts of plants that people eat: flowers such as cauliflower and broccoli; leaves such as lettuce and cabbage; stems such as celery; seeds such as peas and beans; and roots such as onions, carrots, and potatoes.

The menu is divided into parts of plants, with a page of seeds, a page of roots, a page of stems, and so on. Foods are sorted by type in the kitchen. Rather than ordering specific foods, children order by plant part—one root and two stems. The order sheet has a picture of each plant part, with two or three boxes after it for checking how many of each part the customer would like. The cook finds foods from the appropriate groups to put on the plates.

FIGURE 6-2 The customer is checking off his selections on the order form

This style of restaurant gives children an opportunity to use written language in functional ways, as they read the menus, record the orders, and read the orders to select the appropriate foods. They practice classifying foods by the part of the plant. They also hear and use vocabulary related to food and plant parts.

Drive-In Restaurant

In one class, drive-in restaurant play began spontaneously. One child was sitting on a bench shouting, "Hot dogs for sale!" Other children rode up on their bikes and asked for the food they wanted. The restaurant worker handed the child pretend food and received pretend money.

Pretend drive-in play can also be done more elaborately. A box, playhouse, hollow block enclosure, or puppet theater is used as the drive-up window. Signs are posted announcing the restaurant name and the foods that are available. Empty containers from McDonald's, Burger King, or some other fast food restaurant are available.* A large box serves as a recycling bin so that children can deposit their containers when they are finished eating. The restaurant workers retrieve the containers from here to use again.

Order sheets have pictures and names of the foods offered. As the order, is given children check off the appropriate foods and then use the order sheet to select the needed containers. Drive-in restaurant can be played with distinct roles: an order taker, an order filler, and a customer; or one child can play many roles.

Depending on which variation is used, children will be using their imaginations to create food and money; using writing in a functional way; following a sequence of steps; using language to communicate their orders to the counter person, then from the counter person to the cook; and practicing reading environmental print (if food packages of a well known food chain are used).

Ice Cream Parlor

A kindergarten teacher sets this up simply. She wants children to figure out the prices of each order. Heavy cardboard cone-shaped spools from yarn are used as cones. Tag board rolled and taped in a cone shape will work as well. The ice cream is made from colored styrofoam balls. Some balls can have a bite-like chunk cut out of the bottom so they will stack onto the bottom scoop. A small toothpick inserted into the bottom of these

---

*Many fast food restaurants will give you new containers for this purpose. Do not use containers that have had food in them due to potential health problems.

scoops helps to secure them when stacked. Ice cream is stored by flavor in empty cylindrical ice cream containers.

Signs show the available flavors by color and name, and tell the prices for one, two, or three scoops. The prices are simple—one penny per scoop. A can of pennies is provided so children can pay for purchases. For older children the prices can be higher, requiring simple addition to discover the cost. A calculator can be used to determine or check the total. Larger coins or play money can be used for children who are learning the value of coins.

Ice Cream Parlor allows children to use money and numbers in functional ways. It lets them practice one-to-one correspondence in matching the number of scoops to the number of pennies. For those who are ready, it offers practice in simple addition. Children will sort scoops by color, so that the desired flavor is easy to find. Children will use language to communicate their orders. Children use small muscle skills to construct and carry the cones.

Ethnic Restaurant

Restaurants could also be set up for different types of food. Adults could pick restaurants that represent cultures of children in the group, or restaurants that are popular in the area. A visit to a restaurant of the desired type will help the adult plan which materials should be included. Let us look at one of these in more detail.

One class sets up a Chinese restaurant. Children bring in woks, chopsticks, spatulas, and bamboo steamers. The children help the teacher glue rice onto round pieces of cardboard and cut up pieces of brown, green,

FIGURE 6-3 Kitchen of a Chinese restaurant

and red paper to use as stir fry. A cupboard holds two teapots, small cups, plates, chopsticks, napkins, and cardboard carry-out containers.

Two tables are set up in the eating area with an unlit candle on each. A long counter separates the eating area from the kitchen. A cashier sits there with a phone, an order sheet, a cash register, menus, and carry out orders that are ready to be picked up. Signs around the restaurant advertise specials for the day.

Playing in the Chinese restaurant provides a more familiar setting for Asian and Asian American children. It allows them to share their culture with the class. The non-Asian children have the chance to become familiar with one small aspect of another culture. All the children will be able to use language, try on different roles, interact with each other, and exercise motor skills in making the food to use in the restaurant, in cooking the foods, and in serving the foods. Writing is used in functional ways—reading menus, writing down orders, and reading signs.

Dinner Theater

One kindergarten class particularly enjoys restaurant play and puppet theater. A sibling of one of the children had a small part in a local dinner theater, which a number of the families attended. Dinner theater was the

FIGURE 6-4 Dinner theater ticket booth

major topic of conversation after this event. Seeing this interest and their skill at playing both restaurant and puppet theater, the teacher decides to have a classroom dinner theater.

On one side of the room a ticket booth is set up. The ticket seller sets the clock to show when the next performance will begin, writes down the name of the next show on the advertising chalkboard, writes out tickets, and sells them to customers. On the other side of the room, a restaurant is set up, with a kitchen, a reception area with a large sign saying "please wait to be seated", an eating area, and a puppet stage. At a nearby table, children are busily writing and drawing the scripts for today's show. Some of the writers enact their own stories, others serve as directors, telling classmates how to dramatize their script. Some children create puppet shows without using a script (see Figure 6-4 and 6-5).

The children are using written language in functional ways. The written language is central to many of the activities—buying tickets, producing the show, taking orders, and reading menus. Children are using time in a functional way. Children are involved in complex social interactions, with each child having a distinct role. Some roles are less demanding than others, so each child can play at the level that fits his or her needs. The dramatic play builds on and extends favorite themes of the children in this class.

And Still More . . .

These are only a few of the infinite numbers of ways that restaurant can be played. Other possibilities are:

▪ A restaurant that serves three meals a day, with breakfast, lunch, and dinner menus

FIGURE 6-5 Dinner theater kitchen, restaurant, and puppet stage (script writing area is behind the hatrack on the right)

■ An outer space restaurant, serving strange space food, and run by space creatures

■ A restaurant located on some form of transportation: a diner on a train, a restaurant on an ocean liner, or meal time on an airplane

■ A cafeteria

■ A tailgate party before a football game

■ A pet restaurant, so pets can be taken out for a special treat

The restaurants described can serve as a source of ideas for designing your own variation. Perhaps you want to emphasize money, but do not wish to design an ice cream parlor. Payment can be added to any type of restaurant. Remember, if the restaurant becomes too complex, children may become so involved in other aspects that money play does not occur.

If the children in your class are already playing restaurant on their own, consider whether it should be expanded by offering additional props or ideas. Select ones that support what they are doing, and add opportunities to support skills that are being developed in other areas of the classroom. If children are pretending to write down orders with no props, and they are beginning to write in other parts of the room, you might add order pads so they can write in the restaurant as well.

If the class will be visiting a restaurant, use the parts of the restaurant that interest the children most as the basis for designing the pretend restaurant. Children can be included in the planning and designing process. This will help them to recall and organize what they saw on the trip.

The most important thing to remember when planning for and extending children's dramatic play is that it should be the *children's* play. If you wish to stress money, but the children are more interested in ordering and cooking, then this is not be the time or place to teach money concepts. Beware of becoming so wrapped up in designing an exciting play area that you forget the children that you are planning it for.

Evaluate What Really Happens

In the Kindergarten Cafe the children each took distinct roles, fostering growth in many areas. The teacher had hoped this would happen when she designed the environment, but children do not always play in the way that teachers anticipate, nor are the envisioned objectives always met. Careful observation and evaluation of what actually happens in the dramatic play area will show what types of learning are occurring. It will help adults to know what types of adaptations should be made to the area, what types of support should be offered, and when children should be given space to develop the play on their own.

The children playing Friendly's initiated their own restaurant play. Observant adults will see and support this type of play by enjoying it, offering support if needed, and being cautious not to stifle child-initiated play with overplanning.

Many Other Themes

Restaurant is only one of many themes for dramatic play. Like restaurant, each theme can be developed in several different ways. The more children and adults become immersed in dramatic play, the more options they will see. It would be impossible to list all the possible themes, or all the possible directions that any one theme could take.

The remainder of this chapter is a resource list of themes. It is not meant as a definitive list, but as a springboard from which adults and children can create their own variations to fit the special requirements of their settings. Each theme will be described briefly, a variety of directions will be suggested, and general props will be listed. Props that are specifically related to literacy will be listed as well.

A STEP FURTHER   *Are Literacy Props Different from Other Dramatic Play Props?*

Why have I listed literacy-related props separately from other dramatic play props? If dramatic play supports literacy through facilitation of oral language and story creation, then ALL props that support dramatic play will support literacy. Often adults who are just beginning to introduce written language materials into their dramatic play find it difficult to generate appropriate written language props for children who do not yet read and write in conventional ways. A separate list of written language-related props is provided to serve as a springboard for those who are just beginning to introduce this type of material into dramatic play. With practice these beginning teachers will also come to question why anyone would separate literacy props from general props.

Firefighter

Firefighter is a favorite theme for children of all ages. It allows them to take on a powerful role. It is a theme they often initiate on their own. Firefighter is played outside as well as inside. Blocks and water play are other locations where this theme flourishes.

FIGURE 6-6 Firefighting is a favorite theme for young children

Some Possible Focuses

▌ Putting out fires: Children can pretend to douse fires around the room and yard with hoses.

▌ Firetrucks: Children drive trucks and put out fires.

▌ Life in the firestation: The firestation contains a living area, tools for maintenance on the trucks, and cleaning supplies to wash the trucks when they return from a fire.

▌ Communication at a firestation: Provide a table with a phone, and a note pad on which to take down the calls, a map to mark down the calls, and numbered houses to correspond to the map.

▌ Firefighters' tools and clothing: Supply children with real or simulated firefighting props, clothing, air masks, and tools.

▌ Water as a firefighting tool (an outside activity for warm weather): Children pretend to put out fires by squirting water from detergent bottles at flames made of red paper cups placed on a bench or ledge. The water will knock the cups off, putting out the fire.

Note: Firefighter play is something that children tend to play at the simple level of putting out fires. For some of these more detailed themes to develop, children will have had to visit a firestation and/or to have talked about and explored the role of firefighters in detail in class discussions, stories, and activities.

Some Possible Props

- Hoses: Pieces of old garden hose or short sections of flexible plastic tubing from the hardware store.
- Firetrucks: Bikes, wagons, a driving box, a row of hollow blocks or chairs with a driving bench, a triangle or handbell for the siren.
- Air mask: Ski goggles or nose protectors.
- Air tank: A coffee can or large plastic soda bottles can be worn as a backpack when attached to the child with elastic straps.
- Cleaning equipment
- Old boots
- Fire hats
- Kitchen equipment
- Raincoats
- Gloves
- Cardboard axes

Literacy-Related Materials

- Books, magazines, and newspapers in living area of station
- Large map to locate fires
- Small photocopied or dittoed maps to match the large one to mark the fires for the truck drivers
- Cardboard houses that match the numbers on the map
- Pads to write down messages
- Fire report forms used to write down what happened when fire-fighters return from the fire.

Pets

Caring for pretend pets offers children the opportunity to play a loving, nurturing role. It also allows children to deal with fears about animals. For the child who desires but does not have a pet, it offers a chance to be a pet owner. When they play the pet role, the children do not need to use language; being the pet thus provides a comfortable entrance for less verbal children. Being a pet allows children to be loved and pampered. For many children, being a pet is just another forum for family play. Children will often play out familiar family themes in the roles of dogs, cats, or some other pet.

Some Possible Focuses

- Stuffed pets can be added to family play.
- Children can be pets in family play.
- Caring for pets: Provide cans of food to feed the pets, water bowls so pets can drink, leashes for walking pets, brushes for combing pets, and beds that pets can sleep in.
- Mouse play (if the class has a pet mouse to observe): Create a mouse house with shredded paper to nest in, tubes to climb in, wood bowls and a water bottle. This could be done with any type of class pet—rabbit, gerbil, etc.
- Pet store: Stuffed pets and pet supplies can be purchased.
- Pet show: Set up places to display pets and demonstrate tricks they can do, ribbons to be won by all.
- Veterinarian: Examine pets with medical tools.
- Escaping pets: Build enclosures with blocks to hold pets in; engage in chasing games to retrieve pets that escape. This is a common child-initiated pet activity.

Some Possible Props

- Collars and leashes for stuffed pets: String or elastic loops makes collars; ribbon or heavy string make leashes, a paper clip tied on the end of the leash can be used to clip the leash onto the collar.
- Collars and leashes for people pets: Collars made from a belt or a circle of elastic to go around a waist; leashes made from rope or men's ties. (*Note:* Because pets wear collars around their necks, children tend to think they should put collars around their necks when they are being dogs. The dangers of placing things around their necks should be discussed with children. Adults must stress that they should NEVER do this. They will wear their collars around their waists. Since children often initiate animal play on their own, safety discussions of this type at school may prevent accidents by offering children safer alternatives.)
- Plastic dishpan to bathe pets in
- Clear plastic shoe box to use as a fish tank with water and plastic fish
- Food bowls
- Empty pet food cans
- Brushes
- Towels (for beds)

FIGURE 6-7 Intently cleaning the pretend fish tank

FIGURE 6-8 Checking off fish tank cleaning on the pet care list

- Headbands with pet ears
- Stuffed pets
- Bird cages
- Doctor tools
- Plastic pet noses
- Boxes (for pet homes)

Literacy-Related Materials

- Pet food cans with labels (paper labels can be added to other cans if real pet food cans are not available)
- Pet care books
- Pet care checkoff lists to check off if you have given the pet food, water, a bath, a brushing, etc. (see Figure 6-8)
- Name tags to go on the pet collar
- For pet store: Sales receipts, signs, advertisements, price lists
- For vet: Appointment calendar, prescription pad, pet care books, patient charts

Doctor and Hospital Play

Doctor play allows children to become familiar with, and have a chance to control, the sometimes frightening tools and experiences of the doctor's office or hospital. For children who have not had experiences with hospitals, this play creates a familiarity and comfort that could make a future hospital experience less intimidating. This play can be particularly helpful when a peer, family member, or teacher is undergoing medical treatment.

Some Possible Focuses

- Check-up: Children can enact a typical visit to the doctor's office—with a waiting room, scale, and examining room.

- Dolls as patients: Using dolls as patients allows children to play doctor to a doll. For younger children this allows them to have the doctor-patient role without needing cooperative play skills. It allows all children to have control of both roles, which may help those children who find such play frightening.

- Broken bones: Explore the steps that are taken if you go to the hospital with a broken bone—with a homemade x-ray machine, cloth strips to make casts, and/or strips of casting material for making finger casts.

- Ambulance: Moving patients to the hospital with wagons or baby carriages.

- Operating room: Set up a room with operating tables, doctors' tools, bandages, oxygen masks, and IV tubing (attach to wrist with rubber band).

- Maternity ward: Provide dolls and small beds near the moms for the babies.

- Pediatrics ward: Set up this "ward" with fold-down beds (rolled-up sleeping bag or fold-up exercise mat) near the patients' beds so parents can stay with their children, provide trays for meals in bed; and have a playroom.

- Tailor play to current medical experiences of children or their families.

Some Possible Props

- Thermometers (Straws cut into thirds. Have a sealed container with a hole in the lid to dispose of straws after use. They can be sterilized and reused another day.)

- Syringe (toy ones or real syringes without needles)

- Stethoscopes

- Blood pressure cuff

- White coats

- Reflex hammer

- Strips of cloth for bandages

FIGURE 6-9 Oxygen masks for the hospital

❚ Jars for medicine
❚ Dolls
❚ Bed
❚ For doctor's office: Reception area with phone, magazines, and appointment calendar; examining table (table covered with sheet); eye chart, scale.
❚ For hospital: Identification bracelets (Strips of paper taped or stapled into a circle), X-ray machine made of a cardboard box suspended over a table—a foil circle can be attached to the bottom of the box as a lens; anesthetic/oxygen mask; doctor's mask; rubber gloves, foot covers for doctor; operating table.

Literacy-Related Materials

❚ Books for waiting room and hospital patients
❚ Patient charts in folders for doctor's office
❚ Patient temperature/blood pressure chart to hang at foot of bed
❚ Signs indicating where equipment belongs
❚ Doctor IN/OUT signs
❚ Operating room schedule
❚ Meal request form
❚ Books about health and body
❚ Name bracelets
❚ Appointment book
❚ Get well cards

Driving

Driving a vehicle is seen by most children as a powerful grownup act. Driving cars, boats, planes, buses, and other vehicles is something children often include in their play. At times the children will sit in one spot moving steering wheels to indicate motion; at others times they will move around using bikes, trucks, or even their bodies as the vehicle. Driving play is typical of toddlers. It is also often a part of the play of older children, who are more likely to use it as a component of other play themes.

The possible focuses for vehicle play are often similar across the types of vehicles, but some differences do exist. Let's look specifically at airplane play, then explore how the focuses and props for this play are similar to and different from other types of vehicle play.

Some Possible Focuses

- Passenger plane: Set the plane up with pilot, copilot and passengers.
- Passenger plane with more detail: Add ticket sellers and flight attendants to serve food and bring magazines.
- Small planes: Provide radios for talking to the control tower and to other planes.
- Caring for planes: The ground crew uses tools to check out planes before takeoff, and refuels the plane by pumping gasoline.
- Communication: Pilots must talk to the control tower before takeoff and landing to be sure the runway is clear and to check weather conditions.
- Running: Each child can be a plane flying around the play yard; Destinations and speed can be discussed.

Some Possible Props

- Passenger planes made from rows of hollow blocks or chairs— a cardboard side of a plane can be added but is not necessary
- Cockpit and control tower controls—made with a series of cardboard dials and switches, or a box with old electrical switches of various types
- Steering box (such as the one made by Community Playthings®) or cardboard circles for pilots to hold
- Tickets
- Trays and food

FIGURE 6-10 Airplane cockpits and control tower

- Plastic tools
- Luggage
- Hats for pilots
- Bikes as planes
- Control tower: Weather map, radar screen

Literacy-Related Materials

- Flight maps
- Tickets
- Weather maps
- Messages to pilots
- Magazines
- Schedules
- Repair checklists

Other Vehicle-Related Themes

- Going on vacation, including planning, packing, traveling, being somewhere and returning
- Jobs using vehicles, such as police officer
- Going to work using cars, buses, subways, or trains
- Mechanic repairing various vehicles
- Car wash

FIGURE 6-11 Consulting a map book to plan a car trip

▌ Hauling things

▌ Fishing from boats

▌ Map reading, including maps of play yard for bikes; maps to fit the type of transportation, such as street maps for cars, nautical maps for boats, flight maps for planes

▌ Space travel

Hair Salon Play

Hair salon play is a favorite with young children. Both the customer and the stylist roles are popular. The customer enjoys being the center of attention. The stylist is in charge of an array of exciting tools (hair dryer, shampoo bottles, curlers, etc.). This theme offers "adult" roles for all the players, since both customer and hair stylist are usually adult roles.

It is important to design the salon so that boys feel comfortable playing. This can be done by posting pictures of men's hairstyles, and by including a shave as one of the possible services.

Hair salon play encourages social interaction, since children usually do each other's hair, though it does have the flexibility to allow children to do their own hair if they prefer. The social interaction may be as simple as two children trading off the roles of stylist and customer, or it may be a complex system of roles with receptionist, customers, manicurist, hair cutter, and hair setter, each with his or her own responsibilities.

Some Possible Focuses

▌ Children learn interdependence of roles with separate stations in the salon for different services.

- Fixing hair can be part of house play.
- Going to the ball: The salon could be combined with getting ready for a party; children get hair done then dress up for the dance.
- Washing hair: Dolls can be the customers and their hair can be washed with real water, towel-dried, and put up on curlers.

Some Possible Props

- Curlers
- Berets
- Brushes
- Old hairdryer
- Hair clips
- Combs
- Ribbons
- Aprons
- Cardboard scissors
- Cash register
- Water-filled nail polish bottle with brush
- Play sink and hose for washing hair
- Razors (without blades)
- Hair picks
- Wigs with stands (oatmeal containers work well)
- Mirrors
- Shampoo bottles
- Shaving cream
- Dolls with hair

Literacy-Related Materials

- Appointment book
- Bills for services—workers check off the services done
- Magazines for waiting room or to read while under hair dryer
- Signs marking each station
- Hair style posters or books for customers to select desired style
- Signs marking where equipment belongs

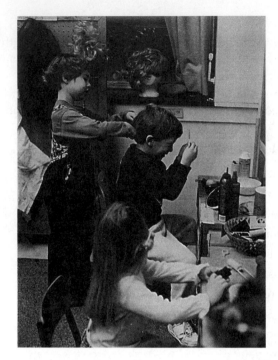

FIGURE 6-12 Hair salon play

Shopping

Store play is popular with children, perhaps because shopping is a regular event in most young children's lives. In shopping, parents have the powerful role. They decide what will and will not be purchased. Playing store allows children to be in control of what is purchased. It also provides a chance to pile merchandise into bags or boxes. Collecting things is a favorite activity with toddlers. Compiling large quantities of objects is a part of play for many older children as well.

The role of storekeeper/cashier is also a powerful one. This person controls the cash register, a favorite toy of many children; decides if the store is opened or closed; and sets the prices of merchandise. Many different types of stores can be enacted. Let us look first at some possible focuses and props for grocery store, then look at some adaptations that could be made for other types of stores.

Some Possible Focuses

▌ Food groups: The groceries can be arranged by food group with breads, milks, fruits and vegetables, and meats each in different areas.

▪ Departments: The food can be divided by types as in the grocery story with areas such as deli, bakery, meats, snacks, soups, cereal, etc.

▪ Farm or factory to store: Beginning with a factory with cans, or a farm with produce, trucks deliver food from farm or factory to the store, stock clerks unload the trucks and stock the shelves.

▪ Jobs at the grocery store: Distinct roles include baker with play dough to make cookies and rolls, butcher with meat trays and paper meat to wrap, truck driver, cashier, manager, etc.

▪ Shopping for dinner: Place the grocery store next to the house so food can be purchased and cooked.

▪ Pricing: Mark price tags on the food and supply pennies or paper money marked with amounts for paying the correct amount.

▪ Shopping lists: Supply paper and pencil so children can write lists before they shop.

▪ Matching foods: Have children match foods with picture advertisements for foods that are in store. Children can select some cards then shop for the items on their cards.

▪ Just like the neighborhood grocery: After a visit to the grocery store, have children design an area for grocery play, including the things they saw on their trip.

▪ Large muscle exercise: Grocery play outside emphasizes delivering things to the store using wagons and wheel barrows.

Some Possible Props

▪ Cash registers (will need more than one as these are very popular)

▪ Shelves, from cardboard boxes stacked with open end to the side, constructed with hollow blocks and planks or with planks and saw horses

▪ Checkout counter with a square of some type to electronically read the code

▪ Empty food containers

▪ Meat trays

▪ Grocery bags

▪ Play dough for bakery

▪ Trucks to deliver

Literacy-Related Props

- Store card with customer's name
- Signs marking shelves or parts of store
- Timesheets (for employees)
- Shopping lists
- Advertising circular
- Checkbooks
- Price labels
- Coupons
- Money
- Sale signs
- Job lists
- Receipts
- Open/closed signs

Other Kinds of Stores

- Clothing store: With mirrors, clothes racks, changing rooms, signs marking where to find different types of clothes or different sizes.
- Shoe store: With rulers to measure feet, shoes, shoe boxes, triangular hollow blocks as foot stool, signs designating men's and women's shoes, colors, and sizes.
- Toy store: With toys to buy.
- Book store: With area where children can make their own books to sell.
- Jewelry store: With a variety of jewelry and a workshop for making extra jewelry.
- Pet store: With cages, stuffed animals, pet supplies, and books about pets.
- Seed store: With planting supplies, seeds, small bags, scales for weighing seeds.
- Appliance store/repair shop: Broken appliances with the plugs removed and tools for taking them apart.

These are just a few possible types of stores. Stores can be modeled after real stores, as those listed above, or they can be designed to fit into what the class is exploring. The kindergarten at the lab school designed a "texture store" in which children collected and sorted things by texture.

FIGURE 6-13 Playing shoe store

The store sold such things as sand, corn meal, foam, and cotton. The children labeled the objects, weighed, and packaged the things for sale. The only limit to the types of stores possible is your imagination.

Putting This List in Perspective

The type of dramatic play that a group of children becomes involved in, as well as the direction that the play will take, depends on many things—their ages, interests, past experiences, skills at pretending, and the materials that are available. The list of themes presented in this chapter is not meant as a blueprint of topics that each group of children should cover. No such blueprint exists, because each group of children is different.

The ideas for the play must originate in children's interests and play patterns. The suggested themes and props can be used to design environments that will extend and expand the children's play. The themes suggested are just a sampling, as are the props and focuses listed under each theme. As adults become comfortable with and excited about dramatic play, they will find that generating, designing, and implementing dramatic play themes become easier and more natural.

CHAPTER 7

Pretend Play beyond the Dramatic Play Area

Hilary is at the easel. She makes a big blob of brown paint at the top of the paper and notices that the brush has dripped drops down the paper as well. "It's raining," she says, shaking the brush to intentionally make more drops. Then she takes her brush and smears the drops over the paper. "Now everything's wet."

* * *

Three children are playing at the rice table. Elsbeth is filling a pot, Jose is measuring rice into a large bowl, Carlos is filling a jar and dumping it back into the rice table. "This is magic soup," says Elsbeth as she fills a pot with uncooked rice.

Jose places a small scoop of rice in his large bowl. "This is the powder," he says. "Now the orange juice," he comments as he adds an orange juice can of rice to the bowl.

"My magic soup makes you invisible," explains Elsbeth.

"My magic pancakes make you bigger," proclaims Jose.

"I know," Elsbeth suggests, "Let's pretend it makes you as big as the school."

"And you can jump over trees," adds Jose.

Carlos appears to be oblivious to this conversation. He repeatedly fills his jar with rice, dumps it out and begins again.

*   *   *

Shawanda pushes a wooden car around in the blocks as she makes engine sounds. The car pushes loose blocks in front of it. She drops them into a corner saying "This is the junk yard." She takes a "one way" sign and places it in front of her stack, declaring, "This says 'Danger—keep out.' " Shawanda places a second car at the entrance to the junk yard. With the two cars facing each other she conducts a conversation between the two. "I'm a police." "You guard the junk yards, don't let robbers come." "Okay." "I'm going to get more junk." She leaves the police car as guard, and zooms the other car off to collect more blocks.

Ian puts some blocks in his truck and drives it back and forth. When a teacher inquires where he is driving, he replies "On the road." The teacher asks some additional questions and talks about how she is going to deliver blocks to the construction site. Ian continues to drive his truck back and forth.

*   *   *

Jameel and Kurt ride their trikes quickly around the play yard circle. When Jameel gets to Ms. Karlitz, he stops and requests, "Fill 'er up." Ms. Karlitz pretends to put gas into the trike and requests payment. "I'm Batman," Jameel announces as the pretend money is exchanged. "I've got to catch up with Robin. We're gonna catch Joker."

*   *   *

Kari and Jason are building with the Mobilo®.* After a while Kari declares she is making a spaceship. Jason agrees that his is a spaceship as well. The two of them begin flying their spaceships around the room.

*   *   *

Regie sticks pieces of drinking straws into her ball of play dough. Then she sings happy birthday and pretends to blow out the candles.

*   *   *

Animal crackers are today's snack. Fillippo is growling loudly as he holds two lions facing each other in threatening stances. He quickly bites the head off one of the lions and declares the other one the winner.

---

*Mobilo® is a plastic construction toy. Some of the connectors spin and others bend, so that once the child has constructed something parts of the object can fold and rotate.

As one can see from these examples, pretend play is not restricted to the dramatic play area. Children can pretend in many different contexts: with blocks, using manipulatives, with sensory materials, while making artistic creations, when outside, or even at the snack table. Pretend play can happen anywhere, and at any time. All that is required is imagination. This chapter will explore pretend play that occurs beyond the dramatic play area. First, it will examine why this type of play is valuable and the nature of this play in general, then it will look more specifically at different areas of the classroom and the types of pretending that occur there.

Facilitating Pretend Play in Many Different Forums

Often when teachers think of pretend play they envision the dramatic play area during play time, yet pretend play can occur in all parts of the early childhood setting, and at all times of day. These additional opportunities for pretend play are an important resource. For the children who do not choose to play in the dramatic play area, there are alternative forums for pretending. For the children who find it hard to leave the dramatic play area, the pretend play options in other parts of the room may entice them to play elsewhere, and perhaps discover neighboring activities or materials that they had not noticed from the dramatic play area.

When teachers look carefully at each area of the classroom with pretend play in mind, many possibilities are evident. Observing the master players in the classroom often suggests additional options for pretending. Once the pretend play forums are found, teachers can structure the classroom environment and their interactions with children to facilitate pretending. Often adding simple props will make the pretend play potential more apparent to all the children.

Similarities between Pretend Play in the Dramatic Play Area and Beyond

Pretend play outside the dramatic play area resembles that which occurs in the dramatic play area in many ways. Let us look at three similarities: the selection of themes, the variation in skill levels, and the integration of literacy.

What Themes Are Played?

As in the dramatic play area, the types of materials that are available may influence the type of pretend play that occurs. Elsbeth and Jose are cooking because pots, mixing bowls, measuring cups, and other "cooking" tools are available in the rice table. If sieves had been available, the pretend play might have revolved around rain or snow, as the children let the rice sift down over the table. If dump trucks had been added to the rice, the play would probably have developed around hauling and dumping rice.

As with dramatic play in the dramatic play area, the themes will also depend on children's past experiences, their interests, their skills as pretenders, and the common themes that the class has adopted. If cooking "magic" food is a favorite activity, as it is in Elsbeth's and Jose's family child-care group, this might be enacted in many different contexts.

Magic soup and pancakes could be prepared at the rice table as in the earlier example. Outside, children might collect leaves, berries, and stones in buckets to make their magic soup. Play dough might be prepared into magic pizza or cake. Sometimes favorite themes will appear in more unlikely places as well. The trucks in the rice table could be used to make truckloads of magic soup.

Some materials tend to point more specifically towards certain types of themes. Trikes are almost always used in some type of transportation play. Animal crackers spark some sort of animal play. Other materials are more open-ended, supporting a wide variety of possible themes. Paint could be used to compose a rain story as Hilary has done, but it could also could be a medium for virtually any theme.

Master Player, Novice, or in Between

In Chapter 2 we looked at master players and novice players in the dramatic play area. The examples at the beginning of the chapter show these same differences in children's skills as pretenders. Elsbeth and Jose are involved in an elaborate story about magic food. Carlos, on the other hand, is exploring the materials. He does not appear to be involved in any pretend play. Shawanda is using the truck to develop a detailed story, while Ian's pretending involves simply driving. Some children are master players, others are still novice players, and many fall somewhere in between. Children who are skilled pretenders in one context are likely to be skilled pretenders in other contexts as well.

Integrating Literacy into Pretend Play beyond the Dramatic Play Area

In the examples at the beginning of the chapter it is clear that children integrate literacy into the pretend play they do beyond the dramatic play area. At the rice table Jose puts orange juice into his magic pancakes because he is pouring from an orange juice can. The "magic" quality of the soup and pancakes was a game the children initiated after reading Steig's *Sylvester and the Magic Pebble* (1969). Playing in the blocks, Shawanda assigns her own personal meaning to a one-way sign, to warn people that the junk yard is dangerous. Hilary is using symbols to tell a story in her painting. Art stories of this type may be purely verbal, as in Hilary's case; however, some children may choose to add their own printed language to the picture, or to dictate the story for a teacher to record.

Literacy can be integrated into the pretend play in the four general ways that we have already seen in the dramatic play area: all-encompassing, enrichment, incidental, and child-initiated integration (see Chapter 5). All-encompassing integration of literacy can be seen when the teacher puts out feltboard pieces or other figures that children can use to retell a favorite story. Chapter 8 discusses book-based play in more detail. Literacy-based dramatic play, such as post office and sign shop, are incorporated into the outside play time.

There are numerous ways in which teachers can enrich ongoing play with literacy materials and ideas. Traffic signs can be added to the block area, placed in the play yard, and used with manipulatives such as the pegboard village or other construction toys. Containers with printed labels (such as the orange juice can) may be added to the sand, water, and other sensory tables. Teachers may also introduce literacy incidentally in response to the moment. If Shawanda had not thought to put a sign on her junk yard, but instead had told the teacher about it, the teacher might then ask if they should make a sign so everyone would know to stay away.

FIGURE 7-1 Traffic signs can be added to the pegboard village

Children may independently initiate the inclusion of literacy. The children cooking magic food at the rice table were playing out a favorite story. Hilary initiated the storytelling on her own, as she made the picture. These are just a few examples of how literacy can be added to the pretend play beyond the dramatic play area. Later in the chapter, when each forum for dramatic play is explored individually, many more examples of integrating literacy will be presented.

Differences between Pretend Play in the Dramatic Play Area and Beyond

Despite these similarities, there are many ways in which the pretend play outside the dramatic play area varies from that which occurs in the dramatic play area. Let us look at four of these areas: the identity of the actor, the level of personal involvement, the need for social interaction, and the balance between manipulation and pretending with materials.

Who Is the Actor?

When children are playing in the dramatic play area, they are the actors in the pretend story. The children are the people who do the cooking, put on the dressup clothes, go to work, or carry out the other actions. The children may take on pretend characters or do these actions without adopting an imaginary role. In some of the examples at the beginning of the chapter, the children are the actors. Elsbeth and Jose are the cooks at the rice table. Regie is the birthday girl with the play dough cake. Outside Jameel and Kurt are the "good guys" in search of Joker.

In some of the other examples, however, the objects are the actors in the story. In the block area, Shawanda and Ian both use their vehicles as actors. Shawanda's cars are building and guarding the junk yard. Ian's truck is driving. The Mobilo spaceships are the actors, while Kari and Jason just manipulate the ships to make the story unfold. Fillippo directs the animal cracker lions, who are the actors in his story. In Hilary's rain story there is no actor. She uses the paper as a forum for telling a story. If the story continues a character may appear as part of the picture.

Some of the materials are flexible, allowing either the child or the object to be the actor. Blocks can be used to create an enclosure where the people can be the actors. The addition of small vehicles and toy people to the block area tend to encourage **object-as-actor play**. Manipulatives can be used to make objects that can be used as characters (as in the case of the spaceships), or to make objects that can be used as props. The Mobilo might have been used to make a bracelet, a camera, or some other prop

FIGURE 7-2 The trucks are the actors in this sand play

that the child-actor could use in a pretend story. With cooking utensils in the rice table, the children are the actors, but if trucks are added, these are likely to become the actors rather than the children.

Level of Personal Involvement

Although pretend play in which the child is the actor and in which the object is the actor are alike in many ways, there also are some significant differences. When children are the actors in the pretend play, they must involve themselves to the point that they have taken on a role, or at least have taken on the responsibility for carrying out the action.

When using objects as the actor in pretending, the individual child can be more removed from the story. It is the lion that has bitten off a head, the police who will not let others in to the junk yard, the spaceship that is exploring the galaxy; the child is merely the narrator and the onlooker. For children who are self-conscious, objects-as-actors pretending allows them to enter pretend play without putting themselves on the line by being actively involved. For these children, using objects as actors provides a less threatening way to enter pretend play.

Is Social Interaction Required?

When children play in the dramatic play area, their play can be social—involving other children—or solitary. A child who is involved in solitary pretending may use dolls or stuffed animals as characters in his or her pretend story, but in general a story with multiple characters will require other children.

When playing pretend beyond the dramatic area, it is often possible to develop multicharacter stories that are enacted by a single child. As she plays in the blocks, Shawanda enacts both roles in her story: police and junk yard builder. In object-as-actor pretend play, it is possible to develop intricate stories with multiple characters without having to interact with another child. A single child can play all the characters.

For skilled imaginers who are just developing social interaction skills, object-as-actor pretend play offers the opportunity to develop long, involved stories that would be impossible if they were required to negotiate the development of the story with peers. On the other hand, children who are skilled at social interaction but less proficient at developing imaginative stories may find it easier to be the actor in the play. By playing along with peers these children can let others set the direction for the play.

It is certainly possible to develop stories with object as actors in which more than one child participates. Jameel and Kurt are using their spaceships as actors. Their ships are traveling together around the galaxy. The path of their play is set by the interaction between the two of them. Children can use objects as actors jointly with peers, or they may engage in this pretending on their own.

The Balance between Manipulating and Pretending with Objects

When children first begin to use a new material, they will explore it and experiment to see what it does before using it in pretend play. If the cash register is out for the first time, children are apt to busily press keys, open and shut the drawer, and take the money in and out. It is not until after they have explored what the cash register can do that they will use it as a prop in their pretend play. This initial exploration will be seen in all areas of the classroom.

In the dramatic play area, most children will move fairly quickly from this initial exploration to using the material for pretend play. The area is designed for pretending, and the children respond to this expectation. Blocks, manipulatives, sensory materials, and art materials are also explored initially. Although some children will then move on to using these materials in imaginative ways, others will continue to explore and manipulate the materials.

This continued manipulation is not surprising, since these materials are designed to be manipulated. Block buildings can be constructed, elaborated, and rearranged without ever moving into pretend play. Rice can be poured, mixed, and sifted without placing this activity in the context of a pretend story. Art materials can be manipulated and explored without creating a story around that exploration.

Unlike other areas, the dramatic play area provides a physical context and suggests a theme or direction for pretending. The pots in the rice table are the only things that suggest that children might want to pretend to

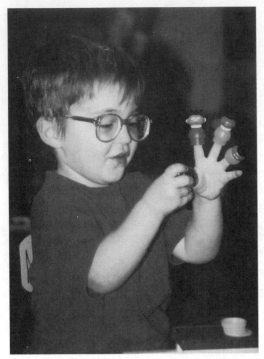

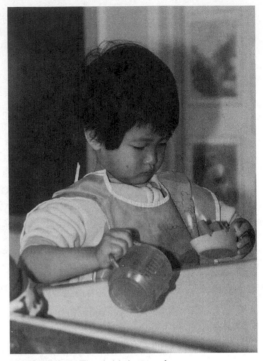

FIGURE 7-3 Creating a story with a handful of characters

FIGURE 7-4 The initial use of sensory materials is exploration

cook, while in the dramatic play area the kitchen appliances, dishes, table, and dressup clothes all suggest becoming a character who is cooking. The children using the Mobilo had to first construct their props before they could begin playing. There was nothing in the block area that told Shawanda to create a junk yard. In order to play, she first had to invent her own theme and then create a space in which the story could unfold.

For children who are not skilled pretenders, this additional step of first creating the context and then playing may be difficult. These children may just use the materials to construct. This is not to say that children will not play imaginatively with the materials—those who are master players will imagine with any props. Those children who are novice pretenders may stay at the manipulative level and not move into pretend play. Certain props will encourage this move to pretend play. For example, the addition of people and wheel bases to Lego® blocks will foster more pretend play than the blocks by themselves.

The remainder of this chapter will look at specific forums for pretend play in more detail, suggesting the special characteristics of play in each area, the types of props that will enhance play, the way that literacy can be

FIGURE 7-5 Playing pretend in the block area

integrated into the pretending, some possible problems that may arise, and the teacher's role in each area.

Pretending in the Block Area

Orion encloses a space about three feet square with a wall of unit blocks.* "This is my castle," he proclaims. As he is off getting additional blocks, Martin sees the enclosure and climbs in. "NO!" shrieks Orion, pushing Martin away from the castle. Martin seems confused by the attack.

"What is the problem?" asks Miss Wells.

"It's my castle. He's in my castle," Orion complains.

"Did you tell Martin?" asks Miss Wells. "He may not know that it is yours." Orion tells Martin, who explains that he wants to come in. The castle is too small for both. They do not seem to know how to resolve the problem. Miss Wells asks if they should build a neighboring castle for Martin, or build an additional room onto Orion's. The boys like the idea of an addition and work together to construct Martin's room.

*   *   *

Cassandra (four years old) and Ronnie (three years old) are building hotels for their large rubber insects to stay at on vacation. Cassandra's is an enclosure of unit blocks.

---

*Unit blocks are the hard wooden blocks often found in early childhood facilities. They are mathematically proportioned. The unit is a rectangle with the length twice as long as the width. The double is twice as long as the unit, and the quad is four times as long as the unit. There are also curves, pillars, posts, and other blocks that are based on the proportions of the unit (Hirsch, 1984). The block area discussion will deal mainly with unit blocks.

She flies a rubber beetle through the air saying, "Now he is going to Disney World. It is a long flight. He meets a friend." She picks up another insect. She conducts a conversation between the two about the trip. Finally they land inside the structure she has built. "It's bedtime now. They turn off the lights." She uses the large quad blocks to make the roof. Meanwhile, Ronnie is piling his blocks in a disordered heap. He balances his beetle on one of the ends jutting out from the pile.

Andy (four years old) is also in the block area. He does not seem to know what to do with himself. He wanders around, kicks a few loose blocks, then picks up the basket of insects and flies it around the block area, just missing the two hotels. Andy collects all the loose bugs in his basket. Then he dumps out the bugs and puts the basket on top of them. He places his hand firmly on the top so no one can take any insects. "I need a grandpa," says Ronnie. Andy ignores him.

Joanne, the teacher, comments, "Andy, it looks like you have all the insects there. What should other people do if they need some?"

"This is an insect store," Andy explains. He makes this clear by hawking his wares. "Who wants an insect? Insects for sale." The other children begin making money out of scrap paper to pay for their insects.

From these examples, and the block example at the beginning of the chapter, it is clear that children can use blocks to create an environment in which they are the actors in the pretend stories (as with the castle dwellers, and the store proprietor), or they can use objects as the actor (as with the insect hotels, and the junk yard builders). The themes that can be played in this area are infinite—anything that the child can imagine can be played.

Props

The props that are available will tend to influence the selection of theme. If fire trucks are in the block area, then firefighter play is likely. But many props are versatile, supporting a wide range of themes. The house boxes* made by Community Playthings take on many different roles: house, cave, prison, apartment building (when stacked on top of each other), store, boat, baby bed, doghouse, or giant's shoes.

Selecting Props

As in the dramatic play area, the number and types of props a teacher selects will depend on the social skills of the children, their interests, as well as their pretend play abilities. When adding things to the block corner, there are many options. It is important not to fill the area with too many different types of materials, as this can be overwhelming and can create so much

---

*These house boxes are sturdy wooden boxes (about 15″ × 8″ × 6″) with a solid floor. Three walls are solid except for a doorway. The fourth wall is open, with just a beam running across at roof level.

clutter that it is difficult to play. The best way to select toys is to observe children's play and add things that will complement and extend that play.

Vehicles.   Vehicles can vary from hand-held to ride-on sizes. In general, it is best to select only one size, either vehicles large enough for the child to ride on and be the actor in the story, or smaller vehicles that can be used as actors or to transport small figures who are the actors in the story. When both sizes are provided, there may be conflict between the two types of play. Teachers can select from a range of transportation modes: trucks, cars, buses, boats, planes, or trains. It is best to begin with one mode of transportation—air, land, or sea—to reduce conflicts. For the youngest children, who still are into dumping and filling, it is important to have vehicles with a cargo area that can be filled.

People.   Many types of people are available to use in the block area. Teachers should select the type that fit the other props. The small Fisher-Price® people easily ride in most vehicles. They are nonspecific in posture, so it is easy to imagine them either sitting or standing. The wooden people (blocks of wood cut along the outside outline of the figure) are often too big for vehicles, and they are definitely standing. Because the wooden people are designed to represent specific roles, it is often difficult for children with less developed imaginary skills to use these figures in stories of their own making, unless the preset role matches the child's intent. Animals also make excellent characters in children's play. These too come in many sizes and types. As with people, select animals so they are the right size to fit the other props being used.

Other Materials.   Miniature furniture and carpet squares will encourage house play in the block area. Adults tend to arrange furniture as it might be seen in a real room. Children tend to fill in every inch of their enclosure with furniture, therefore it is necessary to have a large amount of furniture to avoid conflict, or to develop some criteria with the children for determining how much furniture each child can select.

Many teachers find the best answer is to put out a few props to get the children started, but have some extras that can be added as needed. This way if the first few children in the block area develop stories using all of the people, there will be additional ones for the players who enter later.

Many other props can be added to the block area as well. This short list can stimulate thinking about options.

Hard hats (to go with construction trucks)

Fire hats (to go with fire trucks)

Parquetry blocks to decorate building and floors

Other small colored blocks for building or cargo

FIGURE 7-6 People, furniture, and house boxes can be added to the block area

House boxes

Pulleys (for making elevators)

Pressed cardboard corners (from packing crates)

Small boxes, salt cylinders, toilet paper rolls, or other recycled objects for building and hauling

Traffic signs

The Familiarity of the Props Can Affect the Play

Props such as people and vehicles, which are well known to children, tend to encourage imaginary play even by less skilled pretenders. Developing stories with less familiar objects may require more skilled pretenders. Andy's inability to get started in play may have been tied to the fact that he was not sure what types of stories could be played with insects. Ronnie and Cassandra, who are both experienced pretenders, used the insects to act out a holiday story. They used the insects in the same way they would have used people. For Andy, who is a novice pretender, this was too big a step.

When less familiar props are provided, teachers must observe to see if children need additional support from the teacher, or if they need a few more familiar props. In Andy's case the teacher's question was enough, but for another beginning player some people or trucks might have been needed for the child to find an entrance to play.

Creating a Context for Play

Pretending in the block area differs from that in the dramatic play area because children must first create a context for their own play. For some

A STEP FURTHER   *Using Props to Extend Pretend Play in the Block Area*

When selecting props for the block area, it is important to think about the grouping of the selected objects.

The three-year-old class has been interested in firefighters. Ms. Galaway decides to add firetrucks to the block area. A few of the trucks have ladders and hoses, but other trucks, due to breakage or loss, are missing these important parts. Realizing the importance of these accessories for enacting firefighter stories, Ms. Galaway tapes or ties pieces of heavy string or a shoe lace to each truck. Using a matte knife she cuts numerous ladders out of old cardboard boxes. Small people to fight fires and to be rescued are also placed in the block area.*

Teachers should watch the children's activities to see what props will help extend the play that is underway. The firefighter play in Ms. Galaway's class produced many injured victims. Seeing this, she added dump trucks adorned with red crosses to serve as ambulances, and beds for the hospitals that the children constructed. Maura wanted blankets for the beds. She was sent to the scrap box. Others used cloth scraps for capes or stretchers.

Teachers help children to create props for pretend play that they initiate in the block area.

Teresa and Zarina have built houses in the block area, and they are now inviting each other to birthday parties. Paulo, the teacher, asks if they are going to send invitations. The girls get paper and begin making invitations to deliver to each other. When Paulo asks where the letters should be delivered, the girls decide they need mailboxes. They go with Paulo to the junk closet to get boxes that can be made into mailboxes. They decide to put their names on the outside so everyone knows whose mailboxes they are.

The next day Paulo made available more boxes, with envelopes, stamps, and card-shaped paper so the invitation writing could continue and be undertaken by other children as well. When teachers are observant and sensitive to children's play, they will be able to add props that truly extend what the children are doing.

*For those who prefer to purchase, rather than make, ladders, pet stores have ladders of the right size at reasonable prices. These are made for bird cages or rodent exercise areas.

FIGURE 7-7 In blocks, children build their own context for play

children, like Andy, it is hard to begin play in this area. The teacher's question helped Andy to select a focus for his play. This was the first time that Andy played storekeeper, but this theme was one that he turned to many times during the year, for all types of play. He sold clothing and jewelry in the house area, rides on the climber/boat outside, people in the sand table, and fish in the water table. Selling became a comfortable script that Andy could employ wherever he chose to play.

Integrating Literacy into Pretend Play

As in the dramatic play area, pretend play in the block area offers children functional ways to use literacy. These uses fall into four large categories: signs and labels added to structures or vehicles; using other written language props to support the play, such as maps, tickets, or letters; using books as an impetus for the play; and creating narratives to accompany the story. Let us look at each of these in more detail.

Signs and Labels

At the beginning of the chapter, Shawanda uses a sign to warn others that her junk yard is dangerous. At the beginning of the year, she usually used signs as objects to be knocked over by her truck. Her use of signs as a form of communication, rather than as a target, developed because her teacher, Ms. Potter, spent the first few months of school modeling the use of signs.

Shawanda is building a structure in the blocks. Ms. Potter watches. "This is the school," Shawanda explains.

"Would you like a sign so everyone knows it is a school?" Shawanda agrees, though it seems more to humor Ms. Potter. The teacher gets some scrap paper from the basket on the block shelf and a pencil. "Would you like to write it or should I?" she asks Shawanda. Shawanda wants the teacher to write it, so Ms. Potter asks, "What should it say?" Shawanda tells her to write "school." Ms. Potter writes it carefully, sounding out the letters. She then attaches the sign to a sign stand. Shawanda places it in front of her building. Other children in the area also ask for signs. Some children are disinterested when Ms. Potter asks.

Ms. Potter continues asking about signs for the first few months of school. After a while the children begin to request signs on their own. At times there is no teacher available and the children begin making their own signs. To display the signs, sign holders are made by taping or gluing a clothespin onto a piece of wood. See Figure 7-8 for pictures of these holders.

Once children begin making their own signs, they will often find their own functions for the signs as well. The children in Shawanda's class developed an interesting use for stop signs:

One day three boys were driving their trucks recklessly around the block corner, knocking into many of the constructions. Peter watched nervously. He had built a large house. He needed more blocks, but did not want to leave his building unguarded. He picked up a stop sign and put it in front of his house. "This says stop, no crashing," he tells the truck drivers. They seem impressed with the idea and begin searching for signs to mark their houses as well. Only two could be found, then Jeremy got himself some scrap paper, looked at the stop sign, wrote a series of letters resembling stop, and placed it on a sign holder in front of his house.

This use of stop signs to control the behavior of others became popular in this class. Although none of these children were yet readers, these signs served as an important source of communication. A few weeks later there is again a great deal of crashing in the block area.

The five truckdrivers are banging their vehicles into blocks that are lying loose on the floor. The crashing and the accompanying shouts are extremely loud.

Amanda is looking at books in a chair next to the block area. She looks over in disgust at the level of noise. She gets five pieces of scrap paper and begins to write "stop" (various combinations of s, t, o, p, b, and d) on each paper. She then clips each to a sign holder. She takes them over to the block area and places each on a truck saying, "This says stop crashing. It is too noisy." The drivers seem pleased with their new signs and begin to whisper as they drive around the blocks (see Figure 7-8).

When children have seen signs used by teachers and peers, and have been given the opportunity to experiment with signs, they will often use signs on their own in functional ways during their block play.

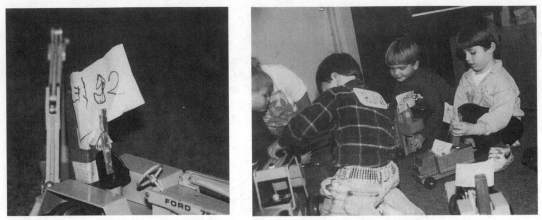

FIGURE 7-8 Child-made stop signs to remind noisy drivers to be quiet

These examples show children using signs to label and to give commands. Signs will also be used to claim ownership. Shawanda might have labeled her school "Shawanda's school." With modeling from the teacher and peers, and materials easily available, children will devise their own functional reasons for making and using signs in their block play. As with the class that often used stop signs to control the behavior of peers, each class will develop its own favorite sign types and uses.

A STEP FURTHER *Beyond Traffic Signs*

Many early childhood programs have commercial traffic signs added to the block corner. Although children do enjoy these, and may use them for personal means as Peter did, they are somewhat limiting, as they deal solely with traffic movement. One teacher felt that other forms of signs would enhance her block area. She cut logos for local stores—McDonald's, Toys R Us, Superfresh Supermarket, Eckard's Drugs—from advertisements and shopping bags. She attached these with masking tape to unit blocks stood on end. These were then spread along the top of the block shelf. She said nothing about the signs. When the children came in they immediately began building stores to go with the signs. The signs added a prompt to suggest what could be built.

When a needed sign was being used by someone else, some of the children copied the sign. Others searched through a box of paper bags for another logo that they could cut out and use. With an older class, the teacher might have involved the children in finding logos and making the original signs. If extra unit blocks are not available, the logo can be attached to toilet paper rolls, empty salt containers, or small boxes filled with newspaper to weigh them down.

Written Materials as Props

Although signs are often the first and most prevalent literacy props used in the block area, many other types of written materials may be used as well. Teresa and Zarina used letters and mailboxes as part of their house play. The children make money to purchase insects at Andy's stores.

Maps can complement transportation play. They can be posted around the area for all to refer to, or can be carried around by the children. It is interesting to provide many types of maps: aviation maps for airplanes; railway routes and timetables for trains; navigation charts of oceans, lakes, or rivers for boats; star charts for rockets; road maps for car trips; and globes and atlases for planning all types of travel.

Children will use maps in many ways. They may just like looking at them or carrying them around. Other children may want to pick places on the map as destinations. Maps with known spots, such as Disney World, a child's house, grandparents' town, family vacation spots, or the school, are particularly popular. Some teachers mark these spots with pictures and labels so children can find desired spots. If needed maps are not

FIGURE 7-9 Consulting his blueprint as he builds

available, some children will create their own maps. One group of kindergartners enjoyed making maps of the roads they had constructed in the
block area.

The possibilities for integrating literacy materials are limitless. As in
the house area, the best approach is to think about the themes that children are playing, then explore the types of writing that are part of these
activities. For example:

- Construction workers might use blueprints
- Police officers might use tickets, or clipboards to make reports
- Air traffic controllers might need flight maps, weather maps, and
  message pads
- Buses might need bus stops, numbers to show where they are
  going, and bus schedules
- Houses might need newspapers, TV magazines, mailboxes, street
  numbers
- Superheroes might need logos taped to their front

The types of props will depend on the interests and play of each group of
children.

Once written materials have become a common prop in the block
area, children and teachers will incorporate literacy as a natural part of
the play. Often one use of writing will blend into another, as children
select the props that are most important for their own play. This personal
response can be seen in the following example.

> *Matt is pushing the ferry boat around the block area calling, "Rides! Who wants
> a ride?" He picks up a few people from the floor and dumps them into his boat.
> None of the children seem interested in getting a ride for their people.*
>
> *"I'd like a ride," says Ms. McTavish, talking for her small block person.
> "Where does one go to get a ride?" Matt points to a random group of blocks in the
> middle of the area. "Is this where the dock will be? I wonder if we ought to make a
> place for the people to wait for the ride?" Matt and the teacher work together to
> make a small dock. "How will other people know that this is where you go to get a
> ride?" Matt decides a sign is needed. He gets the box of colored paper scraps, a
> pencil, and tape. He writes GTRR (get ride here) and tapes it on the dock.*
>
> *Many of the children are now interested in rides and bring their people to
> wait on the dock. Gavin also has a ferry boat. He fills his with paper scraps and
> sails up to the dock to offer rides. "Here's the ticket," he explains as he hands
> each child a scrap of paper.*
>
> *Elsie begins spreading scraps on the floor to make islands for the boats to
> sail around and to.*

Each child uses the paper in a different way. Matt writes and posts a sign
using phonetic spelling. Gavin uses the paper to represent a form of writ-

ing a ticket, while Elsie uses the paper to create islands without any reference to written language.

Books

Books can be used in the block area as a resource for both building and pretending. Books can provide background information. A book about how food gets to the supermarket may introduce children to the idea that trucks deliver food to the supermarket. This may prompt store building and the use of trucks for delivering stock to the stores.

Books can serve as a reference when building.

> *Fiona and Shachar are sailing their cargo ships around the block area. "Where are you taking the cargo?" Miss French inquires.*
>
> *"To South America," Shachar answers. "That's right here," he explains pointing to the corner.*
>
> *"Is there a dock in South America for unloading your cargo?" Miss French asks. The children do not know what a dock is. They get a book on boats from the book shelf and look at the various docks in the illustrations. The children then build an elaborate dock, referring occasionally to the illustrations in the book.*

Teachers can place books on the block shelf for easy reference. Books about building, such as *Building a House* by Barton (1981), or books with many styles of houses, such as *Come Over to My House* by LeSieg (1966), may suggest ways to construct houses. (Further information on these books, and those listed below, is given in the Bibliography of Children's Books.)

Books can also be used to suggest story lines for pretend play in the blocks. A favorite book with many young children is Ron Campbell's *From the Zoo* (1982). A little boy is sent many packages filled with animals. A "from the zoo" label adorns the boxes. Some problem is found with each of the animals and each is sent back to the zoo. One teacher added rubber animals, dump trucks, and small cardboard boxes to the block area. The boxes were labeled "from the zoo." Children used the props to deliver and return animals "from the zoo." When additional boxes were needed, they added their own labels. Other zoo books were available to use as reference for building the zoo.

Children will often use characters from books in their block play. The steam engine might be Marianne from Virgina Lee Burton's *Mike Mulligan and His Steam Shovel* (1939). The train might be Choo Choo the Runaway Engine from the book of the same name (Burton, 1937) or the Little Engine that Could from a book by that name. Careful observation will help teachers to select props and ask questions that will encourage children to build upon favorite books when playing in the block area.

FIGURE 7-10 Delivering
animals as in *From the Zoo*

Narrative as a Component of Block Play

As discussed in Chapter 4 the construction of narrative is an integral part
of dramatic play. The development of oral stories is also an important
component of emerging literacy. The composing of oral stories is similar
to the composing done in written language. Cassandra uses narration to
describe all the events in her story, as she uses the insects to enact it.
Because in the block area children often enact all parts of the story on their
own, this type of narration helps to create the framework and tie together
all the characters.

Some Common Teacher Concerns

Some teachers find supervision of the block area particularly trying. This
area can be problematic for teachers for a number of reasons. Perhaps the
best way to address teacher concerns is to respond to some common comments and questions about the block area.

It Seems Like I Always Have to Go to the Block Area to Quiet Children or Resolve a Problem

During free play teachers often place themselves in other parts of the
classroom, only coming to the block corner when problems arise. With
this pattern most teacher/child interactions in the block area become
adversarial. When teachers spend time in the block area, they can help
children's play to develop in more constructive ways. They can often redirect play before it gets out of hand. Giving block builders the positive
attention of the teacher's presence and interest may discourage children
from using negative means for seeking attention.

FIGURE 7-11 Many problems can be forestalled by giving block builders positive teacher attention

There Never Seems to Be Enough Room

This concern sometimes arises out of a true shortage of space, in which case teachers need to look carefully at their room arrangement to discover how they can allow more room for block play. At other times the area will be large enough, but the children build in ways that conflict with each other. Children do not preplan their buildings. When they start there IS space, but as they continue building, often the structures bump into other structures, block walkways, or make it difficult for other children to get to the block shelves. Teachers can remedy this by helping children find an appropriate place to start their building. Children can be redirected if they begin building in a high traffic area where accidents are likely.

How Do I Stop Them from Knocking down Buildings?

The urge to push over buildings can create a number of problems. When a child knocks over another child's building, or when falling blocks destroy another child's play, problems arise. When a building topples, the setting for the play has vanished and often the children involved do not know what to do next. Some teachers' solution to these concerns is to outlaw knocking down buildings.

But knocking down buildings also offers children a wonderfully powerful experience. Instead of outlawing the destruction of buildings, teachers can help children to find ways to enjoy this powerful experience without interfering with the play of others. Children can choose to knock down their own buildings, as long as they do not fall on other people or their buildings. Once the building is down, children need help to get reinvolved in a constructive activity. Many teachers find that encouraging the children to reuse or put away the blocks insures that other children have room to play. It is important that teachers help with this so it does not become a punishment, but rather, a natural consequence of cluttering the area.

How Do I Get Them to Play Together?

As was discussed in Chapter 3 the reason that children may not be "playing together" is that they may not be developmentally ready for more cooperative play. This may be the reason for lack of interactive play in the blocks as well. However, at times children do not play together in the blocks because they just did not notice other children in the area. Teachers can help children to become aware of each other's play by discussing what is happening in the area.

> Mark, Natasha, and Zabina are all playing in the block area. Mark is working on building a road. Natasha is building a large structure. Zabina is building a smaller structure on the other side of the block area. She is having the Mommy figure tell the girl that it is time to go bed. She then lays the girl on a block inside of the house. Natasha and Mark are also using small people to enact stories that accompany their construction.
>
> Ms. Bakshi comes into the blocks. After watching for a minute, she begins to talk with the children about their constructions. "Zabina, what a lovely house! Who lives there besides the girl and the mother?" Zabina introduces the family.
>
> "Natasha, what an enormous building! Is it something special?" Natasha tells her it is grocery store. "If you let Zabina know when it is done, her people might want to go shopping there."
>
> Zabina has been listening to the conversation and says, "Yeah, I need some more baby food."
>
> "It will be open tomorrow," Natasha tells her.
>
> "Mark, where does your road go?" Ms. Bakshi asks.
>
> "Everywhere." he replies. Ms. Bakshi asks if she and Zabina can drive on the road to Natasha's grocery store. "Sure," he tells them.

Ms. Bakshi's questions alerted each child to the activities of the other children. After this they build a park and school to go to on the road, and houses for Natasha's and Mark's people. At times, discussion of what is happening in the area will prompt children to combine their stories, but at other times children will continue individually. Teachers should respect both reactions.

As a Teacher I Always Feel out of Place in the Block Area.

The fact that children construct their own context for play means that almost any type of play can occur in this area. Because of this, some teachers find it hard to know in which direction to direct children. What type of themes should be suggested or modeled? It takes practice to realize when children are having trouble getting involved and need guidance, when the teacher should sit back and observe, and when the teacher should follow the lead set by the child.

The best way to build teacher comfort in the block area is to spend time there with children who are master players. Playing with children who are skilled pretenders will help teachers to understand what makes rich block play. Observing will also help teachers to know what types of play are used by this group of children.

Pretending with Art Media

Art materials lend themselves to dramatic play in two main ways. First, children create stories to accompany their pictures. At the beginning of the chapter, Hilary tells a rain story as she paints. Although this is not dramatic play in the strict sense, it does offer children opportunities to create and expand upon their own stories. Children accompany their narrations with actions as they extend their stories.

A second way children use art materials for dramatic play is in the construction of props to be used in their pretend play. In the example at the beginning of the chapter, Regie creates a birthday cake for herself with play dough and straws. The children who shopped at Andy's insect store used art materials to create money for their purchases. The boaters used art materials to create signs, tickets, and islands. Some other common props that children make are hats, jewelry, capes, walkie talkies, keys, and food. The types of props that children make will depend on what materials are needed to advance their stories.

Exploration Comes First

When children are introduced to a new medium, they explore what can be done with it. The first time children use finger paint they will swish it, squish it, pile it in the middle, run it through their fingers, make lines in it, and experiment in other ways to see what they can do with this thick wet stuff. It is not until after this exploration that children will begin to use the materials imaginatively. At this point they may begin to create stories as they explore. The lines might be roads. They might draw houses, people, or cars to go with the roads.

It is not until children have become comfortable with materials that they will use them to construct props for their play. Regie will have pounded, poked, flattened, pinched, and in other ways explored the properties of play dough, before she formed it into a birthday cake.

This need to investigate the material before using it to create something can be seen in people of all ages. It is important to know what one can make a material do, to be in control of a material, before putting it to use as a tool to create something. This has important implications for teachers who wish to encourage pretend play. Children must be offered repeated opportunities to use the same type of material so they can move beyond exploration to using these materials in imaginative ways.

Providing Space and Time

If children are going to explore and get to know media, create stories, and design and use props, they will need large blocks of activity time, where they are free to select their own endeavors. A variety of familiar art materials should always be available in clearly marked places. As children explore and get to know new media, these can be added to the area as well. There must also be a place to use these materials, a "free art table" where children can use the media of their choice to make pictures, create props, or write. This table should not be used for teacher-planned activities, but should be dedicated to the children's free choice. With many groups of children, this will be the busiest place in the room.

Encouraging Story Creation

Many children will naturally tell stories as they use art materials. They will use the motion of the paint to be such things as rain, cars, or wind. They will create recognizable objects and create stories about the content of their pictures. Other children will not narrate their work. These chil-

FIGURE 7-12 Children often tell stories about their artwork

dren may be creating internal stories, or may not have thought to tie stories to their creations.

If teachers are an eager audience for these narratives, children will see that picture stories are valued. This will often draw new children into the narration process as well as encouraging those who do narrate to elaborate upon their stories.

> Fernando is swishing the blue paint quickly across his picture. "Your brush is really going fast," comments Mr. Azid.
>
> "Yeah, it's a racetrack so they have to go fast," Fernando explains.
>
> "I see. Who is racing today?" Mr. Azid asks.
>
> "The blue car is the fastest," Fernando says as he paints a brown rectangle with two yellow circular wheels. "This is the finish line." He draws a line across the top of the paper, and decorates each side with flags. "He's gonna win a bank full of money."

Mr. Azid's interest in Fernando's painting initiated the verbal narration. By responding to the initial statement with a question, Mr. Azid encouraged Fernando to expand upon his story. It may be that Fernando was thinking about racetracks and constructing a narration in his head before Mr. Azid approached. On the other hand, Fernando may have just been painting. Mr. Azid's comment about speed may have triggered the idea of a racetrack. In either case Mr. Azid's interest prompted the verbal narration.

For some children who are not yet drawing representationally (they are not yet seeing their art as being something), it may be too abstract a jump to tie the motion of their arms to stories. For these children the inclusion of familiar objects may provide a link to storytelling. Cars can be used to drive through the paint and then create paths, or roads on the paper. Sponges can be cut into the shape of animals, flowers, vehicles, houses, or other familiar objects. Children can stamp these onto the page. They may then tell stories about the objects they have printed.

Pictures from magazines and wrapping paper can be used to create collages. Markers can be taped to the front of trucks, so that driving the truck leaves a mark on the paper. One teacher mounted a rubber spider on a spare marker lid, then inserted a piece of chalk into the other side of the lid. When the children moved the spider along the chalkboard it let out a white chalk-line of web.

Computer programs such as the *Explore-a-Story* series (D.C. Heath & Company) allow children to select objects to add to a background. Drawing programs such a *KidPix* (Broderbund Software) allow children to stamp objects onto the screen. These types of picture creation programs lend themselves to the story telling/picture creation combination. More information is given on these programs in the Bibliography of Children's Literature.

Although these props may encourage storytelling, some children may just prefer to explore and create a visual work. It is not only important to provide opportunities to create stories that encourage children to add narration; but to also provide stories that do not require narration.

Encouraging Prop Creations

Although some children may spontaneously create props to use in their pretend play, many times this idea is first suggested by a teacher. If children need blankets for the beds in their block houses, the teacher might direct them to the scrap box in the art area. If children need crowns to become royalty, or walkie talkies to be spies, they too can be directed to the art area to create the needed props.

Sometimes teachers will model this creation of props. On page 117, when Cheng-Ming wanted to be a police officer, the teacher came to the art area to create a badge for his hat. She realized that it was important for him to enter the play quickly. He did not have time to create the prop for himself, and still be part of the ongoing play. By creating props, the teacher demonstrates an important use for art materials.

Teachers need not, and in fact should not, provide all the possible props. If all the props are there, children have no reason to create their own additions to the play. With modeling and support, children will come to see creation of needed props as the norm. More children will initiate and follow through on their own creation of props.

Integrating Literacy with Pretending

Play in the art area is often rich with literacy. The oral composing of stories for pictures parallels the composing process that occurs in written language. The type of language used for narrating stories also tends to resemble the language used in written stories.

The teacher can add a written component to these stories by recording what children say about their picture. Mr. Azid might have asked Fernando, "Would you like me to write down what you said about your picture?" It is important to involve the child in the process, by his indicating where teacher should place the words on the pictures. If the child prefers, or if the paper is filled with drawing, the words can be put on a separate sheet that will be taped to the back of the finished work. Children will quickly begin to request that teachers come to hear their stories, and write down the words for their artwork.

It is common for art materials to be used to create literacy related props for children's play. Maps are created to be used for finding buried treasure and for traveling in block and dramatic play areas. Tickets are created to be used by police officers, travelers, and movie audiences. Let-

FIGURE 7-13 Making a book
to sell at the bookstore

ters are written. Books are stapled and colored to use in libraries, book-stores, houses, science labs, and many other places. Signs, labels, and advertisements can be added to pretend play of all types. Many times writing will be added to props that are not inherently writing related. A crown might be labeled with the word "KING" to make clear what type of royalty is using this headgear. A puppet created to use in the block area might be labeled with a name, so all will know its identity.

Some Teacher Cautions

The art area offers many opportunities for both pretend play and for literacy. Yet it is crucial to remember that artistic exploration and creation is a meaningful activity in its own right. Teachers must beware of turning the art area into a place where things are created merely to be used elsewhere. While prop and story creation are valuable activities, they should be viewed as only one of the many uses for art materials. Interactions and activities in the art area should be monitored to insure that children are encouraged to use art materials in ways that meet their individual needs.

Pretending with Manipulatives

Most classrooms contain a variety of manipulative toys for children to use such as puzzles, nesting and size toys, board games, counting objects, sorting toys, construction sets, felt boards, replicas (like the Fisher Price village), and objects to explore such as scales and binoculars. Often these materials are found together in the "quiet area" or "manipulative area." In other classrooms they are found in a number of smaller areas. No matter how these are housed, manipulative materials offer many rich opportunities for dramatic play.

For some manipulatives the pretend play potentials are obvious. Construction toys can be used to create props for play in which the child is the actor. They can also be used in object-as-actor play. Children can construct environments in which to enact stories with small figures, or they can build objects, such as spaceships, that can be the actors in the play. Other toys, such as barn or house replicas, are specifically designed to be used for dramatic play. Feltboard pieces are often designed for creating narrations.

Other manipulatives that do not initially appear to lend themselves to dramatic play may also be used for this purpose. Young children will often use puzzle pieces as actors in their pretend play. They will drive the trucks around, create noises and movements for the animals, or use the pieces in the Three Bears puzzle to reenact the story. Children may also use the pieces as props—pretending to eat the food, or using the construction tools.

Some children use board games as a setting for pretending. One group of four-year-olds liked to use the chicken playing pieces from the Discovery Toys® game Are You My Mother to create chicken family stories. The game-board is a garden with winding paths and a chicken coop at each corner. The chickens have magnetic bottoms, and when they wander by the baby chicks they will attract some and repel others. Another group used the Candyland® people to create stories about children who live in Candyland. Since most young children find losing competitive games distressing, storytelling offers a wonderful alternative use for these materials.

Nesting cups make wonderful caves or mountains for the small plastic counting bears or other small figures. These same bears can be com-

FIGURE 7-14 Children help bees and butterflies to collect pollen

bined with many other manipulatives in order to create stories. The one-inch colored plastic counting cubes with an open side make perfect homes for the colored bears. Teachers can also create pretend play materials for the area. One teacher made cardboard bees that could rest on the toilet paper role centers of cardboard flowers (see Figure 7-14).

Moving beyond Manipulation

Although many manipulatives can be used for pretending, they also can be used in ways that do not require pretending. Construction toys can be used for building, size and shape toys can be sorted and stacked, board games can be played according to the rules, and puzzles can be taken apart and put together. For children who are master players the move into pretending is natural; for others it is easier to continue to play with the materials on the manipulative level. Teachers can facilitate pretending by modeling it, by appreciating the pretending that is occurring and drawing other children's attention to it, and by wise selection and arrangement of materials. By arranging the nesting boxes on their sides with small wooden animals inside, the teachers are designing the environment to encourage pretending.

Integrating Literacy into Pretend Play

Signs and labels can be added to constructions in the manipulative area in the same way they are used in the block area. In fact, some manipulatives already include signs and labels. Lego and Duplo® have signs such as POLICE, HOTEL, and GAS printed on some of the blocks. The Fisher Price village has many store signs, traffic signs, and advertisements. Children can also create literacy-related props. Kari and Jason who built and flew Mobilo spaceships at the beginning of the chapter might have created a map for their travels.

Moving Things from the Manipulative Area

Some teachers have asked, "How do we encourage children to keep the manipulatives in that area?" But do these toys really need to remain in this area? Often when children create props they want to use them in other parts of the classroom. Spaceships are flown around to view the world, or are housed on space stations constructed in the block area. Walkie talkies made of bristle blocks are carried into the dramatic play area to be used by police officers and firefighters.

However, when children take these toys to other areas of the room, it may interfere with other children's ability to use the materials. Teachers have handled this in a number of ways. First, if the toy is extremely popular, an additional supply might be purchased to accommodate the many uses that children have for it. Second, the teacher can help the child find alternative materials to construct the needed props, so the manipulative materials will be available for the other children who need them.

Dramatic Play Outside

Children's dramatic play outside will usually be similar to that occuring in the dramatic play area, although because outside play areas are large, this play tends to involve more action. Outside pretend play is often more loosely organized, with children moving in and out of the play more frequently. The physical distance between players often means that subgames and different directions will develop, segmenting the story into many smaller stories.

Props

Creating a base for pretend play is more important outside than inside, where the dramatic play area provides a location for the story. Structures such as playhouses, slides, climbers, crates, or old cardboard boxes can become the focus for outside pretend play. Children will also use bushes, posts, and other stationary objects to define their houses, secret hideouts, or pirate ships.

Often minor changes in the environment will spark a new direction or vitality for the pretend play. If the playhouse is not being used, often

FIGURE 7-15 Climbers offer a base for pretend play stories

adding simple props such as dishes, brooms, or baby dolls will rekindle the interest in house play. Even simple rearrangement of materials can suggest new possibilities. Taking the table out of the playhouse may prompt stories about picnics or moving. Grouping the wooden crates together into a tight cluster to make a larger structure provides a large habitat for superheroes, rabbits, or whatever characters are currently popular with the children.

As in the case of Jameel's and Kurt's Batman game at the beginning of the chapter, vehicles such as bikes, wheelbarrows, baby carriages, and large ride-on wooden trucks and cars are often central to outside play. When teachers place themselves along the road they can talk with the riders as they speed by. In this way teachers can discover what stories, if any, accompany the riding. Teacher questions and modeling can help to initiate or extend this pretend play. Mr. Karlitz's presence allowed Jameel to add purchasing gas to his story. It also gave him the opportunity to verbalize his story to someone.

Integrating Literacy into Dramatic Play Outside

Paulo is standing in the middle of the trike path with his hand up. "STOP," he tells Rosa as she rides up. "You are going too fast. You need a ticket." He writes on his palm with an imaginary pencil, and hands her an imaginary ticket. "That's $500." She takes the ticket, reaches into her pocket, and places some imaginary money in his hand.

Often, as in this example, children will use imaginary props to enact functional uses for literacy. They will read pretend newspapers as they wait for a bus, look at a pretend recipes as they cook in the sandbox, or consult imaginary maps as they pilot their tricycle airplanes to Florida.

Real reading and writing materials can also be added to outside play. Real maps can be taped to the fence for all to consult, or they can be placed in pouches with shoulder straps so children can easily carry them along on their travels. Signs can be added to the play yard as well: traffic signs along the road, labeling signs to turn a part of the yard into a fast food restaurant, a post office, a firestation, or some other needed location. Bringing out paper, markers, and tape will allow children to create their own signs (see Figure 7-16).

The size of the yard affects the types of props to be brought outside. When the small envelopes used for the inside post office are used for the outside post office, they are easily lost in the larger expanses of the yard. The outside post office needs larger mail. The play yard postal workers can deliver enormous packages, huge corrugated postcards made out of sides of boxes, and letters placed in large, page-sized brown envelopes.

FIGURE 7-16 This sign warns people "No cutting down trees"

Playing Pretend in Other Contexts

The dramatic play, block, art, manipulative, and outside areas are just some of the many places that pretend play and literacy can be encouraged. Pretending can occur virtually anywhere and anytime. Observant teachers can discover opportunities for pretend play and encourage these by modeling, supporting, and providing appropriate props. Pretend play and literacy will flourish in a classroom where they are valued, and they will expand to become an integral part of everything that happens.

CHAPTER 8

Children's Books: A Gateway to Emergent Literacy

Two-year-old Daryl is sitting on Miss Hillman's lap talking about the pictures in his favorite book, **Jill the Farmer and Her Friends** *(Butterworth, 1986). They spend a long time looking at Dave the Builder, who drives the dump truck. Daryl makes a BRRRRRMMM noise for the dump truck. When they are done, he walks over to the block corner and puts on a hard hat. "I'm Dave," he says, as he drives the dump truck around in a circle, "BRRRRM-MM."*

* * *

The children listen with rapt interest to **A Visit to the Sesame Street Hospital** *(Houtzig, 1985) during story time in the three-to five-year-old class. In the story Grover is getting his tonsils out. After the story, the children share times they have been to the doctor and talk about new siblings that were born in the hospital. That day a hospital is set up in the dramatic play area. The operations of choice are tonsillectomies and delivering babies.*

* * *

Carl and Eric are making long strings of play dough by squeezing it through a garlic press. "Look, it's rain," Carl announces.
  "Mine's spaghetti," explains Eric.
  Carl giggles and adds, "My spaghetti's raining on the table."

*Miss Kobayashi asks, "Is it raining food in your town like it does in Chewandswallow?", [a fictional town in Barrett's **Cloudy with a Chance of Meatballs** (1978)]. Both boys agree. "Do you need some people for the spaghetti to rain on?" They agree again. Miss Kobayashi gets a basket of small Fisher Price people from the block corner. After a storm of spaghetti covers the people, Miss Kobayashi asks, "What other kind of weather are they going to have?" Eric and Carl spend the rest of play time devising different types of food to engulf their people.*

* * *

Four-year-old Elena is scrubbing the floor in the house area, while Jackie and Patrick are getting dressed to go out. "Can I stop now?" asks Elena.

"No," says Jackie, "you have to keep scrubbing, 'cause you're Cinderella, and we're going to the ball."

All of these children are using books as a basis for their pretend play. Daryl is emulating a favorite character; the doctors and patients are using a setting they have heard about in a book; Eric and Carl are playing with an idea from a book; while the Cinderella family is reenacting the storyline of a favorite book. Playing in this way brings the book closer to the children. They understand better what the book is communicating through making themselves a part of the characters, setting, ideas, and/or storyline. Children play about books that are important and meaningful to them, and through this playing the books will gain still greater meaning for the children.

It is clear that for these children books are an important and meaningful part of their lives. The joy and excitement that comes from hearing books is often what makes children wish to be a part of the reading/writing culture. They too want to be able to uncover the many treasures that books contain.

This chapter will explore the special relationship that children develop with books. Since book reading generally begins at home, we first examine how books are shared at home, and then the role of books in school or other group settings. The end of the chapter will explore ways to encourage the playing with books that was illustrated in the opening stories.

Reading at Home

Books are at the heart of any literacy program. It is generally accepted that reading to young children contributes to their early literacy development

(Teale, 1984). Researchers have found that reading books to young children supports vocabulary development (Ninio & Bruner, 1978; Ninio, 1980), facilitates language development (Chomsky, 1972; Ninio, 1980), increases enjoyment of books (Hiebert, 1981; Holdaway, 1979), and stimulates concept development (Teale, 1984).

Storybook reading also increases children's understanding of literacy concepts and practices. They learn the functions and uses of written language; develop concepts about print, books, and reading; learn about the form and structure of written language; and develop strategies for reading and writing (Teale, 1986). Being read to at home is the strongest predictor of later success in reading (Wells, 1985). How can such a simple activity encourage so much growth? Teale (1986) and Taylor (1983, 1986) suggested that picture book reading has great power because it is a warm, shared experience between parent and child. Holdaway (1979) described it as "among the happiest and most secure in his [the child's] experience" (p. 39).

The Special Qualities of Lap Reading

Family storybook reading, or lap reading as McCracken and McCracken (1972) called it, is different from just hearing a story. As parents read to their children they often stop and discuss the book. These discussions bring more meaning to the story by helping children tie what they hear in the book to what they have experienced in their lives.

This reading is not a passive activity in which parent reads and child listens, but a give-and-take where parent and child tell the story together. The child may, for example, supply the rhyming words at the end of the line, name characters or objects as they appear, or provide favorite lines at the appropriate time.

Children ask to hear favorite books over and over again. The child comes to know not just the story, but the pictures, the rhythm or cadence of the book, and the often repeated discussions that are part of the book sharing experience. This reading and rereading makes the book the child's.

Development of Family Reading Interactions

A number of researchers have studied parents and infants involved in book-reading episodes (Gibson, 1989; Snow & Ninio, 1986). Bruner (1983) gave a typical example of infant-parent book reading. Richard is thirteen months old.

Mother:	Look!
Richard:	(Touches picture)
Mother:	What are those?
Richard:	(Vocalizes a babble string and smiles)

FIGURE 8-1 Children listen to favorite books over and over

Mother: Yes, they are rabbits.
Richard: (Vocalizes, smiles, and looks up at mother)
Mother: (Laughs) Yes, rabbit.
Richard: (Vocalizes, smiles)
Mother: Yes. (Laughs) (p. 78)

This mother is labeling pictures, giving Richard a turn to respond, then taking another turn where she labels or questions. The book reading has a predictable sequence—the mother takes a turn then the child takes a turn.

As children become older, they take a more equal part in the storybook reading process. They repeat phrases and anticipate the storyline of favorite books, and they ask questions about the events in the story or pictures.

Flexible Patterns Develop around Sharing of Favorite Books

One of the joys of repeatedly sharing a favorite book is that a routine develops around the reading. Parents know the lines they will say. Children know what parts they add. Often favorite questions or comments about pictures or actions will become a part of the story-sharing routine. Although there is a set routine, there is still room for child and parent to add new patterns, responsibilities, and questions to the reading routine. Teale (1987) talked about how family storybook readings are both repetitive and innovative. They provide the child with a "generalized framework" within which both parent and child can add their own variations.

As books are read over and over the interaction around each book gradually changes. When books are read for the first time, children tend to label objects and characters. After texts are familiar, the discussions focus more around what the characters are doing and why (Martinez & Roser, 1985; Snow, 1983).

Special Family Book Events

Often special family phrases or discussions will become a routine part of the reading of a favorite book.

Three-year-old Michael and his dad are rereading a favorite book, Ox-Cart Man *(Hall, 1979). In the story a pioneer farmer walks a great distance to take his produce and furs to the distant town to sell them at the market. He sells each of the items he has brought. "With his pockets full of coins, he walked through Portsmouth Market"(p. 20). He buys a few items for the family and walks the long distance home. Today Dad adds his own line. "With his pockets full of coins, his pants fall down." Michael bursts into hysterical laughter. This line becomes a regular part of the reading of* Ox-Cart Man.

Michael and his family will often laugh as they approach the money line in expectation of what is to come. This is a shared experience that has meaning for both parent and child. The family ritual has created a special book culture around this book that is unique to the participants. Others, who have not participated in the ritual associated with this book will not understand why getting money is so funny.

This shared interaction with the book will move beyond just the time when the book is being read. One day, when Michael's dad is about to put a large pile of coins in his own pocket, Michael bursts out laughing. He imagines his Dad's pants falling down.

Voss (1988) described some wonderful examples of how interactions with books spread beyond reading time. Her two-year-old son Nathaniel's favorite book was *Make Way for Ducklings* by McCloskey (1941). One day, while eating baby applesauce from a jar Nathaniel pointed at the label and pretended to read, "Make way for applesauce" (Voss, 1988, p. 272). He was reading the applesauce label in the same way his mother read him the title of the book—by running his fingers under the words, yet he knew that the applesauce was not ducklings, and so changed the wording to fit the situation.

Nathaniel then took his mother out into the back yard to go to the miller and get some bread. He was enacting another favorite story, *The Little Red Hen* (Galdone, 1973). He ended the game in Neverland, the magical place where *Peter Pan* (Barrie, 1911) takes place. This weaving together of favorite stories is typical when children are pretending. They take the elements from stories they like and use them with other favorite pretend scripts.

The type of playing with books that Michael and Nathaniel are doing with their parents is possible because parent and child share common experiences with these books. It is unlikely that anyone else would understand why Michael found putting coins in a pocket so funny. His joke can only be understood in the context of past shared experiences reading *Ox-*

Cart Man with his dad. Nathaniel's mother understood why he was saying "make way for applesauce," and what they were to do at the miller's, because of their shared experiences with *Make Way for Ducklings* and *The Little Red Hen.* These families have each created a shared-book culture around favorite books.

The Value of Playing about Books

McLane and McNamee (1990) suggested that this playing about books has two important values to the child. First, book fantasy playing allows children to reflect on storybooks "to savor their memories, and deepen their understanding of them in fantasy play" (p. 80). Second,

> For children, using literary characters, plots, and language to tell or retell themselves stories may serve as a bridge to reading. In playing with storybook characters and reenacting scenes from books in literary language, children try out the voice of a reader—thus first experiencing reading in the context of play (p. 80).

Story Reading in Childcare Settings

How do we create a shared-book culture in childcare settings? How do childcare programs provide reading experiences that parallel home lap reading? We need to:

1. Reread books often so children know them well.
2. Make book reading part of a warm personal sharing time with others.
3. Change passive reading times, where adults read and children listen, into shared-book times where children can participate in a cooperative give-and-take with the adult.
4. Create a shared-book culture in the early childhood setting where children and adults have their own unique interactions around favorite books.
5. Encourage children to incorporate books into their pretend play.

Let us look at how each of these recommendations can be implemented in early childhood settings.

Rereading Books

Repeated reading of favorite books is a key to all the other recommendations. One of the things that makes family storybook reading such a special time is that the child usually knows and anticipates what will happen in the book, because favorite books are often reread. The reading of a book becomes not just a story to listen to, but a shared ritual.

Children must be familiar with the book in order to be active participants in the book-reading process. The first time a book is read to children, they will often just listen, but as a book is repeated over and over, children can join in the telling of that book. They can become cooperative partners in the book sharing event.

The wonderful shared-book culture that Michael and his dad developed around the *Ox-Cart Man* did not happen quickly. It was the result of numerous readings and rereadings of that favorite book. Nathaniel's pretend play about his favorite books also grew out of hearing the books repeatedly. In order to develop a group or classroom culture around favorite books, books must be read often enough to become favorites. These favorites must then be read often enough so patterns of interaction and play can develop around them.

Daryl's portrayal of Dave the Builder and the Cinderella story playing described at the beginning of the chapter each developed out of repeated experiences with a favorite book. Although it is possible for a single reading of a book to prompt dramatic play, usually it happens when the book that has been reread many times becomes meaningful enough to be used as a basis for play.

Making Times for Reading

In order to have time for repeated readings of books, there must be many opportunities during the day for children to listen to and share the reading of books. Let us look first at adults reading to large groups of children, then explore other times children can listen to books during the day.

FIGURE 8-2 Sharing a special moment as the group listens to a story

Storytimes with the Large Groups of Children

Storytime in the early childhood program brings together the children and the adults to share a warm, special moment with a book. The whole group is focused together on the unfolding of the story. They share the emotions, ideas, and events that the book depicts. At least one regular period should be set aside each day for storytime. In full-day programs a minimum of two or three times is recommended. Additional books can be read to fill in unexpected delays, such as waiting for the bus or when lunch is late.

Can This Time Be Used for Rereading Favorite Books?

Storytime is often used for presenting new books to the children. Can it also be used for rereading favorite books? When I began teaching, I was skeptical about using story time to reread books the children had already heard. As it was, whenever I held up a book there were sure to be a few children who would shout out, "I know that book!" What reaction would I get to a book all the children knew? The first time I reread a favorite book I got the response I expected, "You read that before, aren't you going to read something new?" I was uncomfortable with the rereading and so were the children.

When I evaluated the event later I realized that the problem was my attitude. I didn't believe the book should be reread at group time, and I communicated this to the children. The next time I planned to reread a book, I was prepared for the response. When they all shouted, "You read that before," I agreed. "I picked it because I know it is one of your favorites, and you can help me read it." This time both the children and I enjoyed the rereading. When I presented rereading as a special event, the children saw it that way, too. Rereading became a regular part of group time.

Some childcare workers make one day of the week "Favorite Story Day." Children can request books that they wish to hear on that day. If the list gets long, and the program has more than one adult, the group can be divided. Each adult can read a different book. The children select which story they wish to hear. Old favorites can also be kept fresh by using a variety of formats for presenting them to the children.

Feltboard Stories

Using a feltboard can add a new twist to a favorite tale. Stories that have little physical action are best, because it is difficult to move more than one piece at a time. For this reason, a story such as *The Gingerbread Man* would not translate well into a feltboard story. *The Little Red Hen,* in which it is only the hen that moves from the field, to the miller, to the stove, would be an excellent story to tell on the feltboard. Stories that are particularly suited to this type of retelling included those that are cumulative and that have add-on features such as *Too Much Noise* by McGovern (1971), where one animal after another is brought into the house.

Books where the details of the illustrations are an important part of the story do not make good feltboard stories. For example, much of the charm of *If You Give a Mouse a Cookie* (Numeroff, 1985) comes from wonderful illustrations showing the scrapes the mouse gets into. Telling the story on the feltboard would lose the humor and warmth provided by the details.

A STEP FURTHER   *Making Story Pieces*

There are a number of ways to make pieces for retelling stories.

For adults who are not skilled artists, illustrations can be traced onto thin paper, colored, and mounted on heavier paper. Felt tape can be attached to the back so the figure will adhere to the feltboard. Pellon or other nonwoven interfacing material, available at fabric stores, can also be used for the figures. This is thin enough to allow the picture to be traced, and it adheres to the feltboard. It is best to get a medium- or heavy-weight pellon so the pieces have enough substance.

Puppets for Retelling Favorite Stories

Puppets can be used to reenact favorite stories. It is best to select stories in which the background is not important, where the number of characters is limited, and where simple motions can illustrate the action of the plot. *The*

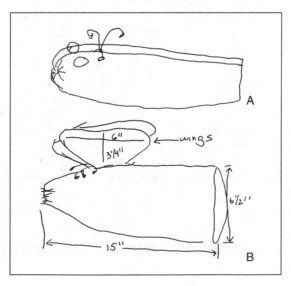

FIGURE 8-3 Drawing of the caterpillar puppet (A) as a caterpillar, (B) as a butterfly

Very Hungry Caterpillar by Eric Carle (1981) makes an excellent puppet story.

A wide variety of puppets can be used for storytelling: store-bought puppets, sock puppets, glove puppets (in which the characters attach to the fingers of a glove), homemade paper bag puppets, or even a traced picture from the book mounted on a tongue depressor. Many books offer ideas for puppet making and puppet stories.

Story Box Stories

Stories can also be brought to life by using small props to reenact the story. The props are all kept in a box, hence the name **"story box."** Often

A STEP FURTHER   The Very Hungry Caterpillar *Puppet Story*

Follow these steps to tell *The Very Hungry Caterpillar* as a puppet story.

To make a caterpillar puppet, make a tube of knit cloth and stitch together one end, or tie the toe of an old kneesock into a knot. Turn inside out. The puckered spot around the toe becomes the mouth. Add button eyes. Pipe cleaners make excellent antennae. To make the butterfly, sew stiff felt wings inside of the sock a bit further up the leg from the eyes (see Figure 8-3).

To tell the story, put your hand in the puppet, hold onto the knot, then fold the leg of the sock back over your hand so that the face does not show. This is the caterpillar egg asleep on a leaf that starts the story. Your other arm, or a stiff paper model, can be the leaf (see Figure 8-4).

To hatch the caterpillar pull the leg of the sock back so it is scrunched around your wrist and the eyes are visible. Now the caterpillar is small. As you tell the story, gradually stretch the leg of the sock further and further up your arm so the caterpillar can grow.

Make the foods in the story, (one apple, two pears, etc.) out of large sheets of laminated construction paper. Make a fist-sized hole in the middle of each piece of food. As the caterpillar eats the food in the story, hold up the appropriate food and have the puppet eat it by sticking its head through the hole in the food. After the food is eaten, pull the sock up to your elbow, where it can remain until the end of the story.

When the caterpillar makes a cocoon, pull the end of the sock back over the caterpillar's head to hide it. Finish turning the sock inside out and the butterfly will emerge.

Make the children more active participants in the story by giving each a food to hold (see Figure 8-5).

FIGURE 8-4 The Hungry Caterpillar puppet is just an egg on a leaf

FIGURE 8-5 Children giggle as the Hungry Caterpillar eats through the food they are holding

the box is turned upside down and used as the stage for acting out the story with the props. When selecting stories to use for story box retelling, it is best to pick ones in which the background illustrations are not important, where the actions are simple, and which present only a few characters. *Martin's Hats* (Blos, 1984) would not make a good story box story, since the backgrounds dictate the type of hat and action that Martin should take. Some books that lend themselves well to story box retelling are: *Too Much Noise* (McGovern, 1971), *The Three Bears* (Galadone, 1972), *The Billy Goats Gruff* (Martin, 1963), and *Nobody Listens to Andrew* (Guilfoile, 1957).

Unlimited Possibilities

As these examples show, the ways of presenting stories are only limited by your imagination. For adults who are comfortable drawing, the chalkboard is often a good prop for telling stories. Adults can draw the story as they tell it to the children. *Harold and the Purple Crayon* (Johnson, 1955) is particularly effective told in this way. Another way of presenting stories to children is with filmstrips, videotapes, or records. Many children's books are available on filmstrip or videotape. Numerous children's books are recorded on records and audiotape.

A STEP FURTHER   Too Much Noise *Story Box*

When telling a story with props it is good to have a stage of some sort: A smooth piece of wood, an upside down box, or the bottom side of a tray all make excellent stages for your story. For *Too Much Noise* I use the stage as the house, and nearby I have a small platform made out of unit blocks or an oatmeal box, for the Wise Person. (The story says "Wise Man," but I prefer to use the nonsexist term when I read and tell the story.)

Wooden animals and people that are often used in the block area make excellent characters. If a certain animal cannot be found, cut out a picture of the animal and tape it to a small box or piece of wood. Wooden furniture can be used for the bed and stove. A bit of reality can be added by using a small tree branch with a play dough base, as the leaves that fall on the roof "swish, swish." A block can be the bed that "squeaks," and a teakettle borrowed from a doll house can be the kettle that whistles "hiss, hiss."

Begin the story with Peter, the bed, the stove, and the kettle in the house. Place the tree next to the house and the Wise Person on the platform. As you tell the story, move Peter back and forth between the Wise Person and the house. Add the animals to the house as Peter does this in the story. It is particularly effective to wave the branch over the house when the leaves go "swish, swish," and to point to other objects as they make noises (see Figure 8-6).

FIGURE 8-6 Telling the *Too Much Noise* story with a story box

Telling Stories without the Book

When retelling a favorite book with props, feltboard, puppets, or other visual aids, it is essential that the adult knows the story well. The retelling must capture the rhythm and flow of the story as well as the plot.

Reading Books at Other Times of Day

Group storytime should be one of many times during the day when children can hear stories. Examine your daily schedule to discover how to increase children's opportunities to hear and share books.

Books During Play Time

Early childhood programs should have large blocks of time in which children are free to select their own activities. This time goes by various names: play time, activity time, free choice time, or even work time. I am using the term "play time" to refer to this part of the day. The space used by the children should be set up with many different areas.

An attractive library area should be available, where children can go to read books, be an author, listen to taped books, use puppets or other oral language materials, retell a favorite feltboard story, listen to a favorite book on the computer, or snuggle in a chair with a favorite book. Morrow (1989, 1993) provided a detailed discussion of how to set up such a center. A wide variety of books should be available. New books should be added to the center often, especially ones that have been read at storytime. It is important to make sure that old favorites remain in the area to allow for repeated readings.

Schickedanz (1986) suggested that it is important for early childhood educators to spend time in the book corner. This communicates to the

FIGURE 8-7 An armchair is a cozy place to read a book with a friend

children that this is a good place to be. It also offers children the opportunity to listen to, share, and discuss books with an adult. However, Schickedanz stressed that the teacher does not need to be there all the time. It is good for children to have some private time with books as well.

Other adults can be invited to the room as "guest readers." Parents, senior citizens, and children from older grades will all enjoy this special role. Remember that adults aren't always necessary to read books. Children can also share and discuss favorite books with peers.

Books need not be limited to the book area. Having a book about gerbils next to the pet, a construction book in the blocks, some songbooks near the rhythm instruments, and storybooks in the dramatic play area to read at bedtime, will allow adults and children to share books in many parts of the early childhood setting.

FIGURE 8-8 Playing a homemade kazoo while looking at the class songbook

Finding Time to Share a Book

As every early childhood educator knows, there is never enough time to do everything that you wish to do. One child may need a lap and a familiar story, while the children in blocks are getting wild and need your calming influence. Try meeting both needs by taking the child and the book into the block area. You can share the book while you help the builders move towards more constructive play.

Book Time

Consider designating a fifteen-to twenty-five-minute period each day as book time. At this time children and adults find favorite books. They can look at the book independently, share a book with peers, or explore a book with an adult. This gives children the opportunity to repeat favorite books by reading the pictures, by retelling the book themselves, or by listening to a peer or an adult retell the book.

At the beginning of the year children who have not had a lot of experience with books may find this time difficult. They may feel that they need to have an adult's constant attention in order to hear a book. Early childhood educators can help children to define themselves as book explorers in many ways.

- Have multiple copies of popular books that have been read to the group, so children can read a book they know.
- Provide many wordless books that do not require reading.
- Provide books geared to the special interests of individual children.
- Help children select books that will interest them.
- Model how to explore new books without reading them.
- Offer books with special things to search for like *Where's Waldo?* (Handford, 1987) or *Have You Seen My Duckling?* (Tarfuri, 1984).

A STEP FURTHER   *Books with Searching Games*

Ahlberg, J. & A. (1979) *Each peach pear and plum; An "I spy" story.* Children search for hiding fairy tale characters.

Baker, K. (1993) *Hide and snake.* Children search for a snake that is hiding among different things on each page.

Cartwright, S. & Zeff, C. (1983) *Find the piglet.* Wordless cardboard book that shows a piglet on first page, then shows it hiding in various locations around the farm. There are other books in this series.

Civardi, A. (1985) *First experiences: Moving house.* A simple book about moving. On each page among the objects moved a little yellow duck is hiding. There are other books in this series.

Demi. (1985) *Demi's find the animal A B C book.* Each page has large outline of an animal, filled with many smaller drawings of that animal. Children must find one that matches the drawing next to the letter.

Dubanevich, A. (1983) *Pigs in hiding.* A book showing pigs playing hide and seek, hiding in all sorts of funny places around the house. Little text.

Handford, M. (1987) *Where's Waldo?* Children need to find Waldo and pieces of this clothing in crowded pages. This is challenging. There are many Waldo books.

Henrietta, (1991) *A mouse in the house.* Simple story of a mouse exploring the house. Children search for the mouse hidden on each page.

Knight, H. (1964) *Where's Wallace?* The story of a monkey who keeps escaping from the zoo, with a little help from the keeper, to explore the city. Children must search for Wallace and other characters after each escape.

Kowitt, H. (1991) *The Fenderbenders get lost in America.* Children search for the family at various vacation spots.

Marzollo, J. (1992) *I spy: A book of picture riddles.* Children search photographs for the objects listed in each rhyme.

Micklethwait, L. (1991) *An alphabet in art.* Children search works of art for objects throughout the alphabet. There are other books in the series.

Raskin, E. (1966) *Nothing ever happens on my block.* Children can search for the witch who moves from window to window.

Tafuri, N. (1984) *Have you seen my duckling?* Children help the Mama duck search for her wandering duckling.

Tallarico, A. (1990) *Where are they? Search for Susie.* Children search for Susie and other objects on crowded pages. There is a series of "Where are they?" books.

Ungerer, T. (1964) *One, two where's my shoe?* A book of pictures that incorporates shoes into the pictures.

Wilson, A. (1990) *Look! The ultimate spot-the-difference book.* Wonderful pictures of different habitats. Children look at each pair to see how they vary.

Yektai, N. (1989) *What's silly?* Children look to see what is silly in each picture.

It is important that book time be a distinct period, not just a holding pattern between one activity and another.

Miss Jackson's class is cleaning up after activity time. As children finish cleaning, they get a book and find a spot on the rug. Laveenia sees children getting books so she drops the dress she was putting away and runs to find a book. Nnamdi and Kyla have been working hard to scrub the paint off the table. They are the last children over to the rug. Just as they settle down with their books Miss Jackson announces, "Time to put your books away so we can go outside."

In this classroom children either help to clean, or have time to read books. They do not get a chance to do both. By using books as a time filler in this way Miss Jackson is communicating to the children that books are not important: Looking at books is something to do when there is nothing else happening. Miss Jackson could remedy these problems by encouraging all children to continue cleaning until everything is put away. After cleanup is completed she could have a book time where all the children get a sufficient amount of time to read their books.

Outside Time

Why not bring books out into the play yard? This is particularly appropriate for daycare centers where children often spend long spans of time outside during the summer. Spread a blanket in a shady spot, and bring out a basket of books. Children's hands often tend to be grimy after playing outside. To protect the books, you may want to have children wash their hands before selecting one to read. A container of wet wipes can also be used to combat grimy fingers. Some adults use outside time to read to children—this way they are handling the books.

Many Opportunities for Rereading Books

As you can see, the early childhood setting can provide many opportunities for children to read and reread favorite books. In order for children to make use of these opportunities, adults must create an atmosphere that values books. If adults value and enjoy books, if they delight in rereading books, if they share their children's excitement over discoveries about favorite books, then rereading books will become an essential group event.

FIGURE 8-9 Book time is a special time of day

Let us now look at the next recommendation for making reading in school emulate family story reading.

Creating Warm Shared Experiences around Reading Books

Family storybook reading is a special time. Families step back from the hassles of the day to share together the joys of books. According to Schickedanz, "The bedtime story may be one of the most positive times of the day for both parent and child" (1986, p. 49). Reading in early childhood programs can never replace this cherished family time, but it can provide additional warm, positive experiences with story reading. This is a second way in which we can make book experiences in group care similar to what children find at home.

Part of the special quality of family reading is the close personal interaction between parent and child. Children are often on the parent's lap, or snuggled up next to them. This same type of one-on-one or small group reading can be provided in childcare settings during free play, outside time, and book time. In fact, in a program where lap reading is the norm, some children will pick a book and climb in the adult's lap because they need that close contact with the teacher. They will sit for a page and then be off.

Group story time cannot provide this same cozy experience, but it can provide an opportunity for the children to unite as a group in a shared pleasurable event.

Children Actively Participating in Book Sharing

A third characteristic of family book reading is the shared nature of the reading event. According to Teale (1984),

> Virtually all analyses of what occurs when parents read to their children (or when teachers read to their students) show that the events are socially interactive ones in which the actual reading of the text and the meaning produced in the reading are constructed through a cooperative negotiation between adult and child (p. 118).

Teachers in Australia felt the interactive reading that parents and children do together was so important that they developed a school approach that parallels the family reading. Holdaway (1979) described this shared book experience. Big books (enlarged copies of books) are placed on an easel where the children can easily see the words and pictures. These books are read many times. Adults use a pointer to follow the text as they read. Child participation in the reading, exploration of print features, and discussion of the story are all integral parts of the shared reading process. Shared book reading makes all the children equal participants in the reading process.

Creating a Group Book Culture

Parents and children develop their own special patterns around the reading of favorite books. Building these types of group patterns around books in childcare settings is a fourth way to parallel home reading. How do childcare providers create patterns that are unique and meaningful to each group of children? How do they ensure the development of a special book culture for each group of children?

There is no formula or set of lesson plans that can be followed to establish a group book culture. Rather, it grows spontaneously from interactions between adults and children as books are shared. First, adults must realize that it is valuable to develop group rituals around books. Then adults must listen to and watch children's responses to books that are read. These patterns are developed as someone adds a personal response during a book-reading event, and someone else adds onto this. Gradually the response builds into a ritual that is repeated with each retelling of the book. When adults are in tune with children, these reading patterns develop naturally.

Each Group Develops Its Own Unique Rituals

Just as Michael and his dad established their own way of reading *Ox-Cart Man*, each group will build its own unique interaction patterns around favorite books. When reading Eric Carle's *The Grouchy Lady Bug* (1977) to

FIGURE 8-10 These children join in the retelling of *Too Much Noise;* one child even imitates the teacher's actions and language

a class, I noticed that the children did not seem to understand the difference between what the lady bug said and what it meant.

The lady bug goes from animal to animal asking, "Do you want to fight?" "If you insist," the animal replies in a menacing fashion. The grouchy lady bug looks at the creature again and says, "Ah, Ah, you're not big enough." The ladybug flies to a larger animal and the whole sequence begins again. The children did not understand that the lady bug was scared to fight the big creature, and used "you're not big enough" as an excuse for avoiding the battle.

The first time I read the story the next year, I wanted children to understand that the lady bug was scared of the big creatures. When I got to the fourth creature, a bird that is noticeably bigger than the lady bug, I asked the children "Which is bigger?"

"The bird," they all replied.

I nodded agreement, "I think he's just scared." When the lady bug told the next creature, "You're not big enough," the children all shouted, "It's big enough. He's just scared." This phrase became a necessary part of the book reading for the rest of the year.

Each group of children is different. Another group may not have found this phrase worth preserving. If one group has developed a special pattern around a book, adults may want to try that pattern on the next group. However, they should not force the adoption of a pattern that is not of interest to the group. An observant, responsive adult will help to develop and maintain interactions around a book that are meaningful to that particular group of children.

Encouraging Children to Share Favorite Book Rituals from Home

Two-year-old Raymond is getting ready to go to bed in the housekeeping area. He puts on a long flowing bathrobe and goes around the house saying, "goodnight table, goodnight chair, goodnight window."

"You sound like one of my favorite books, Goodnight Moon," *comments the teacher Ilene.*

"I have that book," says Raymond.

"Do you think we should have it at school too?" Ilene inquires. Raymond answers in the affirmative and Ilene promises to find the book for tomorrow. Raymond continues saying goodnight to things in the house, then climbs in the doll bed and pretends to go to sleep.

The next day Ilene added the book to the bookshelf. Raymond's enthusiasm for *Goodnight Moon* (Brown, 1947) was contagious. Soon many children were wishing classroom objects goodnight. By recognizing and supporting Raymond's book play, Ilene provided a bridge for Raymond between home and school. She also helped transform his home book play ritual into a classroom book play pattern.

Nathaniel's Mom knew *The Little Red Hen*, so she quickly realized that Nathaniel's trip to the miller was intended to get wheat ground to make flour. In the same way, Ilene recognized that Raymond was playing with *Goodnight Moon* because it was a book she happened to know well. However, the sources of book play are not always that easy to determine. If you have not shared the book with the child, and especially if it is a book that you do not know well, it will be harder to discover the context of the pretend play.

Although two-year-old Raymond might not have been able to verbalize the source of his play, *Goodnight Moon*, without Ilene's question, older children can often tell you the origin of their play. If Raymond had been older, Ilene might have asked, "What made you think to say goodnight to all the furniture?" In that case, Raymond might well have said, "It is like the bunny in the book." If Ilene did not know the book, she could have asked Raymond to tell her a bit about it. If she still did not recognize the book, she could have encouraged Raymond to bring it in to share with her.

Incorporating Parts of Books into Other Activities

Incorporating parts of books into nonreading activities is another way to create a shared book experience for the group. After enjoying *The Gingerbread Man* (Galdone, 1975), offer the children the chance to bake their own gingerbread men. After reading *The Little Fish That Got Away* (Cook, 1956), children can use magnets to catch paper fish with paper clip mouths, or examine a real fish with a magnifying glass. After reading *Corduroy* (Freeman, 1968), children can "find Corduroy's button" by drawing a picture around a button glued on drawing paper (Raines & Canady, 1989, p. 144) (see Figure 8-11). After reading *Growing Vegetable Soup* (Ehlert, 1987), children can make their own vegetable soup, get to know vegetables better by weighing them and examining them with magnifying glasses, or hauling them around in trucks in the block area. After reading *Swimmy* (Lionni, 1968), children could use an outline of a fish and many small fish to create the illusion of a large fish like Swimmy, and his friends (see Figure 8-12).

In each of these cases children are incorporating some part of a book into other activities. The opportunity to have a first-hand experience with a fish, vegetables, and a gingerbread man will make the books more meaningful when they are read again.

If the books are familiar to the children, they may bring their knowledge of the book into the activity. A child making a gingerbread man may give it extra long legs so it can get away from all the chasers. Another child may be the wolf eating the gingerbread man.

FIGURE 8-11 Making pictures around Corduroy's lost button

FIGURE 8-12 Making a big fish with Swimmy and his friends

Adults can help children bring their knowledge of the book to the activity by drawing a connection.

> *Mr. Cooney reads* Corduroy *to his class of four-year-olds. When the book is finished, he asks, "Where do you think Corduroy's missing button is?" The children offer many suggestions about what might have happened to the button, ranging from "The girl found it and sewed it back on," to "A monster took it."*
>
> *"I wanted to draw a picture of my idea," says Mr. Cooney, "so I glued a button onto some paper. Now I can draw a picture around it to show where it is. If you want to help find Corduroy's button there are more button papers at the art table."*
>
> *Dara surrounded her button with many large circles. "This is a button store," she says. Tyrell scribbles randomly around his button, telling the teacher, "It's just scribbles." Sharla draws a garden. The button is the center of the biggest flower. Devon draws an enormous bed over the missing button. Kiesha scribbles blue, red, and brown on the page. "This is the lake I went swimming in this summer, where I lost my red barrette."*

The children differ widely in their way of responding to this activity. Dara's, Tyrell's and Sharla's drawings did not incorporate the book. Some of them drew things that were recognizable, while others did not. Devon and Kiesha did draw a location for the missing button. Devon did it in a way that was recognizable to any viewer. While Kiesha, who is not as mature an artist, drew scribbles whose connection to the book was apparent in listening to her description.

Another way of playing about books is to incorporate aspects of the books into pretend play. This leads us to the fifth recommendation for making school emulate the family storybook reading experience.

Encouraging Pretend Play around Books

Pretending with books is the child's way of contemplating what he or she has heard. McLane and McNamee (1990) suggested:

> When adults read a book that they find interesting or moving in some way, they are likely to talk about it with family or friends. Young children . . . often reflect on situations in story books, savor their memories, and deepen their understanding of them in fantasy play (p. 80)

This chapter began with four stories of children playing with books. What prompts this type of play? If children are to play with books, they must know them well. They must also value books, for children use things that are important to them in their pretend play. If the first four recommendations are followed—rereading books, making book reading a warm personal time, encouraging children to participate in book sharing, and creating a group book culture—then the early childhood setting will be a

---

A STEP FURTHER *Resources on Playing about Books*

Many books now come with suggestions for teachers on how to extend their use. Each of the Scholastic big books comes with a teacher's guide. There are books aimed specifically at helping teachers to extend a wide range of literature.

Story S-T-R-E-T-C-H-E-R-S: Activities to expand children's favorite books by Shirley C. Raines and Robert J. Canady, (1989). Mt. Rainier, MD: Gryphon House.

> Discusses ways to stretch the use of 90 children's books. Activities are suggested for circle time, art, cooking, creative dramatics, dramatic play, music and movement, blocks, science, mathematics and manipulatives, and the library corner. The books are grouped together around some common themes of interest to young children.

More story S-T-R-E-T-C-H-E-R-S: Activities to expand children's favorite books by Shirley C. Raines and Robert J. Canady (1991). Mt. Rainier, MD: Gryphon House.

> Another 90 books presented in the same way as the earlier book.

McElmeel booknotes: Literature across the curriculum by Sharon McElmeel (1993). Englewood, CO: Teacher's Ideas Press.

> Discusses how to use picture books with elementary school children. Although some of the ideas are for older children, many can be adapted for the younger ages as well.

Beyond storybooks: Young children and the shared book experience by Judith Pollard Slaughter (1992). Newark, DE:IRA.

> Discusses ways of using books in the classroom. Specific examples are included with theory.

These resources can serve as a springboard to help you design activities that fit best in the book culture that is developing in your classroom.

place in which books are valued. This will create an atmosphere where book play will flourish.

Integrating Book Play into Children's Dramatic Play

Book play can be integrated into dramatic play in the same four ways that literacy in general is integrated into dramatic play:

1. The book can be a central focus of the dramatic play, as in *all-encompassing integration* of books.
2. Book play may be a part of other dramatic play, as in the *enrichment* mode of integrating books.
3. Adults may spontaneously draw books into ongoing pretend play, as in *incidental integration* of books.
4. Children may incorporate books into their own pretend play, as is in *child initiated-integration* of books.

A closer look at each of these modes of integration follows.

FIGURE 8-13 Taped books offer children a way to rehear favorite stories

All-Encompassing Integration

All-encompassing integration of books into dramatic play occurs when some aspect of a book is the central focus of the dramatic play as in the following example.

> Caps for Sale *(Slobodkina, 1940) is the favorite book of Mr. Thomas's class of four-year-olds. They have been walking around the class with stacks of caps for sale. A group of monkeys tries to steal the caps when they can. Mr. Thomas decides to create a setting for playing caps for sale. He covers one side of an indoor wooden climber with brown butcher's paper, on which he draws a large tree. Openings in the branches are left near the platforms. The brown paper is cut away here, making a space where monkeys can reach down to get the peddler's caps. Many hats are added to the house, so each peddler can have a large inventory.*

Mr. Thomas has created a dramatic play setting, specifically for playing *Caps for Sale*. The setting allows children to immerse themselves in the story. This dramatic play environment was well used by the children, because it had been designed around their interests.

Props can be used to create a pretend play activity in other parts of the room where an element of a book is the central focus of the pretending. The early childhood educator could add a rubber fly, frog, fish, snake, and turtle, along with a net and a small basket to the water table to allow children to enact the story *Jump, Frog, Jump!* (Kalan, 1981).

Story boxes of props that adults use to tell stories during group time can be available for retelling the story by the children. Some children like to listen to a tape of the story being read as they move the figures, while others—like Quay—prefer to tell the story on their own.

> *Four-year-old Quay is intrigued with his teacher's feltboard retelling of* The Mixed-up Chameleon *(Carle, 1975). At play time, he is the first to the feltboard. The teacher starts to put on the tape. "I don't want it," Quay protests, "I want to read the story myself." He opens the book and gives an approximation of the sentence there as he follows along with his finger. He then puts down the book and adds the appropriate felt pieces. He continues in this way until he has retold the whole story.*

One kindergarten teacher placed the big easel with *Jump, Frog, Jump!* near the water table of props, so that one child could read the story, while the other children moved the props (see Figure 8-15).

All-encompassing integration of books has advantages, as well as raising some concerns. When children are pretending in these settings, they must immerse themselves in the books. A possible concern is that if this adult-structured dramatic play is used extensively, it can narrow the type of play that occurs in the area. If adults are not tuned into the children's interests, a structured play setting like the one Mr. Thomas set up could be stifling.

FIGURE 8-14 This child uses the book and feltboard to retell *The Mixed-up Chameleon*

Enrichment Integration

Enrichment integration of books into dramatic play occurs when book play is an option that can be used to enhance play that does not center around the book. For example, many different types of hats can be added to the house area so that children can become different people with the different hats, as Martin does in *Martin's Hats.* Children can play house, as they normally would, or they can emulate Martin: putting on the safari hat and going on an adventure to the jungle, putting on the firefighter hat and dousing fires, or becoming a king or queen by donning the crown.

Incidental Integration

Incidental integration of books into dramatic play occurs when early childhood educators spontaneously come up with ways to incorporate book play, as in the following examples.

FIGURE 8-15 One child reads *Jump, Frog, Jump!* while others act it out

Keesha and Zack are in the house area getting dressed to go shopping. Joanne, the teacher, asks if she can come, too. Keesha and Zack deck her with necklaces, scarves and glasses. Both pick out hats. They each struggle to get a hat on her head first. Joanne reaches up and secures both hats on her head. She begins walking up and down saying "Caps for sale, fifty cents a cap." Keesha and Zack giggle, then they both stack caps on their heads and begin hawking their wares.

* * *

The children are playing family in the house area. Zibby is told by the other children to stay home and clean, while they go to school. She is not pleased with the role she is given and grumbles as she sweeps the floor. Mr. Fahey comments, "You remind me of Cinderella." Zibby perks up, now she can have a prize role. "That's who I am," she proclaims. She runs over and tells the other children. "I'm Cinderella and that's why I can't go to school." The other children become the stepsisters, give out more cleaning orders and head to the ball rather than school.

In both of these cases the adult responded to the children's ongoing play in a way that related to favorite books. Joanne models the book play and the children then follow her lead. Mr. Fahey makes a comment about a book character that Zibby then incorporates into her play. Although these children all used the teacher's suggestions, this is not always the case. If the shopping trip had been important to Keesha and Zack, they would have continued on their expedition instead of becoming peddlers. Zibby might not have adopted the Cinderella role, or she might have met resistance from the other children.

Incidental integration of books is a gentle way that adults can make connections between play and books. It shows the children that adults value and participate in book play. If done right, it is unobtrusive, allowing children to join in if they chose, or to continue their own direction of play if they prefer.

Child-Initiated Integration

Child-initiated integration of books into dramatic play occurs when children initiate book play without prompting from the adult. Examples of this are when Nathaniel pretends to go to the miller to get some grain, and when Daryl proclaims he is Dave the builder. Child-initiated integration of books is an indication that adults have been successful in creating an atmosphere supportive of book play.

When children initiate their own book play, adults may want to help them extend it by joining the play, as Natheniel's mom did or by adding some extra props. Perhaps Cinderella needs more cleaning utensils. The adult can also broadcast what the child has done so others may join in. Adults may design an area around the children's idea, as when Mr. Thomas made a place to play *Caps for Sale*; or they may just observe how the children's play unfolds.

What Components of Books Prompt Book Play?

Often when people think about playing with books they envision the class acting out the story of the book, but plot is only one of the components of books that elicits book play. A look back at the examples in the beginning of the chapter will show four components of books which can prompt book play: character, setting, ideas, and plot. Let's examine the play generated by each of these components.

Characters as a Source of Book Play

When Daryl walks into the block area and puts on the hard hat, he becomes Dave the Builder. In play acting this character, Daryl experiences the power of being a construction worker. In adopting roles, children can become the people they emulate. Trying on roles in this way also builds a better understanding of the character.

Child-Initiated Character Play

Book play based on character is generally child initiated. Like Daryl, children will bring a favorite character closer by drawing that character into their play. Some children will become the character as Daryl has. Other children will imagine the presence of the character as a participant with them in play.

When my daughter was little she had a series of Sesame Street books that she read over and over. At two she would include many of the Muppets in her play. When we drove anywhere, we had to call Oscar, Big Bird, Snuffy, Bert, and Ernie to get in the car. They all had to be buckled up. No matter how many characters we called, she always remembered someone we had forgotten. The last character had to be hurried into the car and buckled up before we could go.

At other times she would include stuffed Muppets in her pretend play. Many book characters are now available in stuffed form: Spot, Corduroy, Clifford, Max and the Wild Things, to name just a few.* If a stuffed replica is not available, children will often use what they have. Many stuffed monkeys have become Curious George, and stuffed rabbits often become the naughty Peter Rabbit. **

---

*Spot is a dog from a series of Spot books by Eric Hill, such as *Where's Spot* (1980), Corduroy is a teddy bear from Don Freeman's *Corduroy* [1968] and *A Pocket for Corduroy* (1978). Clifford is a dog from a series of books by Norman Bridwell, such as *Clifford the Big Red Dog* (1986). Max and the Wild Things are from Maurice Sendak's *Where the Wild Things Are* (1963).
**Curious George is from a series of books by H.A. Ray. The first entitled *Curious George* (1941). Peter Rabbit is the hero of Beatrix Potter's well known *The Tales of Peter Rabbit* (1902).

Incidental Character-Related Play

Although character play is usually child initiated, early childhood educators can introduce this type of book play as well. Adults can do this incidentally as when Mr. Fahey commented to Zibby, "You remind me of Cinderella." In order to do this effectively, teachers must know which characters have meaning for the children. Adults can also draw characters into the book play by taking on the role of a favorite character.

Enrichment Integration of Characters into Dramatic Play

Although this is done less often, early childhood educators can use enrichment integration to draw book characters into dramatic play. In the same class where Daryl played Dave the Builder, many of the other two-year-olds reread the page about Jill the Farmer. In response to this interest, the adult added rubber animals and tractors to the block area. The area next to the house was turned into a farm by adding paper bag heads and cloth coverings to saw horses, and adding brushes and food bowls to care for the animals. Some children on their own declared they were Jill the Farmer. Others followed their lead, or responded to the teacher's comment about what Jill the Farmer might do. Still other children played farm without any interest in Jill. This setting allowed children to integrate the character if they desired, but also allowed those who chose to develop the play in their own way.

All-Encompassing Integration of Characters into Dramatic Play

Adults would not design all-encompassing integration of characters into dramatic play during free play, because it is too adult-structured for this time of day. But this mode might be used during group time. Early childhood educators might design a creative movement activity where the children try on a certain character. The children might be the peddler from *Caps for Sale* and walk through various terrains without losing their caps. They might explore what it would be like to be the troll from *The Billy Goats Gruff*. How does a troll move? How does he hide under the bridge? (See Figure 8-16.) They might become Imogene, the girl in *Imogene's Antlers* (Small, 1985), who woke up one morning with antlers and the next day with a peacock tail, and experiment with how they would move with different types of animal parts.

Settings as a Source of Book Play

Books can provide information about a setting that can later be the basis for pretend play. The children at the beginning of the chapter listened to *A Visit to the Sesame Street Hospital*, then pretended in a dramatic play area

FIGURE 8-16 How does a troll move?

designed as a hospital. The book provided the children with a common hospital experience as a basis for developing their play.

Although all of the children had past experiences with doctors, not all had past experiences with hospitals. The book showed children that familiar doctors and medical procedures are part of the unfamiliar hospital event. The book extended the children's knowledge about doctors and hospitals, and in turn the dramatic play helped children to better comprehend what they had heard in the book.

At times, books about more familiar settings, such as the supermarket, can be used to create a shared expectation of what might happen in the dramatic play area. However, if the setting is too foreign to the children, the book alone may not provide enough background to support playing the theme.

When observing children's play, it is sometimes difficult to determine when a theme has been generated by a book, or when it has been derived from another source. Adam loves boats. He likes talking about them, and usually chooses boat books at book time. When playing on the climber outside, Adam turns it into different types of boats, on a wide variety of exciting missions. It may be that the play grew out of the books he reads, or it may be that the books and the play both indicate a deep interest in boats.

Early childhood educators can employ two modes of integrating book settings into dramatic play: enrichment integration and incidental integration. The first mode is used when adults use a book to introduce the theme for a dramatic play area, or read a book to extend themes that children have been playing.

Adults may draw book settings into dramatic play incidentally by commenting on the connection between the children's play and a book.

Shahid and Sonja crawl around the play yard growling. Then they creep into a large cardboard refrigerator box and curl up against the back wall. Miss Maceroli comes over and peers into the box. "We're bears," the children inform her.

"Is this the cave that Beady Bear tried to live in?" Miss Maceroli asks, reminding them of the Don Freeman (1954) book by that name.

"Yeah," agrees Shahid, "and it is really dark, and bumpy like Beady's cave."

The teacher's comment helped the children envision better the environment they were imagining for their pretend play. At other times children may choose to ignore the adult's comment. It takes an observant adult to know how to draw book settings into play in this way and when to leave the play to develop on its own.

Book Ideas as a Source of Dramatic Play

At the beginning of the chapter, Carl and Eric make play dough food to rain down on the people of their town, as in a favorite book *Cloudy with a Chance of Meatballs*. They are playing with an intriguing idea that they heard in a book. They are not acting out the plot, but rather an idea—"food raining down from the sky." Let's explore the ways that ideas from books are integrated into children's dramatic play.

Child-Initiated Integration of Ideas

Adults explore ideas they find in books through discussing them; children do it through playing with them. Therefore, it is not surprising that children often initiate dramatic play based on ideas they have heard in books. When Raymond said goodnight to objects, he was using an idea that he had heard in *Goodnight Moon*.

When children are playing with ideas, it may not be immediately apparent that the source of the play is books. Adults will need to listen carefully to children's play, asking probing questions occasionally, if they want to discover the connection between the play and books. Although it is not necessary to know the source of the play, this knowledge will allow the adult to share the child's engagement with the book.

Incidental Integration of Ideas

Early childhood educators can draw children's attention to the relationship between their play ideas and books by asking questions or making comments pointing out the similarities. Carl and Eric had not thought about *Cloudy with a Chance of Meatballs* until Miss Kobayashi mentioned

Chewandswallow. Adults and children must share a knowledge of many favorite books in order for this type of reference to be successful.

Enrichment Integration of Ideas

Books are a wonderful source of ideas for enrichment integration of literacy into dramatic play. The idea from a book can be the stimulus for a wide variety of open-ended play. *The Berenstain Bears' Moving Day* (Berenstain & Berenstain, 1981) may lead children to pretend they are moving, perhaps packing up all the clothes and dishes and moving to another part of the room. Adults can provided boxes and wagons to expedite the moving.

Rod Campbell's *From the Zoo* (Campbell, 1982) might lead to play about shipping things back and forth to the zoo. Large boxes could be provided to ship children who are pretending to be animals. Children could affix signs saying "to the zoo" or "from the zoo." Smaller boxes could be used for sending stuffed animals or wooden animals to the block area zoo.

An inventor's workshop and store could be set up after reading *Bert's Hall of Great Inventions* (Dwight, 1972). The children could make outlandish inventions in the same way that Bert does. *Christina Katerina and the Box* (Gauch, 1971) tells how Christina uses her imagination to turn a refrigerator box into many different things. This can be the starting point for children to turn their own boxes into many different things (see Figure 8-17).

FIGURE 8-17 Using a box to become a Jack-in-the-Box

These are just a few examples of how to use the ideas from books as a trigger for dramatic play. The possibilities are endless.

In each of these examples an idea from a book is the spark that motivates the pretend play. Adults can use books to create a group excitement about an idea, then provide materials for children to explore the idea in their dramatic play. Some children will connect their play to the book: "I'm going to make a castle like Christina." Others will play with the ideas without reference to the books, and still others will develop their play on their own theme rather than incorporating the idea at all. It is important that adults respect all of these play options.

A STEP FURTHER   *Moving Day*

Three of the eighteen children in Joanne's four-year-old class are moving to new houses this spring. Yuri is excited about the move, Nicole is worried, and Darice does not talk about it. Joanna wants to create an opportunity for children to talk and play about this event. She begins to read books such as *Moving Day* (Tobais, 1976) during storytime, followed by class discussion of moving. She adds large trucks and wooden furniture to the blocks. To create houses to move to and from, she collects cardboard box bottoms from the soup section of the grocery store (they are about ten by fourteen inches in size). She paints the boxes and then cuts out small doorways.

After reading *The Berenstain Bears' Moving Day*, where the bears move from a cave to their familiar tree house, Joanna puts out two sets of materials for playing these events. Two small tables each hold a cave made out of a small box covered in black paper and turned on its side; four colored counting bears (each set has a different color to differentiate the two families); a tree house; furniture; and a truck to move the furniture.

Finding a Tree House: When Joanne did this she used a Weebles® Tree House and a Fisher Price Tree House that she found at garage sales. (They are no longer made.) If you cannot locate one, you can construct your own out of a sturdy cardboard box (about 10 to 12 inches square), and a coffee can. Decorate the coffee can to resemble the tree trunk. Place the opening of the box to the front. Cut large arched openings in the two sides. Be sure to leave a sturdy two-inch column at the front of each side and a one-inch border at the top of each wall. Place the box on top of the tree trunk and fasten securely. Decorate the outside of the box with paper leaves and small sticks.

All-Encompassing Integration of an Idea

Free play would not be the time for all-encompassing integration of a book idea into dramatic play, because it involves too much adult structure.

However, this mode might be used during group time. The adult might lead a movement activity in which children plant and care for a seed the way the little boy does in *The Carrot Seed* (Krauss, 1945). They could be different animals hatching out of eggs after reading *Chickens Aren't the Only Ones* (Heller, 1991). LeSiegs *I Wish I Had Duck Feet* (1965) could lead into a exploration of how to move with different types of animal parts.

Plot as a Source of Book Play

Children often reenact the storylines from favorite books. The children at the beginning of the chapter were playing Cinderella. The story provided a framework for their pretend play. It was a familiar story that they could play without having to negotiate the plot line. Playing books in this way allows children to rehear the book in a more active way. It allows them to bring the story closer by becoming part of it.

Is the Plot Faithfully Reenacted?

When reenacting stories in this way, children will often use only parts of the story, combining them with favorite pretend play episodes. Cinderella and the Prince may go on a plane trip honeymoon to Hawaii. The stepsisters might go on a shopping expedition to get ball gowns. Cinderella might have a twin sister who stays home and cleans with her. In this way the children can model the story to their own needs and interests.

Some children find it hard to vary the plot of a well known story. They insist on a literal reenactment. If this is done during play time in a school setting it can create some problems. Often other children do not want to stick so closely to the story. The story might require too many or too few characters for the available players, or props that cannot be found. If a child insists on only playing "the right way" this might lead to arguments and bring the play to an end. Adults may want to help these children to be a bit more flexible.

> *A department store is set up in one area of the classroom. Arianne and Juanita are shopping. Arianne sees a teddy bear on the shelf. "I know, let's play Corduroy. I'll be the little girl and you can be my mother."*
>
> *"No, I want to be the girl," insists Juanita. Helen offers to be the mother. The girls argue over who Juanita can be.*
>
> *Ms. Keenan comes over to mediate the dispute. "Could you be sisters who are going shopping together?" she inquires.*
>
> *"But there aren't sisters in the book," protests Arianne.*
>
> *"That is true," agrees Ms. Keenan. "How can we find a place for Juanita in the story? Maybe you can play your own story, one that is sort of like Corduroy, but in this one sisters go shopping together." Arianne grudgingly agrees. Now that she knows it is no longer the real book she will allow some flexibility in the plot.*

It is not always as simple as in this example. Sometimes the children do not want to change the story despite the teacher's intervention. Over time these children will learn that insisting on an exact replication of the story usually leads to the end of play. These kinds of conflict and negotiations play an important part in children's development of social competence.

TV and Movies as the Source of Stories

Some of the children playing Cinderella at the beginning of the chapter had the book, others had seen the movie, some had heard the story in both ways, and a few learned of the story from being included in the reenactment. Movies, TV, and videos are often a source for both plots and characters that become part of children's pretend play. Early childhood dramatic play areas suddenly contained an abundance of Michaelangelos, Leonardos, and Raphaels after a Turtles movie was released, and children quickly adopted the roles of Belle, Lumiere, and Chip when *Beauty and the Beast* was in the theaters. In many cases, as with the Cinderella players, children will experience the story in both film and book form.

These stories are used in children's play because seeing them enacted on the movie screen or TV makes the story and characters so vivid. Unfortunately this vividness also tends to make children more rigid about their portrayal of the story. They have seen how the character looks, acts, and moves and may expect these traits to be incorporated into their pretend play. Adults may have to work hard to get children to stretch their play beyond the limits of the movie plot. Sometimes suggesting new scenes to the story, like playing when Belle was a little girl, will provide a way for children to be flexible without violating the sanctity of the plot they know.

Movie stories can provide a strong shared plot that will allow children to become involved in dramatic play with complex social interactions and rich language. In this way movies are fulfilling the same need as books. However, book play has the added advantage of helping to build a love for books. This type of book play is particularly helpful to children who come to school without many past experiences with books.

There are also many children's movies that portray two dimensional characters, stereotypical good-guy versus bad-guy plots, and a great deal of violence. Adults will need to use their judgment about which themes to encourage and which they should try to redirect into other channels.

Children Spontaneously Playing Book Plots

When book plots are used in free play, they are usually introduced by the children. These stories become part of the repertoire of pretend play episodes that children pull from when they decide what to play.

Incidental Integration of Book Plots

Early childhood professionals might draw book plots into play incidentally when they comment on the parallels between children's play and favorite stories. Adults can also begin playing a favorite story if the moment seems right.

> An obstacle course is set up outside with a wooden plank spanning the space between large wooden crates. The children have been going across a number of different ways. Carly taps her heels on the wood as she walks across. Ms. Mooney, the teacher, asks in a deep voice, "Who's that crossing my bridge? Is it that billy goat again?" Carly answers yes. The billy goat story continues as various goats cross the bridge. In this version there are red goats, and giant goats, and skinny goats, and sister goats, as well as the more traditional little, middle-sized, and BIG billy goat brothers.

Here the teacher responded spontaneously to the setting and the tapping heels to introduce a favorite book into the children's play.

Using Book Plots as Enrichment

Adults may add props to the dramatic play area that will support a book plot that children have been using in their pretend play. If many children in the group have been playing Cinderella, the adult might add cleaning utensils to the house, and provide a clear area with music that can be used for the ball. If Shahid and Sonja continued their interest in playing Beady Bear, the adult might add flashlights, pillows, and newspapers that can be carried up to the cave as Beady Bear does in the book. Children are then free to use the props as part of their book play, or to play act other themes if they prefer.

All-Encompassing Integration of Book Plots

It is rare that adults will plan a dramatic play setup that revolves around the plot from a book, since this would be too adult-directed for free play. If the story from a favorite book is already the center of children's play, then the adult might design an environment where this could expand, as Mr. Thomas does with *Caps for Sale*.

Group time offers many opportunities for more formal play acting of plots from favorite books. There are many resources discussing ways to use books and poems as a basis for formally acting out plays. There are many ways to organize this type of play acting. The early childhood educators can read the story with the children doing the motions, or adding simple repetitive phrases that the characters say.

This type of formal play acting requires quite sophisticated social skills. Children must be able to accept that they will not always have a role in the play, and that when they do have a role it may not be the one they want. Children must be skilled at cooperative play. Therefore, this formal reenactment of books is generally more appropriate for children in kindergarten or primary grades. Some four-year-old classes could handle this type of play acting late in the year, or if it is done in small groups.

A less demanding way to enact stories at group time is to have all the children try on one role at the same time. All the children can be very small billy goats. They can explore how it would move, what its voice might sound like when scared, and how quickly it would trip-trap across the bridge. They can then try on each of the roles in turn. To make the reenactment more storylike, the adult could be the troll for the group of billy goats.

This format includes all the children, does not raise problems of who gets what role, and does not require cooperative interaction of characters. It can be done with children as young as three, and for older children it provides a good lead-in to the more formal story dramatizations.

Adults could gradually move to reenactment where children take individual roles by moving from whole group portrayal of roles to small group portrayals. When doing *The Billy Goats Gruff* the children could be divided into four groups. One quarter of the children would be the little billy goat, one quarter the middle-sized billy goat, one quarter the big billy goat, and the last quarter would be the troll.

Some stories, such as *Too Much Noise* can be expanded to allow all children to have parts. The adult can be Peter, another adult can be the

A STEP FURTHER   Too Much Noise *Reenactment*

After the children have heard *Too Much Noise* many times, Jane has the children help her act out the story. The children sit in a circle. She spreads a large frayed brown blanket in the middle of the circle to be Peter's house. The children comment on the holes in the blanket—she tells them it is because Peter has a very old house. She puts on an old vest and cap to be Peter. A student teacher dons a flowered hat and shawl to be the Wise Person.

Jane asks for volunteers to be the various parts. Each child gets a prop to signify his or her role. The floor gets a piece of wood. The bed gets a doll house bed. The person being the noisy leaves gets a branch with leaves on it. A teakettle goes to the person with that part. Each of the children portraying animals gets a wooden replica of an animal. There are multiples of most animals.

The Wise Person stands to the side. The bed, floor, kettle, and leaves stand on the blanket, then Jane begins telling the story. The children make the noises for their object. Peter walks to the Wise Person who tells him to "Get a cow." Peter does not understand why, but invites the cow into his house anyway. The cow(s) then come onto the blanket. The story continues with the blanket getting more and more crowded. The animals are then let go, the children go back to the circle, and only the quiet sounds remain.

FIGURE 8-18 Creating a lifelong love of books

Wise Person. Individual children or pairs of children can be each of the objects or animals that make noise. This ensures that all children have parts, and it allows children to pick a more demanding role—such as the swishing leaves that are in the story from the beginning—or a less demanding role like the cat that only comes in once. More confident children can pick a solo role, while the less sure can share a role with a friend.

Building a Love for Books

It is clear that books and pretend play complement each other. Playing with books extends children's understanding of books, as well as increasing their enjoyment of books. Creating an early childhood setting where books are read, enjoyed, and lived will provide children with the basis for a lifelong interest in books.

CHAPTER 9

Creating a Literacy-Rich Environment

Tanya writes a message to her daughter reminding her to feed the cat. She places the note prominently on the front of the refrigerator where it will be seen. Tanya thinks about how important this form of communication is at her home, and wonders if it would also be important to the group of four-year-olds she teaches.

Tanya purchases a small bulletin board for her classroom. She makes a label, "Messages," for the top of the board. An open envelope filled with blank paper and a pencil is attached to the board as well. The board is placed on the wall where the class meets for circle time. Tanya writes a message with large print to inform the children that today is Hannah's birthday. Tanya folds the message in half, draws a birthday cake on the outside, and pins it on the board.

When the children are gathered at circle time, Marco asks, "What's the birthday cake for?"

"I'm so glad you noticed that message, Marco," Tanya replies. "I sometimes forget things so I decided to put up a message board so I could write down things I want to remember. What do you think this message might be about?"

The children call out, "Birthday cake!"

"How did you know that?" Tanya asks.

The children tell how they looked at the picture. Tanya shows how impressed she is with their skill at figuring out her messages. "Should we see what it says inside?"

Tanya opens the message so the children can see the writing. "That's me!" says Hannah, pointing at the message.

"That's right!" Tanya agrees. "It does have your name on the message right here. Why do you think that your name is there?"

"I'm five!" Hannah answers.

"So maybe this message is about Hannah's birthday." Tanya points to the first word. "Hannah told us this is her name, I wonder what the rest says. This word starts with a B," Tanya makes the "b" sound a few times.

The children shout out, "Birthday."

"What great readers!" Tanya says admiringly. She reads the message following under the words with her finger. "Hannah's birthday is today."

"What's the other message?" children inquire eagerly pointing at the "Messages" label on the top of the board.

"This message is a label to tell us what this new bulletin board is for," explains Tanya. With Tanya's help they figure out that it says "messages." The class talks about what the board can be used for.

The message board becomes an important feature of the classroom. Children eagerly look for messages on the board each day at circle time. They try to guess the content from the picture on the front. Some messages say what will be happening in the room that day. Some messages tell of trips to be planned. Some messages are letters from a vacationing teacher.

Many messages are added during the course of the day. Tamir is distressed when clean-up time comes and he has not finished creating his secret cave in the sand table. Tanya suggests writing a message for the board to remind him that he wants to work on that first thing tomorrow. When a new computer program is introduced, it is so popular that a list of people who want a turn is started. The list is stored on the message board so the next day children who were waiting can have their turn.

Brayonna wants to know how long snakes can be. None of the books in the classroom have the answer. Tanya writes herself a note to go to the library to get a book on snakes for Brayonna. Tanya discusses with Brayonna what the note should say, and sounds out the words slowly as she writes them. "If I don't have time to go tonight the message will help me remember to go tomorrow," Tanya explains. Pictures without names are put on the message board so the artist can be found and his or her name can be added to the picture.

The board is used to communicate with other people who use the classroom. A message is left for the cook saying that Micah wants crackers and peanut butter for snack again soon. A message is left for the morning class asking them to look for Casey's missing blue mitten.

Children also write themselves messages about things they want to do, to remember, or to tell the rest of the class. Some children even put pictures on the front of their messages so the class can guess the content.

The children in the Tanya's classroom turn naturally to literacy as a tool to communicate, remember, claim ownership, and organize events. They work together to tease the meaning out of written messages. The message board provides a wonderful impetus for reading and writing.

Should All Early Childhood Settings Have Message Boards?

What is the "message" of this example? Should a message board be a staple of all early childhood settings? Will this addition insure that this same involvement with literacy will occur? No. It is not the individual activities or materials that create a literacy rich environment. Rather, it is an attitude or philosophy about literacy. It is a shared group culture in which literacy is an integral part of everything, where children are encouraged and supported as they explore written language. Reading and writing are seen as tools to be used by both children and adults in order to expedite communication.

A Message Board in Another Classroom

Let us look at how a message board is used in another classroom, one that has a different philosophy about how children learn to read and write.

The children in Ms. Micco's kindergarten are assembled at circle time. A message with a large letter B on the outside is on the board. Ms. Micco checks the jobs list for the day, "Let's see. Who is our message reader today?"

A number of children shout out, "Carmen!"

"Please raise your hands if you want to say something. Kendra, your hand is up. Can you tell us whose turn it is to read the messages?" Carmen is identified as the message reader and comes to the front of the room. "Carmen, what do you think this message is about?" Carmen seems unsure. Other children shout out help, but are quieted by Ms. Micco. She encourages Carmen to look at the alphabet chart to see if she can find the letter and figure out what it is. While Carmen is looking, children start giggling and whispering about how THEY

know all the letters. Ms. Micco tells them to give their attention to Carmen. Two children start tickling neighbors and are reprimanded.

Finally, Carmen figures out the letter. "That's wonderful, Carmen," compliments Ms. Micco. "That is a B to tell us that today is B day. Who can think of a B word?" Children take turns suggesting B words, which Ms. Micco writes and pins up on the board. Circle time is over. Ms. Micco asks all of the children to find three B things and make a picture of each for the message board before finding an activity for the day.

"Do we have to?" Anthony groans. "We did that yesterday."

"We want to see how many B words we know," explains the teacher. "Yesterday we made K words."

This teacher has turned the message board into an assignment that must be completed before children can do the things they want to do. Reading and writing messages has become something that HAS to be done, rather than something that children are driven to participate in because of their inner desire to communicate and to organize their lives through literacy.

Ms. Micco discourages group response. Children are expected to arrive at the answer independently, unlike the first classroom where discovering the meaning of written language was a community endeavor. Ms. Micco will not allow others to help Carmen, whose lack of knowledge about letters becomes a liability and a matter for teasing, rather than just a natural stage in the process of learning.

The children in this classroom do not exhibit excitement at being part of a literate community. They interact with print because it is a requirement. It is clear from these two examples that it is not individual activities or materials, such as the message board, but an overall atmosphere, a philosophy about literacy, that creates a literacy-rich environment for children.

How Is This Literacy-Supporting Atmosphere Created?

How do adults infuse their early childhood setting with this literacy-supporting atmosphere? The atmosphere arises from a set of principles about children's learning and literacy that influences the way adults set up the environment, the types of activities that are designed, and the way in which adults interact with the children in their care.

Let us look at the principles that comprise this philosophy about literacy, and how these principles guide the behavior of adults who espouse them. These principles are based on the discussion of emergent literacy presented in Chapter 4.

FIGURE 9-1 Literacy becomes an integral part of all activities

Principle 1: Reading and Writing Are Tools

Early childhood educators view reading and writing as tools that are used to accomplish many outcomes. Adults spontaneously incorporate literacy into numerous everyday activities. Children are encouraged to use written language as a tool to accomplish their goals as well. The message board in the first classroom is a catalyst for writing with a range of purposes: to remind, to announce, to organize events, to claim ownership, to communicate from far away, and to request information or objects. When literacy is seen as a tool, it becomes an integral part of all activities, rather than isolated skills to be taught.

Principle 2: Children Learn about Written Language by Being in an Environment Where It Is Used

Just as children learn oral language by being surrounded by people who are talking, they learn about literacy by being surrounded by people who use written language. Seeing the power that written language has for the adults around them makes children want to have this power as

FIGURE 9-2 Learning to write is a social endeavor

well. At home children see their parents using written language in diverse contexts. The home provides many naturally occurring opportunities to model reading and writing.

Often teachers do not use written language in the children's presence, since most young children cannot yet read or write conventionally (Dowhower, 1989). However, if adults believe that it is important for children to observe adults engaged in literate tasks and that children's literacy is emerging, then it is crucial that adults model their use of written language for the children in their care. In the first classroom, Tanya uses written language to announce Hannah's birthday, to remind herself to go to the library, to ensure that Tamir has the chance to finish his sand cave tomorrow, and to communicate with the cook. Not only does Tanya model her use of literacy, but she also verbalizes what she is doing. When she writes the note to look for the snake book, Tanya talks about why she is writing the note, what should be in the note, and models how letters can be matched to the sounds words make.

Principle 3: All Young Children Explore and Construct Knowledge about Literacy

Children strive to make sense out of the written language that is in the world around them. They gain knowledge of written language through exploring and experimenting with print. As children write messages for the board, they experiment with various ways of writing. They are exercising and refining their knowledge about how written language works. As children practice reading messages, they see that written symbols can communicate, and they stretch their knowledge of how to gain meaning from these written symbols.

Children develop their knowledge about written language at different speeds and in individual ways. As they try to make sense of writing, they will arrive at their own unique hypotheses, gradually modifying the hypotheses to coincide with conventional writing. Adults realize that children will be at different levels, and that children will use different levels of skill depending on the context in which they are using literacy. For example, children will often sound out words when making a message for someone who is not there, or when writing brief texts, but use random strings of letters or pseudo cursive writing when writing more lengthy pieces, and when incorporating the act of writing in pretend play.

The childcare setting is arranged so children have large blocks of time, space, and materials where they can be involved in activities of their choice. This allows them to explore writing as it applies to their interests. Adults express interest in children's writing and encourage children to verbalize their developing knowledge about literacy. This helps children to synthesize their ideas, it helps the teacher to know what types of support are useful, and it encourages children to compare their hypotheses about written language.

It is the adult's role to observe the children's current knowledge and to help children to consolidate and extend this knowledge. Adults will vary their interactions in keeping with the children's level of literacy knowledge. If Tamir is just building his concept that print conveys meaning, Tanya will talk about how a note can remind him to finish his cave tomorrow. If Tamir is beginning to connect speech sounds with letters, she can elicit his help in figuring out what letters are needed to write the message. If he is an eager writer she can encourage him to write the message himself, whether it is at the scribble stage, at the conventional writing stage, or somewhere in between. Whatever stage Tamir is in, the adults should respond to him as a member of the reading/writing community. In other words, children learn the specific skills needed for reading and writing through their own exploration, together with scaffolding provided by teachers to help children expand their understanding. Schickedanz (1989) illustrated beautifully how specific skills are taught as teachers facilitate children's emergent literacy.

Principle 4: Literacy is a Community Endeavor

Written language is a form of communication. Harste and Woodward (1989) suggested that "reading is not so much taking meaning from texts as it is sharing meaning about texts" (p. 154). For young writers who are just beginning to explore written language, the communication often comes through talking about what they are writing, rather than from the symbols themselves (Dyson, 1993). Children are encouraged to discuss ideas with each other. They share the content of what they write, as well as their strategies for creating print. Sounding out words often becomes a group process with many children offering suggestions. The writer may take any or all of the suggestions, or none.

Principle 5: Rich Verbal Language Supports Emergent Literacy

Rich verbal language is the foundation for the development of emergent literacy. Children use and develop oral language in environments that provide time, stimulation, and encouragement. Adults recognize that group lessons provide little opportunity for individual children to exercise their oral language skills, so large blocks of time are available for less structured, more child-directed activities.

Principle 6: Using Symbols for Communication Contributes to Emerging Literacy

Written language is a system of abstract symbols. Children's ability to use these symbols derives from experiences with a wide range of **symbolic representation**. Dyson (1993) suggested that "written language emerges most strongly when firmly embedded within the supportive symbolic sea of playful gestures, pictures, and talk" (p. 39).

Therefore, early childhood settings should offer children many opportunities to talk, play pretend, dance, and create pictures. Our world is also filled with written symbols that are not words, such as arrows and pictorial signs marking such things as restrooms and telephones. Even nonreaders can easily interpret these signs. Providing many opportunities to read **pictorial symbols** allows children to become confident in their ability to interpret written symbols before they can read words that are written.

FIGURE 9-3 Picture symbols on a recipe

Tanya's use of the birthday cake on the outside of the note allowed a class of nonreaders to easily discern the content of her message. Pictorial symbols can be used in such things as recipes, games, and directions.

Seeing This Philosophy in Action

A good way to illustrate this philosophy more concretely is to observe a number of events that occurred in a preschool where it is put into action.

> *Juan watches his mother's car pull away from the play yard.*
> *"NO! NO!" he shouts, then begins sobbing. Ms. Billie gives him a hug.*
> *"Juan, what is making you so sad?" she asks him.*
> *"My Mom forgot to kiss me goodbye," he sobs.*
> *"No wonder you are so sad. Do you think that we should write a letter to her to let her know that you were sad, and remind her to kiss you tomorrow?"*
> *Juan nods. They go into the classroom to get paper and pencil. Juan dictates, "Dear Mom, I don't like it that you didn't kiss me goodbye. Don't ever forget again! Love, Juan." Ms. Billie writes down the words, letting Juan write his own name. Juan gets an envelope from the writing center. He seals the letter inside, and attaches a stamp (the kind that come in magazine advertisements). He takes the letter to the shoe bag pockets that hold papers to be sent home. He looks carefully at each name to make sure he has the one that says "Juan" and not the one that says "Julius." When he is satisfied that he has the right pocket, he drops the letter in, and runs out to play with his friends.*

Writing the letter offered Juan a way to do something about what had upset him. Now he is ready to join his friends. The teacher helped Juan deal with his emotional distress by using writing. This illustrates Principle 1. Juan saw the uses of written language for communication to his mother and for self-expression. It also illustrates Principle 3. The teacher encouraged Juan to use his reading skills to find his pouch, and his writing skills to sign his name. Because of Juan's level of distress, the teacher wisely did not use this time to demonstrate how sounds and letters fit together, but took over this part of the task herself.

A STEP FURTHER *Preparing Mom for the Letter*

Ms. Billie helped Juan to deal with his sadness at not being kissed by writing a letter to Mom to express his feelings. Ms. Billie realized that the letter was strongly stated, and that it might upset his mother to receive it without an explanation. Later in the day she took a moment to write a letter to Juan's mom explaining the context of Juan's letter, assuring her that the distress the letter expressed was only momentary. She emphasized to Juan's mother that writing the letter had helped him to deal with his emotions.

It is snack time at a family daycare home. Three-year-old Tonisha places a pretzel vertically and puts another pretzel across the top. "Look that's my name."

"That's my T, too," Tommy proclaims.

These children are excited about letters. They feel ownership of the T. They feel knowledgeable about letters. It does not matter that they do not yet realize that it takes many letters, not just the T to make their names. In accordance with Principle 3 these children are exploring and constructing knowledge about written language.

In this instance literacy is a community event, as Principle 4 asserts. The social atmosphere in the family childcare home encouraged children to share their knowledge of letters and names. Many discussions like this will cause children to see not only the similarities in their names (the T) but also the differences.

Four-year-old Will goes to a half-day preschool in the afternoon. He tells Ms. Schultz that his best friend Ramiro comes to the school in the morning. "I wonder where his cubby is," ponders Ms. Schultz.

"I know, we need to find his R," Will says. He looks carefully at each cubby label. He finds "Rachel," but moves on when Ms. Schulz reads the name for him. When he finds the right cubby, Ms. Schulz asks, "Would you like to write a message and leave it for Ramiro to find in the morning?" He doesn't respond, so Ms. Schulz adds, "It will be like a treasure."

Will gets paper and markers and carefully draws a long winding line that goes off the end of the paper. "This is the map. It says to go this way and then this way." Will turns the paper over and continues the line. At the end he makes an circle, then covers it completely with black marker. "That's the treasure," he explains. "It's buried." Will puts it in Ramiro's cubby then asks what the name says on the next cubby. It is Maria's. He gets a paper makes a series of squiggles and puts it in Maria's cubby. "I'm going to write letters for everyone!" Will spends the rest of the afternoon making treasures for the morning class (see Figures 9-4 and 9-5).

Will is excited to discover that the labels on the cubbies all stand for people. He realizes that letters are messages to people who are not present. He sees two important functions of print (Principle 1)—claiming ownership and communicating with others. He recognizes letters, but his own writing is still a series of scribbles.

It is clear that Will is exploring and constructing his own ideas about print (Principle 3). This incident also illustrates Principles 5 and 6. Will uses verbal language to explain and elaborate on his map. He uses drawing symbols to communicate the concept of "treasure."

Kelvin, who is four-years-old, and his teacher, Mr. Cohen, are making roads in the sandbox. Kelvin notices Ms. Jasper, the director of the center, walking around the yard with the clipboard taking notes. She takes a few broken hollow blocks and places them to the side and attaches a note. "What's she doing?" Kelvin

FIGURE 9-4 Making the treasure map

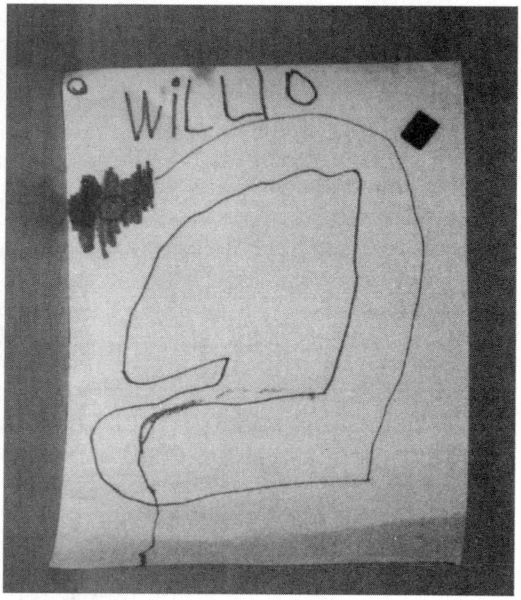

FIGURE 9-5 The finished map

inquires of Mr. Cohen. Mr. Cohen suggests that Kelvin go and ask. When Kelvin comes back he says, "She's writing what needs to be fixed."

Kelvin continues to dig roads. His bulldozer keeps getting caught on buried sticks. As he impatiently pulls out yet another stick he declares, "We need a sign saying no sticks in the sandbox."

"What a fantastic idea!" replies Mr. Cohen. "It is almost time to go in now, let's remember to make it during play time."

FIGURE 9-6 Attaching the sign to the sandbox

At the beginning of play time Mr. Cohen reminds Kelvin that he had wanted to make a sign. Kelvin gets out paper and marker and makes a row of +'s and o's. When it is done, Kelvin reads the sign to Mr. Cohen, pointing to one letter for each word he says. "No sticks in the sandbox." Mr. Cohen asks if he can also write the words. Mr. Cohen writes the phrase conventionally under Kelvin's +o writing. Kelvin gets the tape and rips off a long piece. "Make it in a circle," he requests, handing of Mr. Cohen the tape. Kelvin then draws a large circle on the back of the sign to show where the tape should go.

When the sign is done Mr. Cohen and Kelvin go out to the sandbox to attach the sign. "Now I'm going to make a sign telling people to leave sand in the sandbox." When they return Nathan inquires about why they went outside. Mr. Cohen encourages Kelvin to tell about what they did. Nathan is impressed. He immediately starts making his own sign. It is a warning for the tall ladder leading to the play house roof. Nathan carefully sounds out his words. He makes the F sound a number of times, unsure what letter to put down. Frankie, who is making a play dough snake next to Nathan, offers a suggestion "F—that's for Frankie." When the two new signs are done, Kelvin and Nathan go to hang them outside (see Figures 9-6 to 9-8).

This incident illustrates all six principles. Kelvin and Nathan use writing to communicate commands and warnings to other people (Principle 1). Kelvin observes Ms. Jasper using written language (Principle 2). This is what prompts him to make his own sign.

Both children create writing at their own level (Principle 3). Kelvin uses the two letters to spell whatever he wants. He seems to believe that

FIGURE 9-7 Attaching warning sign to house

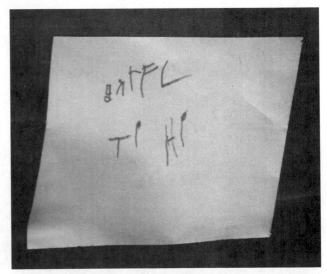

FIGURE 9-8 "Be Careful, It's High"

each word can be represented by one letter. When he makes his second sign, it is clear that this hypothesis about writing is not firmly held. His first reading of the sign matches one letter to one word. "Don't put sand out of the sandbox." Then he fills up the whole page with +'s and o's. When asked to read the page with the additional writing, Kelvin rereads the same message despite the extra letters. Nathan uses phonetic spelling to create his sign.

Literacy is a community endeavor (Principle 4). Kelvin's interest in signs draws Nathan into sign writing as well. Nathan's sounding out of words draws in Frankie. The signs on the playground attract attention, and prompt more signs from the children in other classes in that school.

Verbal language is a key part of what happens (Principle 5). Kelvin uses oral language to discover and communicate what Ms. Jasper is doing, to discuss his plans for his sign, and to describe to Nathan what he has done. Finally, Kelvin uses a symbol, a circle, to communicate where the tape should be placed (Principle 6).

Creating an Environment to Support This Philosophy

Although it has been stressed that the literacy-rich atmosphere in the early childhood setting is more important than specific materials or activities, this atmosphere does not exist in a vacuum. What type of early childhood environment do adults create to support this literacy philosophy? These environments contain a number of components:

1. Materials, time, and space to support pretend play in the dramatic play area, blocks, and many additional areas
2. An abundance of environmental print
3. Books of all kinds, used in many ways
4. Materials, time, and space for children to create their own print
5. Materials to create and interpret symbolic representations
6. Encouragement for oral language and word play.

Let us look more closely at each of these components.

Supporting Pretend Play

This book has already described how adults can support pretend play in all areas of the early childhood setting, as well as the importance of dramatic play as a medium for encouraging emergent literacy. This is only one component of a literacy-rich early childhood setting. The literacy activities that occur during dramatic play can support and encourage literacy activities in other parts of the room, which in turn support and encourage literacy activities during dramatic play.

FIGURE 9-9 Puzzles can be a source of print

Providing Abundant Environmental Print

If children learn about literacy by being surrounded by print, then the early childhood environment should contain ample environmental print. Words and letters should be found on such things as signs, labels, directions, messages, charts, games, puzzles, posters, and lists.

Insuring That Children Attend to the Print around Them

Schickedanz (1993) pointed out that merely having print present in the room does not assure that children will pay attention to the print. She described different ways that children interact with attendance charts (a chart where children post their names, often with a symbol picture attached for identification). When children can identify their name cards by color, symbol, or pictures, they often do not heed the printed names. The color and picture matching are so easy that children do not need to focus on the print.

By placing just the names on the attendance chart cards, children cannot register their presence without finding their names. Adults help the children to develop strategies for identifying their names. This provides a context in which children seek clues from adults about interpreting print.

Names, Names, Names

Their names are often the first words that children are able to recognize, as well as the first word they can write. Early writing often consists of strings of letters from the child's name (Temple, Nathan, Temple, & Burris, 1993). Names can be used on attendance charts, to mark cubbies, to list birthdates, to designate jobs on a chart, to make list of children waiting for turns, to label mailboxes (so children can send each other letters), and to indicate preferences, hair color, family size, or other things of interest on charts (Levin, 1994).

Children should be encouraged to write their own names on their artwork and other creations. Even if children scribble (which is a legitimate form of writing), they begin to see that they can make marks that proclaim ownership. Adults can assist children who are unsure by having a container of name cards that children can use as reference. Children go through a stage in which they can identify their names when they see them and can recite the letters, but have trouble visualizing the individual letters in order to reproduce them. A container of name cards will remind children how their names look.

Adult guidance will show the child how to use the name card. For example, if Mark is not sure how to make his name, the adult could ask him to find his name in the box. Suggest that Mark start with the M. If he is unsure how to make it, the teacher can suggest making a line going down. "Now let's make this sliding line," said while tracing the line that goes down.

A STEP FURTHER   *Becoming Someone Else*

At the University of Delaware Laboratory Preschool, children wear name tags year-round so the child development students who observe the classes can identify children. Each day begins with children picking their own name tags to be attached to their backs. Children would often identify their friend's tags as they looked for their own.

One year, two girls, who were inseparable friends, decided to change names for the day. Marybeth wanted to wear Sarah's name tag and vice versa. The teacher felt that this would confuse the observers, so she suggested the girls make new name tags for the front with the name they wanted to be called. They got the name box out and copied each other's names, then taped their new names to their fronts. This continued for many days.

Other children were intrigued with the new names and begin copying other children's names as well. One boy made a big S for his front, since he was Superman. As the name changing group grew, it became hard to decide who to be each day. Marybeth solved the problem when she added more than one name to her front. She became Sarah, Christina, Sachi, Maria. By the end of the month the name writers could read all the names in the class.

The adult can encourage Mark to name the letters if he knows them, and to make them if he knows how. For the letters he does not feel he can make, the adult can break down the letters into simple lines and circles. The "r" might be described as "a line with bump on it." By breaking down the name-writing task into small segments it becomes more manageable.

These verbal descriptions will give the child something to think about when trying to make the letters at a later time. Adults can make the harder letters such as "s" and "e" until the child is ready to tackle these on his or her own. The adult should stand beside or behind the child when writing so the child can see the left to right progression of the name writing. When children are searching through the name box for their names, they will often be excited to find the name of a friend. More adventurous writers will often reproduce friends' names as well as their own.

Labeling the Room

Labels are another common form of print found in early childhood settings. Often adults attach written labels to objects in the room such as chairs, tables, clock, windows, crayon boxes, and so on. This provides a written word to go with the things that children see and use every day. The theory behind the labeling is sound; however, often these labels become like wallpaper—something you see every day, but do not really attend to.

This does not mean that adults should avoid labels, but rather that they should find ways to generate children's interest in the labels. This can be done in a number of ways. A sign shop could be set up where children can create their own labels to place around the room. A treasure hunt could be designed where children search for different words around the room. Children could help create labels for toy shelves so everyone knows where to put toys away.

The message board could contain a word for the day. Children can try to discover what the word says by searching for it somewhere in the room. Labels can be changed on a regular basis. Children are more likely to notice them if they are in a new location or on a different colored paper.

The Alphabet

Besides providing printed words, the early childhood setting can also provide individual letters in many forms. Alphabet strips—long strips of sticky-backed paper with the alphabet on the front—can be placed on tables for children to refer to when writing. The strip reminds them of how needed letters look. The pretzel letter makers might have used such a strip as a stimulus for producing other letters with their pretzels. Other sources for letters are alphabet blocks, alphabet puzzles, alphabet cookie cutters for play dough or damp sand, ink pads with rubber letter stamps, alphabet charts, alphabet books, or magnetic letters.

FIGURE 9-10 Using letter cookie cutters with play dough

And More Words

Words can be present in many other places as well. Some puzzles have words as part of the picture, or hidden under the pieces. For example, a person puzzle has body part names under each piece of the body. The word "head" is printed under the head, the word "arm" is under the arm, and so on. With prompting from adults, children find they can read each word by identifying the body part that covers it.

Directions for experiments and recipes for cooking can combine picture clues and words. As children become more skilled at reading these recipes, adults can encourage them to decipher more of the words. When children are cooking, the picture recipe can show two tablespoons from the blue bowl, which is labeled sugar. Encourage children to figure out what that word is. (Some children will use initial letters to discover the identity of the ingredient. Other children will find that tasting what is in the blue bowl is often a good way to discover the word's meaning.)

Words can be incorporated into bulletin boards. In one four-year-old class, the bulletin board display is changed when some new project or unit of interest is begun. The children eagerly try to guess what the new topic will be from the pictures, and then figure out what the words must say.

Poems and songs can be posted on chart board for children to read with the adult. Schickedanz (1993) pointed out that children often read these by reciting the poems from memory without really attending to the print. She suggested turning these into puzzles with key words on removable cards. Children, with the help of an adult, can try to replace the missing words.

Calendars are another source of print. Unfortunately in many early childhood settings, calendar time becomes a dreaded routine to be plowed through each day. Some teachers have replaced the group calendar time with a "living calendar," which is used to record important events such as birthdays, field trips, a child's trip to visit grandparents, and so on.

If teachers turn to the calendar to find birthdays, to see how many more days to a trip, to see why Mark was absent last week, then children will often take the calendar to browse through as well. If words and pictures are used to designate events, children may try to read the words that go with familiar pictures. Instead of checking the calendar every day, it can be checked when an important event is approaching, or a new month is beginning.

Consider adding print to hallways, storage areas, the play yard, the bathroom, as well as to the regular inside play spaces. The sources for print are limitless. Besides those mentioned above, posters, messages, letters, a rolodex dictionary (with each card having a word of interest and a picture to illustrate the word*), traffic signs, and of course books all add print to the environment.

Providing Materials for Creating Writing

If children are to write, many writing tools and materials should be available. They need tools to write with, paper to write on, and tables or other surfaces to work on. Often other materials are added to make writing more appealing.

Writing Tools

Thin and thick markers, crayons, plain and colored pencils, and chalk can all be available. Be sure that the pencils have soft lead so that marks can easily be seen. Lighter colors such as yellows are not recommended, as they are often hard to see. Markers should be discarded when old. It is frustrating for children to write and not be able to see what they have written. Typewriters and word processors are also excellent tools for writing. These often appeal to children with less refined motor skills. With these tools recognizable letters can be produced easily.

---

*This is an excellent accompaniment to a typewriter—children enjoy finding favorite words and copying them on the typewriter or computer.

Papers

Provide an assortment of papers to suit different needs. Large unlined sheets of newsprint 9″ × 12″ or 12″ × 18″ give lots of space for writing and drawing. Copier paper and drawing paper show the marks more boldly and clearly. Long narrow strips of paper will often foster long single lines of print. Small pads can be used for messages, writing tickets, and taking orders. Index cards and small scrap paper make good signs and labels. Paper folded in half can be used to make cards.

Stapling paper together will create a book. Books can be rectangular or cut into many different shapes. Long skinny books will elicit different drawings and writing than house-shaped books, or boat-shaped books. Books can also be cut into the shape of letters or numbers.

Other Materials

Often the addition of other materials will entice children to the writing area. Staplers, string, paper clips, tape, and brads all can be used to fasten papers together. The area can also contain envelopes and stamps (from magazine advertisements) for writing letters, and paper punches, rulers, carbon paper, and other office supplies for children to use as they desire.

Places for Writing

Tables should be available where children can write. A table that is near writing and art supplies can be used jointly by children who are writing and drawing. Since drawing is often an integral part of children's early writing, combining the two areas makes sense for beginning writers. Clipboards, either full paper size or small notecard size, are appealing to chil-

FIGURE 9-11 Flat smooth boards for writing on the floor

dren. These also encourage children to carry the paper around, adding writing to a wide variety of activities. Flat smooth boards, cut from pieces of masonite, provide a hard surface for children who wish to work on the floor.

Where Should the Writing Materials Be Located?

Morrow (1989) suggested that separate writing centers be set up to house the writing materials. This works well when the children see themselves as writers. However, many three-, four-, and even five-year-olds do not begin the year viewing themselves as writers. They are unlikely to seek out a writing area. For these children it would be wise to integrate the writing and drawing areas. Since most young children do see themselves as people who can create drawings, they will come to the area and might discover writing materials that intrigue them.

Some teachers find it helpful to have writing materials in many parts of the room so children will have tools readily available to write such things as signs in the blocks, letters in the house area, or treasure maps in the play yard. This duplication of materials in different parts of the room could be augmented by a writing area or writing shelf that houses a larger collection of all these materials. As the year progresses, this can increasingly become the area to turn to for writing materials. Thus, children will find writing materials easily available when they are just beginning to explore writing. Once they clearly see themselves as writers, they will search out the writing area for needed tools, and in so doing may discover other writing options that they had not considered.

Researchers have not yet explored which way of presenting writing materials is most effective (Schickedanz, 1993), so teachers will have to experiment to see which designs best meet the needs of their groups of children. Once an area has been established, it should be reevaluated periodically. Changing the arrangement and the available materials may draw fresh interest to an area that children had begun to take for granted.

Providing Opportunities to Create and Interpret Many Symbolic Media

As Principle 6 asserts, learning to connect meaning with different symbolic media contributes to children's emerging literacy.

Art

The early childhood setting should provide daily opportunities for creative art. It is important that art be viewed as a way for children to explore and express with a variety of materials, rather than as a craft project to be completed in a set way. If children are free to use materials in their own manner, they can create their own symbols. They often make pictures to represent stories or events. They also often move freely between the creation of pictures and designs and the production of letter forms.

Creative movement

Children should be given opportunities to dance and to use creative movement to communicate (Pica, 1995). At group time, children can explore what it feels like to inch along like a caterpillar, to remain still inside a cocoon, or to float gently like a butterfly. During play time children will often use their bodies to create other creatures or characters as part of the pretend play. Again, these experiences allow children to create symbolic representations, which are cornerstones of literacy development.

Recipes

The early childhood setting should also offer children opportunities to decipher written symbols. Picture recipes are an excellent source of pictorial symbols. Recipes for making small individual portions will allow children to follow the recipe once, then repeat it a number of times. This way children will get many opportunities to practice using the symbols. (For teachers who are not skilled at drawing, there are cookbooks that present the recipes in pictorial form. A particularly good one is *Cook and Learn*, by Beverly Veitch and Thelma Harmes [1981].)

Trail mix can be made out of cereals, nuts, pretzels, and dried fruits. Children can be asked to measure or count out the ingredients. In the recipe in Figure 9-12, the children count out 6 Rice Chex®, 6 Wheat Chex®, 6 pretzels, and one-eighth cup of Cheerios®, shake them in a bag, pour them into a serving bowl, and begin again.

Adults can design the recipe to fit the skills of group. Children who do not count rationally can match ingredients to pictures on the recipe to get the right amount. Figure 9-12 shows a recipe of this type. Fruit salads, vegetable salads, powdered drink mix, and vegetable soups all allow adults to design the recipe to fit the skills of the children in their care.

Treasure Hunts

Treasure hunts can require children to follow picture clues (another form of symbolic representation). The hunt might begin at the play yard gate where there is a picture of the swing set. When the children get to the swing set they find a picture of the sandbox, the sandbox has a picture of the shed, and so on. The last picture can be of an adult who has stickers for prizes. Children should be encouraged to do the hunt as often as they would like, gathering many prizes. It is interesting to watch experienced hunters showing friends how to decode the pictures along the path.

FIGURE 9-12 Trail mix recipe

There are many variations on the treasure hunt. Instead of following a set path, children could have a number of items to locate. They can have a treasure map that shows a number of items to be found. The items can be large things such as the swing set, or things to collect such as leaves, sticks, and pine cones.

Other Sources for Pictorial Symbols

Pictorial symbols can be used in many ways with children. Computer software often uses picture symbols on the menus of programs for non-readers. For example, *Color Me* (Mindscape), a drawing program, uses a long crayon to depict the color choices. The point of the crayon becomes the color the child chooses. Board games require children to use the dots or color on a die to decide how many moves to make. Many sorting games ask children to match objects by category. All the animals go by the animal picture, all the vehicles by the car picture. Picture symbols can be used along with words to mark where toys belong on the shelves.

Picture symbols can be used to give movement directions. Adults can use picture signs to tell children which body parts to move during a group movement activity. These can be pictures of body parts cut out of magazines and mounted on cards. Children can use the signs on their own to orchestrate their motions or to direct a friend's motions. Picture directions of this type can also be used to indicate the path to take on an obstacle course, or the order in which to play instruments in a song (Davidson, 1989).

Encouraging Oral Language and Word Play

Principle 5 asserts that rich verbal language supports emergent literacy. Oral language develops in an environment filled with language, an environment filled with things worth talking about, an environment where children are given time and encouragement for talking with both adults and peers.

Children talk most in relaxed unstructured times, when they are involved in activities of their choice. Teachers should observe the children in their care to see when and where talk flows most prolifically. These situations can then be expanded and extended to provide more opportunities for language. Different materials and situations will spark conversation in different children. With observation, adults will learn to provide appropriate stimulation for each child.

Although all forms of oral language support emergent literacy, let us look more specifically at two aspects: Playing with words and telling stories.

Playing with Words

Four- and five-year-olds enjoy the silliness of playing with words. Nonsense rhymes such as "Frankie-Bankie" and nonsense phrases such as "chair-head" will bring peals of laughter from four- and five-year-olds. Part of the enjoyment of these silly phrases comes from the child's power over words. These children have such a good command of language that they can play with it and make it do crazy things.

Playing with words in this way also adds to the child's metalinguistic understanding. As discussed in Chapter 4, metalinguistic awareness is children's conscious awareness of how language works. In the case of rhyming, it is their growing awareness of how phonemes fit together to make words. Listening to and creating rhymes helps children to separate the initial sound of a word from the rest of the word, an essential skill for writing phonetically.

Circle times offer many excellent opportunities for hearing and using rhyming words. Numerous children's books are written in rhyme. When the book is familiar, children enjoy adding the final rhyming word to the phrase.

Songs are another excellent source of rhymes. "Willoughbee Wallabee Woo," a song Raffi sings makes rhymes with children's names. It starts with a silly name where all 3 parts start with a "W". Then it sings the child's name starting first with the "W" and then correctly. This allows children to hear rhymes, gradually identify the rhyme for their name, and then for other names.

As children become skilled at knowing which name will rhyme with the W-name, the activity can be made more challenging by changing the first letter. If the chosen letter is a "T," the new version would have all parts of the silly name start with "T." If the class is studying bees, the letter "B" can start the words. If grapes were for snack, then "G" might start the words. After the adult has talked about why certain letters have been selected, children can be encouraged to suggest letters as well.

Many others songs can be used for creating rhymes as well. The song "Jenny Jenkins" rhymes clothing types and/or colors with reasons why this clothing would be wrong. For example, "I won't wear red 'cause I'll fall outta bed." "Hickory Dickory Dock" can be sung with additional verses as the clock strikes two, three, and so on. When the clock strikes, the mouse will do something that rhymes with the time; for example: "The clock struck two. He got stuck in the glue."

When the songs are first introduced, adults can model how they select rhyming pairs. When singing "Jenny Jenkins," the adult might comment, "Green. Let's see what rhymes with that? Deen, teen, bean. I won't wear green, cause I'll look like a string bean." As children begin helping the adult come up with rhyming possibilities, they can be given turns to provide rhymes. It is important to realize that in any group some children will easily come up with rhyming words, while others will not have a clue as to what a rhyme is. To avoid putting children on the spot, adults will need to make the rhyme creation a community event.

Rhymes can be used more spontaneously as well. Once they begin to rhyme, children will often turn friend's names or objects into rhymes.

> *Mark, who loves rhymes, rides up to Ms. Saracho, who is standing by the bike path and proclaims, "I need gas-bas."*
> *"How much-buch?" she responds.*
> *"Ten dollars-bollars," he answers.*

By joining Mark's rhyming game in this way Ms. Saracho shows him she likes his ideas, and she extends the play. Often when adults join in children's rhyming play, other children will enter the game as well.

Creating Stories

Storytelling uses a different type of language than just conversing. It is a language that is closer to that used in books. Storytelling need not be a formal event. The recounting of something that happened last night is a form of storytelling. Adults can encourage children's narratives by being good listeners and by asking questions that make children extend and elaborate on their stories. When telling events, children often begin in the middle and leave out crucial information. Appropriate questions will elicit this missing information.

A STEP FURTHER *Keeping the Joy in Rhyming Games*

It is important to remember that for many children the concept of rhyming is unfathomable. For these children, rhyming can be frustrating, especially if right answers are emphasized and praised. Rhyming play should be done in a fun relaxed way that allows children to enter or not enter as they choose. Adults should find ways to use all suggestions, whether they rhyme or not.

When suggesting a rhyme for "Jenny Jenkins," a nonrhymer might gleefully suggest, "She won't wear green 'cause she'll look like a sink." If adults find a way to use the child's idea and still create a rhyme, then the nonrhymers will know that their contributions are valued. The adult might suggest an extension to this child's verse. "She won't wear green 'cause she'll look like a sink and feel mean."

By making rhyme creation a competitive event where correct or quick suggestions are valued, children who are not skilled come to dread this type of play. On the other hand, providing many opportunities to listen to rhymes, and allowing children to experiment and make errors will lead them to gradually understand what it is that the rhymers are doing.

Children also enjoy creating silly narratives.

While playing with play dough a group of four-year-olds make pizza. They begin naming silly toppings.

"*Mine is a chicken pizza.*"

"*I gotta spaghetti pizza*"

"*I got a rocket ship pizza.*"

"*What will happen if I eat a rocket pizza?*" *inquires Mr. Cohen.*

"*It'll go all around your body,*" *Missy suggests.*

"*No, I know! It will turn you into a rocket!*" *suggests Tonika.*

"*How do I steer it?*" *asks Mr. Cohen. The children all make suggestions, then continue the story elaborating on the suggestion that they seemed to like the best.*

Children enjoy this type of spontaneous group story. At times children will develop these on their own. At other times judicious questions from the adult will start the story unfolding.

Storytelling can also be done as children create pictures, use the computer, play pretend, and build with blocks or manipulatives. Jones and Reynolds (1992) suggested that teachers write down these stories. Rereading the stories at circle times will usually spark a flurry of storytelling from other children in the group. Paley (1990) described how children's narrated stories can be the basis for group reenactment.

Weaving Literacy and Dramatic Play into Other Areas of Learning

We have looked at many of the individual materials and activities that can support emergent literacy in the early childhood classroom. Often these are organized around a general theme or topic of interest. This is often called the "integrated approach" or "integrated curriculum." Children pull together skills and knowledge from many areas as they explore a broad body of knowledge. Literacy activities and dramatic play can both make major contributions to such units of study. Let us look at how literacy and dramatic play are woven into a month-long study of eggs and birds in a four-year-old class.

A Unit on Birds and Eggs

Jennifer's parents had found some snake eggs under their porch steps. She brought the eggs, which looked like tough leather pouches, to share with the class. Greg and Zack's favorite outside game was being eagles speeding around the play yard and nesting on the top of the climber. Robbie was a dinosaur expert, often adding information about dinosaurs to whatever discussion was underway. Because of these interests, the teacher decided to begin a month-long exploration of eggs and birds.

Besides the snake eggs, many real eggs were explored. Bird nests with eggshell remnants were examined. Frog eggs were added to the aquarium. Spider egg sacks were examined. Whelk egg sacks were shared. Whelks have spiral seashells, the type often used to listen to the ocean. The egg sacks for these sea creatures are a series of leathery disk-like containers attached along a stiff spine. Inside each disk are many tiny shells. Some egg sacks were opened so children

FIGURE 9-13 Watching the incubator to see if the eggs have started to hatch

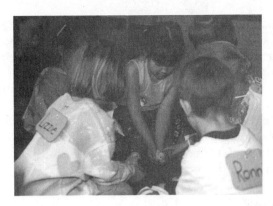

FIGURE 9-14 Petting the chicks

could see the tiny shells that made the rattling sounds inside. A trip to the local natural history museum allowed children to see eggs from different animals, as well as birds of all sizes and colors. Birds were observed in the play yard. An incubator was set up with chicken eggs so children could watch the hatching process. The real eggs and birds were supplemented with bird and egg books, a video of eggs hatching and of birds learning to fly, puzzles showing what is inside of eggs, and posters.

These experiences with eggs were supplemented by many activities that allowed children to consider and use what they were learning about eggs and birds. The next sections will present some of the many literacy-and play-related activities that supported children's exploration of birds and eggs.

Egg Bulletin Board

To introduce the many different types of eggs, the teacher designed a bulletin board to show a meadow and pond with the many different types of eggs that can be found in such a scene. A sandy beach was made from pieces of grayish sand paper. Turtle eggs were cut from sandpaper and glued together into a cluster. They were nicely camouflaged on the beach. A sheet of grey paper, on which was drawn some baby turtles, was cut to match the egg cluster. A brad was used to attach the eggs to the turtles like a cover. This was then mounted on the beach so that the eggs could be rotated on the brad to reveal the turtles.

Hatching eggs of this type were made for butterflies, spiders, birds, fish, and frogs. The frog eggs were made of the bubble paper that is used for packaging. It covered tadpoles, which in turn covered frogs. The butterfly eggs covered three layers, first the caterpillars, then the cocoons, then the butterflies.

The teacher used this to tell the story of Beatrice Butterfly who was lonely in the field because no other creatures were around. She finds each of the egg groups and watches it hatch. The children are encouraged to help Beatrice guess what might hatch from each set of eggs. At the end she finds Bernie, another butterfly, and is no longer lonely. During play time the children often retold the story, moving Beatrice around the board and helping the eggs to hatch. This gave children the opportunity to exercise their storytelling skills, as they rehearsed the knowledge they had gained about eggs. This bulletin board was created by a teacher who found artistic work satisfying. For teachers who have less interest, skill, and/or time for artwork, the bulletin board here can be created on a much simpler scale, using photos or traced pictures.

Hatching Eggs

The interest in the bulletin board eggs led to children making their own hatching eggs. Children fastened two oval pieces of manila paper together with a brad and drew various creatures inside. This activity generated much oral language about the inhabitants of eggs. For some children it led to storytelling. One child even cut out a butterfly so he could retell Beatrice's story when he got home. When the oval paper was all gone, children created their own by cutting off the corners of manila paper to make egg shapes.

The activity provided an opportunity to use oral language skills, to represent creatures with drawing, and to exercise small muscle skills in drawing, cutting, and attaching the brad. Children also used what they had been learning about eggs. Some children made "silly" eggs with cows and dogs emerging from eggs. They would show these to the teacher, barely suppressing giggles over how silly they had been.

Egg Books

Homemade books were stapled and cut into egg shapes. Some children just decorated the pages. Some children drew rainbows, people, or other current drawing interests, but most filled the books with creatures that hatched from eggs. Some children labeled their creatures with strings of letters, others used phonetic writing, still others dictated information about the creatures for the teacher to record. These books were shared at circle time, encouraging other children to be authors and have their work shared on following days.

The books elicited both oral and written language from the children. Children wrote at differing skill levels and felt comfortable with whatever their level was. The book production was a social event. Group discussion and peer drawings often influenced the content of the books and helped with the phonetic spelling.

Pretending to Hatch Eggs

Plastic eggs that open were used with small rubber creatures to allow children to support pretend play around eggs and hatching. Eggs with rubber and wooden snakes, frogs, dinosaurs, birds, spiders, and turtles were added to the block area with many trucks for hauling the eggs and creatures around. Children built nests, hideouts, and apartments for their creatures. One child built a store that sold unhatched eggs, creatures, and eggs "to crawl back into at bedtime."

The aquatic creatures, along with rubber fish and bits of bubble paper (to be fish or frog eggs), were added to the water table. A bin of birdseed was put out with eggs and birds to hatch and feed.

The children found it hard to wait the twenty-one days for the chicks to hatch, so a small play incubator was made out of styrofoam. The children could turn the eggs in this, just like the teacher turned the real eggs. The children could have the plastic eggs hatch whenever and as often as they wished.

Bird Forest

A dramatic play area was designed to allow children to be birds. Brown package wrapping paper made trees. The tops were attached to the ceiling, and the bottoms were fastened to wooden steps, or table legs. The space under the table became a nest in the tree. A board between two pairs of steps was a branch to perch on or fly from. Barrels become hollow logs that offered other places for nesting. A piece of blue carpet was used as a

FIGURE 9-15 Bird forest

pond. Beanbag chairs and wooden crate boxes each served as additional nesting spots.

Eggs cut out of foam filled many of the nests. Children became birds with rubber beaks and homemade wings. They each painted their own wings using cake tempera paint on old sheeting material. Loops of elastic attached to the tips of the wings held the wings on wrists. A strip of cloth velcroed loosely across the neck held the wings on the shoulders.

In the forest the children played bird family; as they played they used the information they had learned about birds during group time and from books. Some birds slept squatting on the plank, gripping hard with their hands. They had learned that once birds sit, their muscles clamp shut and will not loosen until the bird stands up again. They invented danger calls and food calls. These songs differed as the calls had on the bird song record they had heard. While drinking, the birds tilted their heads back so the water would run down their throats, just like the baby chicks did when they drank (see Figure 9-15).

Bird Calls

The group listened to recorded bird calls in which the call was like the bird's name: Bobwhite, whippoorwill, and chickadee, for example. The children then made up calls using their own names. This offered the children a chance to play with language, to hear the many different ways that the same name could sound.

FIGURE 9-16 Playing "What Colors Are the Eggs?"

Egg Math

Counting children at the snack table was a favorite pastime of this group of children. They would often count the total number of people (6); then count the boys (3) and the girls (3); the adults (1) and the children (5); the people with pants (4) and the people with shorts (2). To follow up on this, the teacher adapted an activity from *Math Their Own Way* (Baretta-Lorton, 1976).

Five blue eggs were cut from blue mat board that was white on the other side. The children put the eggs in a cup, shook them, then dumped out the eggs, looking to see how many white and how many blue eggs they got. On a sheet with five egg outlines, the children colored in with blue crayons the number of blue eggs they had shaken. Children would repeat this many times to see the different results. Children did the activity in different ways. Some children counted the number of blue eggs. A few children used numerals to record the number of blue eggs. One child even phrased the findings as a math problem: 2 + 3 = 5 (see Figure 9-16).

A STEP FURTHER   *Each Child Will Approach Activities in Individual Ways*

Activities should be designed to allow children to approach them in a variety of ways and at a variety of levels. The egg math game is a good illustration of this. Children who cannot count can play this type of game. They merely need to match the eggs to the outlines and then color. The game can also provide a challenge for children who want to experiment with simple addition.

Damien found his own unique approach to the activity. He watched the teacher's demonstration at group time. He shook the cup and 3 white eggs and 2 blue eggs came out. He put the eggs back in the cup. To Damien's amazement, the next time only blue eggs came out. He spent ten minutes dumping out eggs, each time amazed that the number of blue ones changed. As he was putting the eggs back in, one flipped over, changing from blue to white. An excited grin spread over Damien's face. Racing up to the teacher, he declared, "I know how you do it!" He then showed her how the egg was a different color on each side.

For Damien, the point of the activity was to discover the mystery of the changing colors. He worked hard at finding the solution, and was justifiably proud of his accomplishment. What he gained from this was as important as the math skills that other children developed.

Measuring an Albatross

When talking about how different birds can be from each other, the teacher showed the class a small paper hummingbird and a large paper albatross. The children were intrigued with the length of the albatross. Its wing span almost reached across the length of the classroom. It was left on the floor for children to color. Some children decided to see if they could make a string of chain links as long as the albatross (see Figure 9-17). When it was finished, they dictated a label to the teacher. "This is as big as an albatross." The chain and label were posted in the hallway for other children to see. These children used written language to communicate to others. They also used the chain links to represent the size of the bird.

Soap Eggs

A favorite activity during this unit was making soap eggs. Children followed a picture and word recipe to make soap eggs. The eggs were made with powdered Ivory laundry soap and water. A small plastic dinosaur or turtle was enclosed inside the soap, to emerge as children washed with the soap.

This activity provided practice in following picture directions. Children refined their small muscle skills. The activity generated a good deal of talk, especially about what type of creatures could come out of eggs.

Egg-Hatching Game

The teacher developed an egg-hatching game to go with the unit. A cardboard tray designed to hold 36 eggs is used as a base. One row is colored

FIGURE 9-17 Measuring the albatross

blue, one yellow, one pink, one purple, one green, and one white. Plastic eggs are placed on the tray matching the color of eggs to the rows. A small rubber animal is placed inside of each egg. Next to the egg tray is a poster of an outdoor scene (see Figure 9-18).

Children roll a color die and "hatch" an egg that matches the color rolled. The animal that emerges is placed on the poster where it might like to live. When all of one color is hatched children can either refill an egg if they roll that color, or roll again.

The color spots on the die are symbols that children must interpret to know what color egg to hatch. As they play, children hear and use color names. Discussion arises about where animals should live, and what color eggs each animal should be returned to at the end of the game. Children often use the props to develop pretend play about the animals.

Embryo Chart

Next to the incubator is a chart showing twenty-one eggs which are labeled day 1, day 2, and so on until day 21. Inside of each of the outlines is a drawing of what the embryo inside the egg looks like after this many days of development. The day the incubator arrives, all the eggs but day one are covered with post-its™. Each day the next post-it is removed, uncovering one more egg. The children can lift the bottom of the post-its to see what the embryo will look like on future days.

The children often discussed what new parts the chicks had developed that day, or would be developing tomorrow. Being able to see what was happening inside the egg, and seeing the twenty-first day getting closer made the waiting a bit easier.

FIGURE 9-18 Egg-hatching game

FIGURE 9-19 Birdhunt

The chart generated oral language. Some children read the numeral that indicated the date; others counted the uncovered eggs to help them decipher the number of the current day.

Bird Watching

Children enjoy searching games. Birdwatchers often search for birds. The teacher put these two ideas together and came up with a bird hunt. Six distinctive photographs of birds were posted around the room. Some were suspended from the ceiling, others were on the backs of shelves, still others were on walls. Each was mounted on dark blue paper. Each was next to a numeral from 1 to 6.

Smaller versions of the six pictures were drawn onto a ditto along with the numeral. Next to the numeral was a small box to check when the bird was found. The name of each bird was printed below the illustration (see Figure 9-19). Next to the birdhunt sheets was a tray with binoculars made from toilet paper rolls and string. Children used the binoculars to search the room for the birds. When a bird was found, they would check it off.

Children would repeat the activity many times, excited with how fast they could become. Each night the teacher would move the pictures to new locations so a new hunt could begin the next day. One child carefully wrote the numeral in the box when the bird was found. Another child took the can of colored pencils and a writing board to the first bird and carefully colored the ditto to match the photograph. Children were using symbols (the outlines of the birds and the numerals) to indicate which birds they should find.

The ideas described in this unit show how science, math, dramatic play, and emergent literacy can all be pursued as children extend their knowledge about eggs and birds. In the study of eggs and birds literacy was a tool for exploring and learning. It was a natural component of many of the unit's activities.

Even with a Supportive Literacy Atmosphere, No Activity Is Magical

The beginning of this chapter stated that it is not individual activities that create a literacy rich environment, but rather a philosophy about literacy that permeates all that happens. Even when this atmosphere *is* present, the above activities are not guaranteed to be successful in all childcare settings. Developmentally appropriate practice in early childhood settings involves responding to the interests and needs of each child (Bredekamp, 1987). The success of dramatic play or a literacy activity depends on the interests of the children in the group.

> *Tanya, the teacher from the beginning of the chapter, was so pleased at the excitement the message board had generated that she planned to use it as a central part of her classroom the next year. Her first message was a birthday announcement as it had been the year before, but this time the children seemed bored and restless.*
>
> *When messages appeared on the board, children didn't notice. When Tanya asked if children could guess what was in the message from the picture, a few of the children responded, but others didn't seem to care. The only use the children found for the message board was pinning up drawings without names for identification. This became a favorite clean-up activity.*

Even though Tanya's philosophy about literacy remained the same, and although the activity was recreated the same way, this group of children did not find the literacy tied to the message board appealing. The message board became simply a place to hang unclaimed and unnamed pictures. This particular group of children explored literacy through sign making, book authorship, and letter writing.

In light of this, it is important to keep in mind that the suggestions given in this chapter are just possible activities, approaches, and materials to foster literacy. Each teacher will have to select, try, and evaluate ideas to see what helps the children in his or her care explore literacy.

CHAPTER 10

Creating Continuity

Michael began reading around his fourth birthday. Now although he reads avidly at home, including challenging books like **My Visit to the Dinosaurs** *(Aliki, 1969), he never shows his reading skill to teachers. When his parents ask if he ever reads to teachers at his daycare, he replies, "No, kids don't read at school."*

* * *

Zachary, who is five, scribbles lines of cursive-like marks on long thin strips of paper at home. They are tickets that are handed out to everyone in the family for a variety of crimes. He eagerly reads the ticket to the offender as he issues it.

In Zachary's kindergarten a different kind of writing is expected. When students are asked to write he begins making the scribble cursive lines that he makes at home, narrating the content as he writes. His teacher tells him, "This is writing time. You need to copy the words from the board, not scribble."

* * *

Tiffany has always enjoyed writing. At home she scribble-writes, makes long strings of letters, and lists words she knows. In first grade she began with the writing techniques she brought from home, but then moved on to doing phonetic writing as she made advertisements for the school grocery store. During writing workshop she made elaborate pictures with a few phonetically spelled labels. Stories were long strings of random letters to accompany a verbal narration about the pictures. At the parent conference Tiffany's mother expresses concern over the fact that Tiffany is not writing correctly. Mom feels that too much time is spent in play. First grade should be a time for work sheets and "real learning." At home Mother begins pushing Tiffany to write "correctly." Tiffany's writing at home decreases.

* * *

Springside Elementary School has a developmentally appropriate kindergarten program where children are helped to construct knowledge of literacy, and other things, through play. However, the first grade teachers still use skill-based reading readiness programs. They complain constantly about the kindergarten program. "All they do is play. The children have a hard time when they come to first grade. They expect to play. They do not know how to do worksheets. They do not think it matters if words are spelled correctly." These teachers feel that children would be more successful in first grade if the kindergarten prepared them better. These children feel like readers and writers in kindergarten, but find that in first grade they are viewed as beginners.

Each of these vignettes illustrates discontinuity between the child's construction of literacy in one setting and in another. Michael felt that the knowledge he had constructed about literacy at home was irrelevant at school. School learning was something separate.

Zachary quickly learned that the scribble-writing that was valued at home was looked down upon at school. Although he found writing at home a joyous event, he learned that writing at school was a meaningless, laborious task.

Tiffany was an eager writer both at home and at school. She had confidence in her ability as a writer. She was building her skills at phonetic spelling, but slipped back into use of random letters for longer pieces of writing. The constant pressure from her parents to "write correctly" made writing a chore where she was always making mistakes, instead of something over which she had mastery. Her parents were concerned because they did not recognize the learning that was occurring at school.

The Springside children are treated as readers and writers in kindergarten, but when they get to first grade they are viewed as unready for reading and writing. This schism between teachers creates a discontinuity for the children. The attitude of the first grade teachers also reinforces parents' concerns about what is occurring in kindergarten.

Why Is Continuity Needed?

Children do not segment their lives. Two settings at variance may place stress upon the child (Powell, 1989). According to Henderson (1988), "If schools do not make the effort to include parents in the learning process, children can find it difficult to integrate the separate experiences of home and school" (p. 152). Two classroom settings that differ significantly can create integration problems as well. Continuity between home and school, and from one class and another, is important for a number of reasons.

Children Need Faith in Themselves to Construct Knowledge

Children learn about literacy from the world around them. They learn from what they see at home, at school, and in the community. From their experiences, children begin to create an understanding of reading and writing. Children must feel comfortable to be daring, to create and act upon ideas about literacy, even if the ideas are incorrect (Calkins, 1986). If they feel that their efforts to construct knowledge are always faulty, then children will be less willing to make guesses, less willing to trust their ideas, and less willing to stretch their knowledge bases.

When children like those in the opening stories are confident in their skills in one setting, but meet with criticism in another setting, they begin to doubt their skills. This uncertainty undermines their ability to learn, making the acquisition of literacy more difficult. When continuity exists between different settings, children will take the confidence they have gained in one setting and apply it to their construction of literacy in other settings.

FIGURE 10-1 Children must feel comfortable to act upon their ideas about literacy

Children Come to School with Literacy Knowledge

Children do not learn about literacy as a set of individual skills; literacy learning is not a step-by-step process. Rather, children construct their knowledge of literacy by gradually making sense out of the writing and language around them. They come to school with a wealth of knowledge they have already accumulated about literacy.

Taylor and Strickland (1989) stressed that literacy instruction must build on the knowledge that children bring with them. When schools ignore that knowledge, they not only undermine the children's faith in themselves as learners, but they must also reteach what children already know about literacy. When there is continuity between home and school, the schools can build upon knowledge children bring from home and move children towards further understanding.

Literacy Is a Lifelong Skill

Although schools ask children to answer comprehension questions, analyze poetry, compose essays, and do other academic reading and writing, the ultimate aim of education is to produce adults who comfortably use reading and writing in their everyday lives (Fox, & Sarcho (1990). To meet this goal, children must see the connection between school literacy and their lives outside of school.

Building this connection is especially important for children whose home cultures are different from the middle-class white culture upon which most schools are based. Children from nonmainstream cultures often do poorly on standardized assessment tests and school tasks that mirror these tests. Providing activities that are linked to the community offers these children more opportunities for success.

As Taylor and Strickland (1989) explained,

> We cannot replace family life with classroom experiences, but we can recognize the legitimacy of children's social existence and use it as a basis for curriculum and instruction. Children are at risk when meaning is lost in the expensive rigmarole of artificial reading and writing activities. There is no doubt in our minds that children are disenfranchised when excluded from genuine literacy learning (p. 275).

Building a connection between home and school may be especially important to children whose homes differ from those that researchers defined as "literacy rich." These children may come to school with fewer literacy skills. They need, even more than other children, to see the reason for literacy. They need to find the joy, excitement, and purpose of literacy. They need to see the value of what they already know, and to see how new skills can be used in their home community.

Building continuity between home and school ensures that literacy developed in schools can be meaningfully applied in the community. It assures that cultural differences will not create road blocks for learning.

Supporting the Learning That Occurs at Home

By building on the learning children bring to school, teachers validate the importance of learning that has gone on in the home both for the children themselves and their families. When teachers celebrate the literacy learning that children bring to school and childcare, they help parents see the value of the simple everyday activities that contribute to children's construction of literacy knowledge.* Supporting parents' skills raises the self-esteem of parents, which is integral to the development of the child (National Association of State Boards of Education, 1988).

A strong connection between home and school will allow teachers to extend parents' techniques for expanding literacy through everyday events. It will also allow teachers to share what is happening at school so parents can extend school learning at home.

Impediments to Continuity between Home and School, Classroom and Classroom

Although it is widely held that strong relations between home and school are important (Bredekamp, 1987; National Association of Elementary School Principals, 1990), there are unfortunately many impediments to building these partnerships. This section will explore some of the impediments, and suggest techniques for circumventing these and building strong school/home and classroom to classroom continuity. The last part of the chapter will discuss the techniques suggested here in more detail, and discuss how this bond can be used to support emerging literacy.

Parental Expectations

Parents want what is best for their children. They often do not know the newest educational philosophies or methods. They may watch the phonet-

---

*This book has avoided the use of the word "school," since many children are in early childhood settings that are not "schools." However in this chapter, where relations between home and childcare facilities are discussed, the use of these longer terms becomes unwieldy. Therefore, in this chapter the word "school" will be used broadly to refer to any childcare setting.

ic spelling and play-oriented program with concern. To them this does not look like learning. This does not look like school as they remember it. "Their first memory of school is of learning in the elementary grades. They remember structured lessons and rigid routines and assume that such practices are necessary for learning to occur" (Bredekamp, 1987, p. 85). They may question whether the school is really helping their children to learn.

Parents who do not understand the learning that is occurring may ask such things as, "Why do the children play so much?" "Why don't they bring home worksheets like the children in the other class?" "Why don't you teach them the right way to spell words?" It would be easy for teachers to see such questions as criticisms and become defensive, a reaction that may strain parent/teacher relations.

To circumvent this potential problem, it is important for early childhood professionals to see these questions as legitimate parental concern for their children, which is tied to a lack of understanding of the learning that IS occurring in the classroom. The early childhood educator can help parents to recognize the way in which the play-oriented classroom supports emergent literacy and other learning (Bredekamp, 1987). Some mechanisms for explaining school philosophy to parents are things such as newsletters, workshops, slide shows, inviting parents to spend time in the classroom, and regular descriptions of children's progress.

Parental Distrust of Schools

Many parents had unhappy experiences with schools when they were children (Kostelnik, Soderman, & Whiren, 1993; Hendrick, 1992). These parents come to school or childcare with negative preconceptions of what will happen. They may distrust both teachers and schools (Powell, 1989). To such families school is a place where you are belittled and where you meet failure. These parents put up walls to protect themselves and their children. Teachers need to demonstrate that school is a warm, caring place, that children and parents are respected, and that it is a place where both children and parents can succeed.

Teachers' Negative Views of Parents

No one likes to feel in the wrong. If the teacher blames the parents for children's poor language skills, lack of literacy knowledge, or other deficits, this negative evaluation is sure to be sensed by the parents (Hendrick, 1992). Teachers may not make the effort to involve parents because they feel that "today's parents (especially low-income, single-parent, and dual-career families) would be unwilling or unable to participate in program-related activities" (Kostelnik et al., 1993, p. 376). Many others have also cited the unfortunate tendency of teachers to doubt parental interest, time, or ability to support their children's learning (Goldenberg 1989, Powell 1989, and Rasinski 1989). When the teachers do involve parents, it may be in programs to remediate what is not being accomplished at home. A parent/teacher bond will be difficult to create when parents feel that teachers look down on them.

Early childhood educators must believe that parents are working for the best interest of their children. It is true that low income, single parenthood, and dual careers in a family can make life more difficult. Early childhood programs should work to support these families, by understanding and providing flexibility in order to facilitate a better bond. These parents often cannot attend meetings because of busy schedules, lack of transportation, or need for childcare. In order to involve parents, notice for meetings must be given far in advance. Transportation and childcare should be arranged when necessary.

If children do not go directly home after childcare or school, or if they ride in a carpool, notes may not get home. If parents are unresponsive, early childhood educators should telephone to see if messages are actually getting home. For parents who are not skilled readers, phone calls may be preferable anyway. By communicating in a variety of ways, early childhood professionals are more likely to find a method that meets the need of each family.

Structures That Limit Parent/Teacher Interaction

Often the way the early childhood programs are structured inadvertently creates barriers to parent/teacher relations by limiting the chances for parents and early childhood educators to interact. When children ride buses to school, parents have fewer occasions to speak informally with teachers. They also cannot observe how the classroom is set up and the many challenging things that are planned each day.

In some early childhood facilities, parents are asked to leave and retrieve children at a central spot. This is done because it is more convenient for parents and less disruptive for the early childhood educator. However, building a strong parent/teacher relation is essential, and it is worth a bit of inconvenience and disruption.

Early childhood educators will need to work harder to build relationships with parents when the school structure limits the informal contact. Personal contact with each family should be made early in the year. Such things as phone calls, newsletters, personal notes, and parental visits to the classroom can maintain the contact through the year. Although structural problems may make it more difficult to create and maintain contact with parents, these relations can still flourish when teachers view them as a high priority.

Dissension between Educators

When teachers in successive grades hold differing philosophies about how children develop literacy, the children can be the casualties of the discontinuity. Not only can this dissension undermine the children's faith in themselves, it can also undermine the parents' understanding and acceptance of the school program. Administrators, who are often trained to work with older children, may not understand the developmental needs of younger children. They may pressure teachers to use standardized programs and to limit the amount of play that occurs. This attitude may also undermine parent/teacher interaction by contradicting what is happening in the classroom.

Although negative comments from other teachers and from administrators can be upsetting, it is important to view these in the same light as negative comments from parents. These professionals are concerned about the best interests of the children; they just view learning differently. It is the early childhood professional's responsibility to educate colleagues through such means as sharing children's work, distributing newsletters, making available professional literature, and inviting colleagues to share in classroom literacy events.

One class particularly enjoyed the rhythm of *Over in the Meadow* (Wadsworth, 1986). They decided to turn it into a play. They made costumes, posted advertisements around the school, and sent out child-made invitations to parents (see Figures 10-2 and 10-3).

No matter what the challenges, each early childhood professional is still responsible for ensuring that what happens in the early childhood

FIGURE 10-2 Advertisement for a kindergarten production of *Over in the Meadow*

FIGURE 10-3 The teacher reads *Over in the Meadow* while children act it out

setting is developmentally appropriate. Bredekamp (1987) stressed that "no early childhood professional should abdicate this responsibility in the absence of support from colleagues or supervisors" (p. 87).

Ingredients for Building Strong Teacher/Parent Partnerships

Building strong teacher/parent partnerships depends on three main ingredients: rapport, individualization, and communication. Let us look at each of these ingredients.

Rapport

Comfortable rapport is the foundation for positive relations between people. Since rapport often develops with familiarity, the more opportunity there is for contact between early childhood educators and parents, the more likely rapport is to develop.

Rapport is also based on sharing of similar interests and concerns. Since children are the joint point of interest for both parents and teachers, expressing enjoyment of, affection for, and interest in their children is an easy way for early childhood professionals to build rapport with parents. Teachers demonstrate their feelings about children by the way they interact with them, by smiling at what children do, by offering a lap to sit on, by being excited about what the children are doing and saying. Parents can observe the warmth and affection that is part of daily interaction between teacher and their children.

People talk about things that interest them. Doting parents often recount cute anecdotes about their children. These parents seem to be bursting with pride over the marvelous things their offspring do. Early childhood professionals who eagerly share the many wonderful things that children do at school communicate this same feeling of pride and caring. The fact that these stories are remembered and passed on demonstrates involvement with and interest in the child. The tone of what is said demonstrates the feeling for the child.

When children are picked up at the end of the day, teachers can describe something interesting that the child did or said during the day. Comments that show how the child contributes to the overall warmth and demeanor of the classroom are particularly welcomed by parents, such comments as: "I was so proud of what Keely did today. When Eric fell off his bike, she was the first one there to comfort him. She even gave up her own bike to go in and help him get a bandaid." Or "Angel made my job easy today. She got her classmates interested in writing. She made a big sign for her grocery store in the blocks announcing a sale. All the other block builders, not to be undone, had to have signs as well."

Written communications are particularly useful in situations where parents and teachers do not see each other on a regular basis. But even when the contact is regular, parents enjoy seeing their children's actions captured in writing. Newsletters can include descriptions of the early childhood setting showing individual children's activities (see A Step Further, [page 263]). "Happy notes" (Bundy, 1991; Kostelnik et al., 1993) can be sent home occasionally describing something the child did at school.

Rapport grows out of mutual respect and concern. It is important for early childhood professionals to express interest in the child's family, as well as in the child, by such things as admiring a new baby, expressing concern about an ill grandparent, and sharing excitement over a parent's promotion. Support and interest in the family should be communicated in ways that are not pushy or prying.

Individualization

A key dimension of developmentally appropriate practice for early childhood programs is seeing each child as "a unique person with an individual pattern and timing of growth, as well as individual personality, learning style and family background" (Bredekamp, 1987, p. 2). Curriculum and adult-child interaction should be tailored to fit each individual child.

Individualization is equally important when working with families. No two families are the same. They have different interaction patterns, goals, interests, and needs. Some parents seek out information from early childhood professionals and will chat for hours. Other families may be less verbal with teachers. These differences in communication styles may be due to personality differences, or they may be caused by differing cultural norms. Teachers must find ways to communicate with all families.

Some parents will attend meetings and volunteer in the classroom. Other families may have crowded schedules that interfere with such participation. Other families may have cultural values that make them uncomfortable with these kinds of relations with professionals. Alternative ways must be found to share information with these families.

Some families will have overly high expectations and not see the many small accomplishments of their children. Early childhood educators can lead these parents to see their child's many strengths. Other families will have low expectations for their children. These parents can be helped to expand their views of what young children can do.

The types of literacy events that occur in each home will be different. Taylor and Dorsey-Gaines (1988), in a study of black inner-city families, found the integral part writing played in the lives of all the families.

> The families used print to fulfill requirements for assistance, to build and maintain social relationships, and to create a socio-historical context for their everyday lives (Taylor & Strickland, 1989, p. 255).

Teachers must find ways to support, extend, and celebrate diverse literacy patterns. General goals can be set for parent/teacher interactions, but each teacher will need to discover the techniques for reaching this goal that best support individual families.

Communication

Communication is the heart of all personal interactions. Communication is two-way interaction. Many times teachers see their role as telling parents things; listening to and learning from parents is equally important. Families can share information about the child at home. In the area of literacy they can share such things as their children's favorite books, their interest in environmental print, and the way they write their names. Teachers can share similar information about the children's interests and actions at school.

Information from One Setting Can Explain Behavior in Another Setting

Sharing information often explains behaviors that are unclear from just the home or school perspective.

Many afternoons, four-year-old DayQuon comes to childcare grumpy. He sits by the wall for the first half hour scowling at anyone who approaches him. For the rest of the day he is happily involved in a wide range of activities. A phone conference with his grandmother reveals that DayQuon often falls asleep in the car on the way to childcare. He is grumpy when awakened. The teacher and grandmother discuss ways of readjusting DayQuon's sleeping patterns. Because of current family pressures, there are not many good options.

After talking to DayQuon's grandmother the grumpiness makes more sense to the teacher. She realizes that DayQuon needs some space and time to wake up when he arrives at childcare. She also offers DayQuon many techniques for communicating his need for private time to the people around him.

Pooling Knowledge Can Lead to Deeper Understanding

Communication is more than just sharing information. By pooling and comparing their different perspectives on the child, parents and teachers can come to a fuller understanding of that child.

Five-year-old Aneshka's home language is Polish. She spends a great deal of time writing both at home and at school. When children are trying to sound out words at the art table, she eagerly offers suggestions. She knows many of the consonants but consistently misnames the vowels. She is beginning to feel unsure of herself due to the constant disagreement with other children over vowel names.

At home Mom and Aneshka are making a Polish alphabet book. Mom notices that Aneshka is hesitant to identify the vowels that she seemed to know before she started school this year. The teacher and Mom discuss Aneshka's writing at pick-up time one day. When they look at some of Aneshka's writing and discuss what is happening at home and school, they realize that Aneshka is confused because although the same letters are used in English and Polish they are called by different names. A is called ă, E is called ĕ, and most confusing I is called ē. When Aneshka calls the letter I "E" at school, she is corrected by her peers. At home she is unwilling to name letters because she is now uncertain of her knowledge.

Once Mom and the teacher realize the source of the problem, they devise a plan for helping Aneshka to be more successful. They decide it would be best to discuss with Aneshka that the two languages use different names for the letters, and then to concentrate on learning the letters in one language at a time. Since helping peers at spelling is considered a high-prestige activity among this group of children, it is decided to concentrate on the English letter names first.

Personalizing Information Makes It More Meaningful

Many times teachers see their role as giving parents information about child development. Yet, even information that seems straightforward is often better presented in a sharing, rather then a telling, format.

> *Brad is one of the few children who is still three in a class of four-year-olds. It is his first time in a group setting. He finds it difficult when he cannot have the toy he wants immediately. He will often resort to hitting or biting to get what he wants. With the help of teachers, he is beginning to use words. He is now sometimes able to shout angrily at the children in his way rather than being physically aggressive. Dad is particularly worried about what he calls Brad's selfishness. He feels that strict rules, enforced by spanking, will straighten out the behavior.*

In this situation a parent meeting, newsletter, or shared professional article on children's social and emotional development may not present information so that Dad can easily relate it to Brad's behavior and language skills. A more effective technique would be a conference in which the teacher presents Brad's behavior as typical for children his age, along with outlining the growth that he has made so far this year. The teacher should encourage Dad to talk about how Brad deals with frustration at home, especially the times he does it successfully.

From this the teacher can construct parallels between home and school behavior and provide some guidelines for better understanding and dealing with the behavior. In the context of this dialogue the teacher may include comments like those that follow.

- Like many children his age, Brad finds it hard to wait for things that he wants. At this age many children do not yet have the language or social skills to ask for what they want in more adult ways.

- Communicating when we are angry is difficult, even for adults. It takes a long time, and adult support, for children to develop this language skill.

- I have been impressed with how hard Brad is working to control his frustration when he does not have what he wants. He is now often able to use words to tell peers what he wants, or to come to teachers for help rather then hitting or biting.

- Often having a teacher agree that it is hard to wait when you want something reassures Brad that others know how hard he is trying.

- He is starting to yell at children who have what he wants. I am pleased to see he is learning to recognize the effectiveness of words. With time he will learn to make requests in politer ways.

By describing Brad's behavior in relation to child development research, the teacher reassures Dad that his child's behavior is not aberrant or malicious. By describing techniques used at school, the teacher models ways to help Brad develop more mature methods for dealing with frustration.

Dad was not convinced immediately, though he did feel that the teacher knew and cared about his child. After many conversations of this type coupled with clear signs of Brad's social maturation, Dad began to relax and be more understanding of Brad's behavior. Dad occasionally sought additional suggestions and information from the teacher.

What Information Should Be Shared?

There can be no communication without something to communicate about. Every child and family is unique, so the communications between each teacher and parent will also be unique. There are, however, certain broad topics that are covered at some point between each parent and teacher: Knowledge about the child, descriptions of the child's home and school environments and activities, general child development information, and realistic goals for the child linked with techniques for helping the child reach these goals. A Step Further, which follows, describes some of the information that can be included in parent teacher discussion about emerging literacy.

Formats for Communicating

This section will describe some of the many formats for home/school communication and highlight the ways they can be used to communicate about emerging literacy.

Initial Contacts

Teachers' contacts with families and children before the child begins school demonstrate an eagerness to begin a relationship. This first contact can be made in a number of ways. Visiting the early childhood center allows both the family and the child to gain a sense of what the setting is like, to have their questions answered, and to begin to become comfortable and familiar with the staff and center. Having a preadmission time when children can visit the school with their parents reassures the children that this is a fun place to be, a place where they and their parents are welcomed.

Phone calls, welcoming letters to parents and children, and home visits also demonstrate interest in the child and family. These initial encounters set the tone for later interactions, as well as allowing parents and teachers to share a variety of information. Teachers can share information about the program, such as what a typical day looks like, how discipline issues are handled, what kinds of things are usually of interest to children in the first month of school, and what types of oral written language learning are likely to be occurring.

During these initial contacts, teachers and parents can discuss ways they can work together to facilitate the child's development. The framework for each parent-teacher partnership can be established, and the parents and teachers can discuss the best ways to get in touch with each other: Phone, letter, meeting, or at pickup or dropoff times.

A STEP FURTHER   *Possible Literacy Information to Share*

Obviously communication between parents and teacher will be tailored to each child, but the following list highlights some areas of literacy information that are important for mutual sharing between early childhood educators and parents. The list should be adapted to better match specific early childhood settings, children, and families.

About the child

▎Uses of oral language: To express needs, to narrate games, to name things, to express feelings, to organize interactions, to resolve problems, to talk in small or large groups with adults or peers

▎Description of oral language: Vocabulary, clarity, length of utterance, complexity of sentence structure

▎Interest in word play: Rhyming, making jokes, inventing silly words, group chants

▎Favorite books, songs, poems

▎Interaction with print: Interest in print, attempts to decipher print, recognition of letters, matching letters to sounds, reading words conventionally, techniques used to retell books, awareness of conventions of books.

▎Description of written language: When it is used, understanding of the way print works, spelling strategies used, physical ability to produce writing

About home and school settings

▎Times when reading and writing are used by adults and/or children

▎Activities and materials that encourage literacy

▎Play activities that generate abundant language

About child development

▎Description of how oral language develops

▎Description of emergent literacy: The importance of "mock writing," the value of making children feel like readers and writers, the alternating of growth spurts with plateaus while children integrate their new knowledge, the importance of errors in constructing knowledge, the need to use literacy functionally

About individual goals and techniques to reach them

▎Discuss goals for the child's further literacy development

▎Discuss techniques for supporting the child's current literacy skills: Ways to include children in retelling of books, ways to support current writing levels, materials, ways in which child explores literacy in pretend play, and events that will encourage reading and writing

Describing age-specific developmental trends can sometimes forestall misunderstandings later. Although parents enjoy their children's mastery of new words, there are exceptions. For example, four-year-olds often like to try out "bathroom language" and other risque words. If teachers describe this tendency at the beginning of the year, along with why it happens and how teachers deal with it, parents are not so shocked when their children begin trying out this language. This also allows teachers and parents to begin a dialogue about how to handle such issues.

Parents can discuss their goals for their children and share information about their children that will help the teacher prepare for the child's first few days. For example, if a child likes to explore machines, the typewriter could be a good place to direct the child. If a child tends to be disoriented when awakened in new places, parents might mention a favorite song that may help the child feel at home at the end of naptime.

Informal Interactions

Many little things can be shared on an ongoing basis through informal contact when children are dropped off or picked up from school. This informal time contributes to the familiarity and rapport that makes for a good relationship.

When possible, staff and classroom schedules should be arranged to insure that there is time for a parent/teacher chat at the beginning and/or end of the day. For childcare centers with long hours, it is good to have one of the main teachers from each class available at the beginning or end of the day at least a few days a week. When children come to school by bus or carpool, teachers should make a point of frequent phone contact with parents. A regular time should be set when the early childhood educator can be reached by phone.

It is often through these informal interactions that educators find out about such things as an illness in a family, a favorite neighbor moving away, the death of a pet, or the beginning of toilet training. Adults can share current information about the child: A new favorite book, frequent play themes, and emerging friendships. A regular part of such interactions are the priceless anecdotes about the child.

Lengthy conversations and discussions of major concerns should be avoided when children and other parents are around. These topics should be deferred until more private times, when both adults can give full attention to the conversation.

Written Communications

Written communications can range from the formal to the informal, from the general to the personal. These can be used to follow up verbal communications, or to reach family members who are rarely seen. It is important that written communications use simple, non-jargon language. The early childhood educator must be sure to consider the language abilities of the family in the same way that the abilities of children are considered. A few types of written communications are described below.

Policy Statements, Parent Handbooks, and Curriculum Guides

Some early childhood facilities provide parents with written material about such things as the school's philosophy, curriculum, and policies. These materials could include a discussion of the value of play, and a description of how emergent literacy is facilitated.

Newsletters

Newsletters sent home on a regular basis share such things as current classroom events, favorite books and songs, as well as child development information. Unfortunately many schools distribute schoolwide newsletters in place of the more personal ones from individual classrooms. Like the practice of having all children picked up at the front door, this may be easier organizationally, but it decreases the interactions between parents and teachers. A Step Further below provides an example of a classroom newsletter.

A STEP FURTHER *A Newsletter*

AFTERNOON NEWS

FAMILY NIGHT

Maggie Jones wanted everyone to know about the family night at the Northwest Community Center. There are games for children of all ages, even a room for infants. Part of the time is for parents and children to play together, and part of the time is for parents to relax and talk to each other, while children are supervised by the center's staff.

A BURST OF WRITING

In January we noticed a burst of interest among many of the children in "writing." Because so many children have been interested in "writing" I thought I would take a few minutes to discuss the development of "writing" in young children.

Many researchers and educators have become interested in studying beginning writing in the last few years. They have found that children begin to become "literate," or become people aware of writing, much younger than was originally thought. Just as talking starts with a babbling stage, literacy also has a "babbling" stage. When babies begin to talk, you can see that they are experimenting with when to talk, and are seeing that talking will get certain results.

In the "babbling" stage of literacy development, children are becoming aware of the print around them. They see that books have print and that the same story comes out of the same book each time it is read. They may try out "reading" the book themselves.

They are aware of the writing around them in the world, and may ask "what does that say?" When playing pretend grocery store, they may check to see what the label says if they see their parents doing this. They are beginning to realize that the print says things that are important to read and respond to.

Children will also begin to do pretend writing. At first pretend writing may be random scribbles. As children get a better idea of letter forms, their pretend letters will tend to be constructed of lines and circles like ours.

Not all of their "writing" will use real letters, but the letters will look similar to our real letters. It is all right that the letters are not made correctly. Beginning writers are trying out letters, just as beginning talkers try out sounds. Both will eventually learn to be more accurate. But both need the time to be inaccurate as they are learning.

Children enjoy "reading" their writing to you. It is interesting how three or four marks can be used to represent a paragraph-long story.

What have I seen at school to show me that some children are excited about literacy?

- Many children enjoy "reading" books to teachers or friends at book time. They will repeat stories that they have heard read to the class.
- Almost all the children are beginning to help write their names. Some children write the whole name. Some will do the name as we talk it through: "What does your name start with? A 'J' is a line with a loop at the end. 'a', that's a circle and a line." Others will help with one letter, or write it with us holding their hands. Still others will make a series of scribbling marks. We do not push children to write their names. But we get VERY excited when they do it, which makes them pleased with themselves and eager to try again.
- In January we had clipboard with paper and pencils out with our grocery store, the hearing doctor, the eye doctor, and the "animal study center." Children eagerly used these to write shopping lists, make money, write prescriptions, and record about animals.
- A few of the children are adding writing to the their art work.

What can you do as a parent to nurture your child's excitement in writing?

- Most important, realize that all children develop at different stages. Although some children in the class are interested now, your child may not be interested until next year. That is fine.
- Have paper and pencil around so that if you are writing—letters, bills,

shopping lists, etc.—your child can write along with you.

- Be excited about your child's writing. Your interest is the best way to encourage the child's interest.
- Do not worry about correct letter formation. If a child is unsure how to do a letter, and is concerned, you can describe how to make it. Sometimes just having letters around to look at is helpful.
- Encourage the use of written language in pretend play—reading to baby, writing messages.

LET'S TALK

Feel free to call me if you have any questions, concerns, or comments about your child or about school. My school number is 555-4518. I can be reached during nap, from 1:30-3:00 every day except Wednesday. If I am not in, please leave a message and I will return the call. I can be reached at home in the evening at 555-8027.

HICKORY DICKORY DOCK

Mark asked me to include his favorite new song—"Hickory Dickory Dock." We have been singing the nursery rhyme and adding other verses with silly things for the mouse to do. When the clock strikes two he gets stuck in the glue. The children like helping to make up the rhymes. Although most still do not know how to make rhymes, they enjoy helping me choose among some possibilities.

The newsletter will be even more personal if it serves as a forum for families to communicate with one another. Parents often know about places to get bargains on used clothing, local children's concerts, great parks for children, or other resources of interest to all families. Newsletters can be used to share such things as the birth of a sibling, requests for help with transportation, or invitations to join a babysitting co-op. Children are another resource for newsletter topics. By including them in the selection of topics and the dictation of stories, they participate in a functional use for literacy.

"What I Did Today" Notes

One of the reasons that many parents like worksheets is that these papers show what their children are doing in school. In play-oriented classrooms, children may not take home daily papers showing what they have done. Regular newsletters can help to fill this void. "What I Did Today" notes also fill this void. These notes describe individual activities that happen in school. They may explain what children learn from doing puzzles, from building in the block area, from playing at the water table, or from working in the classroom grocery store (see A Step Further, on [page 281]).

A STEP FURTHER *"What I Did Today" Notes*

By writing one or two of these a week, teachers can gradually build up a large collection of "what I did today" notes. Children playing in a literacy-related or other area take a "what I did today" note describing the activity. These can be taken home daily, or on some regular schedule. Here is an example.

Today I Used the Typewriter

What: Today your child used the typewriter. The children explore how the typewriter works. They like to make the bell ring at the end of the line. Some of the children have been exploring the shift key, which changes the letters from lower case to upper case. They discover that the letters look different when the shift key is up and when it is down. Some of the children have been searching for specific letters to write their names, others prefer to type random letters, then hear the teachers read their new words like: "lakjfnnnennn." Other children will read their typing to teachers, with long elaborate stories to go with the random letters.

Why: Although it seems like "just play," the children are learning about how the typewriter works. They use problem solving to figure out what the different keys do. They are also becoming familiar with letters. Children are often excited when they discover "their letter"—what many children call the first letter of their name—on the typewriter. Typing is perceived by children as an "adult activity." Typing makes them feel like writers.

Extending at Home: When your children bring home typing ask them to share it with you. They may want you to read the "funny words," or they may want to tell you the story they have written. If you have a typewriter or computer at home, you may want to set it up so your child can use it. At school we have a "one finger at a time" rule for our manual typewriter so the keys don't get stuck. The children work hard to maintain this limit.

Personal Correspondence to Families

Newsletters provide an overview of what is happening in the classroom, but individual notes tell parents about their child. A note saying, "Wow, today Wendy wrote her name all by herself," shares a happy event with Wendy's parents. As Wendy observes the teacher writing this note, and later listens to her parents reading it, she sees literacy in use.

Individual Child Notebooks

An alternative to notes is a notebook for each child (Kostelnik et al., 1993). Teachers can record children's activities, language, and accomplishments, as well as questions for parents. Parents can read the notebook when they come in to pick up their child, or take it home and return it the next day. These notebooks can serve as a forum for dialogue back and forth about the child.

Written records of this type allow grandparents, or other family members who do not have regular contact with the school, to share in the school/family interactions. For children who are in remedial or therapeutic programs, or are in more than one early childhood setting, these notebooks provide the various professionals who work with the child a forum for communicating with each other. If notebooks are used by a number of professionals who work with the same child, it is important to keep in mind what information is privileged and what can be shared.

Parent Meetings, Picnics, and Other Get-Togethers

Parent meetings can take many forms. Slide shows or videos of the program give parents a glimpse of what happens at school. A film about emergent literacy can initiate a discussion about the emergent literacy of this particular group of children. Workshops for making materials to use at home give parents something to do, but leave time for informal conversations.

Family events such as picnics, field trips, or fun nights bring families and teachers together in relaxed enjoyable ways. For example, family fun nights are a great favorite with the families of children in Nadine Heim's two- and three-year-old class at the University of Delaware Preschool. Activities that might be available are creating murals, fishing, making and eating a snack, searching for buried treasure in the sand table, and building ramps for small cars to race down. Children can try these with their parents and siblings.

Families can be invited to participate in important classroom events. Children can make the invitations. After a class of four-year-olds visited the art museum, they designed their own art museum and invited parents to the grand opening. When the chicks hatched in a three-year-old class, parents and siblings were eager to observe their growth.

Parents of two-year-olds were invited to make a date to join the class for lunch. The class had space to accommodate two visiting parents. Parents would reserve their "meal with the twos" far in advance. Videotaping such events allowed absent parents to enjoy the events at a later time. A class of five-year-olds enjoyed acting out the poem *Over in the Meadow* (Wadsworth, 1986) and decided to invite parents and administrators to watch the performance (see Figure 10-4).

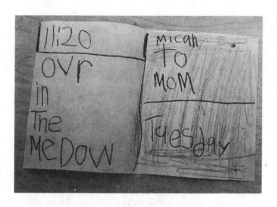

FIGURE 10-4 Invitation to Mom to come see *Over in the Meadow*

Spending Time at School

When parents spend time at school they can see what is happening, as well as the many things that children are learning. Watching an early childhood professional respond to a child's scribble writing and help another child to sound out a word shows parents how literacy can be facilitated. Unfortunately, many schools restrict parent volunteers to cutting out shapes for projects or other menial tasks. This is not the way to make parents feel welcome or needed. A parent can be invited to school to be a guest reader, an expert chef to assist with a cooking project, or to participate with children in other ways.

Parent Conferences

Parent conferences give parents and teachers extended time to discuss what they know about a child, to pose questions, and to set goals for facilitating the child's further development. Conferences are most effective when teachers can illustrate their observations with stories about the child, videos or photographs of the child at school, or samples of the child's artwork or writing.

Children Sharing School Activities with Their Parents

Children's excitement about what they have done at school demonstrates to parents the powerful learning that is occurring.

> *Evan is making his seventh batch of finger paint. He looks at the recipe card and then picks a remnant of blue chalk to put in his baggie. He takes a wooden mallet and hammers the bag until the chalk is dust. After checking the recipe again, he dumps the chalk dust into a small bowl, adds a spoonful of liquid starch, and stirs. He likes the way the blue first makes swirls in the starch and then gradually colors all of it. When the paint is ready, he mixes two more colors, then makes his*

picture. "I wish I could show my Dad how to make this." Ms. Goetz, his teacher, offers to make a copy of the recipe to go home. She copies the recipe onto a ditto with a note saying that Evan asked that it be sent home. When he is done painting, Evan helps her to run off the ditto, and puts a copy in each cubby.

When he gets home, Evan eagerly explains the note to his Dad. He explains the recipe by pointing to each group of words and pictures as he explains what it says.

Children enjoy taking home favorite books to share with parents. Some schools have book kits that can be taken home. The kit might contain a book, a tape recording of the book, and materials to play about the story. For example, materials to make "Wild Things" masks might accompany Maurice Sendak's *Where the Wild Things Are*. Children like to sing songs they have learned at school to their families, but often cannot remember all of the words when singing on their own. Although typing out the words will help, a better way is to make a tape of favorite songs that children can borrow.

Communication Techniques Are Merely Tools

Because each parent/teacher relationship is unique, the forms and content of communications will also be unique. One might assume that communicating in all the ways mentioned above would assure strong relationships. In fact, it would likely prove overwhelming for both educators and parents. The communications methods suggested are tools that can assist in creating the unique partnership that exists between each educator and each set of parents. The appropriate tools should be selected to use with each family. You would never use all of them. These tools will be useless without true teacher interest and regard for each child and family.

Building Partnerships with Administrators and Other Professionals

It is easy to build partnerships with administrators and fellow teachers when they understand what developmentally appropriate practice is for young children. These partnerships are harder to build when this understanding is missing. Many times teachers retreat into the safety and comfort of their own classrooms when met by criticism from colleagues. Although this may be an easy way out for the educator, it is not in the best interest of the children. Bredekamp (1987) stressed that

The lack of understanding about developmentally appropriate practices on the part of many parents, teachers, and administrators is largely a

result of the failure of early childhood educators to clearly articulate
what they do and why they do it (p. 87).

Early childhood educators must maintain positive relations with colleagues in order to communicate what they do and why.

Many of the communications techniques described for parents are
also successful with colleagues. Informal conversation in the teachers'
lounge provides an arena for sharing anecdotes that illustrate how children construct literacy in a play-oriented classroom. For example, a
teacher might recount something like this:

> *I put out signs in the blocks last week, but the children had just ignored them.*
> *Today Tony had built a large building, he watched other children driving their*
> *trucks around the blocks recklessly. He kept himself between them and his build-*
> *ing, but he wanted to leave to get some more blocks. He picked up the sign, put it*
> *in front of his building, and said, "This says stop, no crashing my building."*
> *Then of course everyone wanted signs. There were not enough, so some of the*
> *children made their own. Tony got the children to do what I had been trying to*
> *have them to do all week!*

This story illustrates for colleagues the wonderful literacy that develops
during play.

Children can also be encouraged to use writing to communicate
beyond the classroom. One kindergarten class was concerned about conservation. They made placards to carry in a parade, and flyers to hand
out. While they shared their conservation ideas with others in the buildings, colleagues saw the types of writing that these children produced.

Newsletters can be shared with fellow teachers and administrators.
Early childhood educators need to work to broadcast the achievements

FIGURE 10-5 Anti-pollution
flyer says "No" to pollution and
"Yes" to a pretty earth

FIGURE 10-6 Placard for "Protect the Earth" parade

that occur in their classrooms. A note proclaiming "What has been happening in our class," which describes relevant learning events, can be posted on the classroom door or on a staff bulletin board. Early childhood teachers can lead in-service for other teachers demonstrating the type of literacy activities that occur in their classrooms.

Invite administrators and fellow teachers to visit the classroom and to attend special classroom events, but be aware that visitors may need help interpreting what they are seeing. As visitors watch a child who is scribble writing in the house area, the teacher might offer a brief description of this child-literacy development, and the value of this type of writing. This description will emphasize to the visitors that learning is occurring and that teachers know how to facilitate it.

Just like parent/teacher relationships, professional relationships must be two-way interactions. Early childhood educators must listen to and respect their colleagues' ideas, even when there are differences in philosophy. Looking for common ground will help educators build the continuity that is important for the children in their care.

Isn't This Continuity a Frill?

Building home/school and teacher/teacher partnerships is obviously not a simple task. Wouldn't educators' time be better spent in teaching children? Even if schools could successfully develop children's literacy by cloistering it within the school setting, only half the purpose of education would be accomplished. The children might have the skills to read, but they would not know how to use these skills to best advantage in their lives outside the school. Building partnerships between home and school, teacher and teacher, is not a frill. It is an essential ingredient for the effective development of emergent literacy.

Glossary

Active role play center: A term used by Shipley (1993) to describe a play area that combines large muscle equipment with pretend play.

All-encompassing integration: One of the four modes for integrating literacy into dramatic play, when teachers design a dramatic play setting for children where literacy is the focus of the play. Post office, library, and newspaper are all examples of this type of integration.

Associative play: One of Parten's (1932) levels of social play interaction. Associative play is loosely organized play in which children adopt a shared theme, but within that theme each child continues with his or her own play. An example of associative play is when children decide to play house. They all pick roles: One child is the big brother making dinner, another is the grandma going to a wedding, while a third is the mom going to work. They interact by saying goodbye to each other when people leave. The play of each child tends to move in its own direction, only loosely affected by the play of the others.

Child-initiated integration: One of the four modes of integrating literacy into dramatic play. Child-initiated integration occurs when children spontaneously incorporate literacy into their play without adult intervention.

Constructive play: A type of play where children use materials to construct, build, or create something: Such as when a child constructs a building with blocks, creates a painting of something at the art table, or stacks sand into a castle in the sand box. Children may move back and forth between constructive play (where they are building a house) and imaginative play (where they are using dolls to act out stories within the house).

Cooperative play: One of Parten's (1932) levels of social play interaction. Cooperative play describes the play of children who are working jointly to develop a mutual story. Children take distinct roles. The game is based on children's interactions with each other.

Coplayer: One of the teacher's roles in facilitating pretend play. As a coplayer, the teacher takes a role in the children's pretend stories. The teacher is one of the players, but does not take a leading or directive role.

Decentration: The process of learning to see beyond self and realize that other people exist in the environment, each with unique needs.

Dramatic play: A type of play in which children or adults use their imaginations to create and enact pretend events, characters, and/or actions. Dramatic play can be as simple as pretending to drink out of a play glass, or as complex as a story using many characters, props, and actions. This type of play can also be called "pretend play."

Dramatic play area: A place in the early childhood setting where children can take on and enact roles in pretend play. Some refer to this area as the "housekeeping area," but since it can be set up to support themes other than house play—such as grocery store or firestation, the use of the term housekeeping area is misleading.

Egocentric: Being focused on self and one's own needs.

Emergent literacy: Children's process of developing awareness and control of written language. It particularly includes the exploration of written language that occurs before children begin reading conventionally.

Enrichment integration: One of the four modes of integrating literacy into dramatic play, when literacy materials are added to enrich a theme that does not center around literacy: Pads can be added for messages in the house, prescription pads can be added to the doctor's office, or menus can be added to the restaurant.

Environmental print: Writing that is part of the world around such as signs and labels.

Exploration: When children manipulate objects in the environment to gain knowledge about these objects, and how they can use them.

Flexibility principle: According to Clay (1975), this is one of the principles of writing that children discover as they begin to learn about written language. The flexibility principle maintains that small collections of lines and curves can be combined in different ways to make new letters, although not all symbols created are real letters.

Generative principle: According to Clay (1975), this is one of the principles of writing that children discover as they begin to learn about written language. The generative principle sees written language as generated from a group of symbols arranged in different ways. This can generate a never-ending amount of written language.

Incidental integration: One of the four modes in which literacy can be integrated into dramatic play. Incidental integration occurs when the teacher initiates literacy activities as a spontaneous response to the unfolding play.

Interpreter (as a role of the teacher): One of the teacher's roles for facilitating dramatic play. As interpreter the teacher helps children attend to and understand the meaning of other children's actions and words.

Master player: Children or adults who are skilled at playing pretend.

Mediator: One of the teacher's roles for facilitating dramatic play. As a mediator, the teacher helps children learn to deal with conflict by acting as an arbitrator when conflict arises.

Metacommunication: Talking about how people will talk. For example, in dramatic play a child might say, "pretend you are the mother and are yelling at us. Then we tell you we aren't going to listen."

Metalinguistic awareness: Conscious awareness about how language works.

Narrative: Language that tells a story. Narrative usually refers to written language that tells a story.

Object-as-actor play: When children play pretend using an object such as a doll or car as the actor in the pretend story.

Observation: Observation is an important role of the teacher in an early childhood program. They watch the children's play to understand the individual styles and needs of each child.

Oral language: Spoken language.

Parallel play: One of Parten's (1932) levels of social interaction. This is play in which two or more children are engaged in the same activity next to each other. Although children are aware of each other's presence, the play is still independent. An example of this type of play is when children put pretend food on the table together, enjoying the presence of the other child, and perhaps imitating each other's actions.

Parallel player: One of the roles of teachers for facilitating pretend play. As a parallel player, the teacher plays alongside the child. The teacher's level of play imitates that of the child.

Phonologic system: The science of speech sounds. This includes what sounds are used in a specific language and how they are combined with each other.

Pictorial symbols: Drawings or signs which are used to communicate. The international traffic signs use pictorial symbols to communicate to people with different language backgrounds. Recipes or other directions can be written with a series of picture steps for nonreaders.

Play training: When adults help children to increase their pretend play skills through such methods as modeling and questioning. This is also called "play tutoring."

Play tutoring: When adults help children to increase their pretend play skills through such methods as modeling and questioning. This is also called "play training."

Pragmatics system: The relation between language and the way in which it is used for different functions.

Pretend play: When children use their imaginations to play out pretend events, actions, or people. It can be as simple as pretending to put the baby doll to sleep by rocking it, or as complex as enacting long involved imaginary stories. Children can be the actor in the pretend play, as when they eat an imaginary dinner, or they can use objects to be the actors as when they drive a car making motor sounds. This is sometimes called "dramatic play."

Props: Toys and materials used while playing pretend. Such things as dressup clothes, telephone, dishes, cash registers, pads and paper, or any other material that is used in the process of playing pretend.

Psychoanalytic theory of play: A theory which sees play as a forum for children to deal with life issues that concern them, such as the birth of a sibling, the divorce of parents, or a trip to the doctor.

Reading readiness model: An older model for viewing the way children learn about written language. This approach assumes that children have to be "ready" and have mastered a set of skills before they can begin learning to read.

Recurring principle: One of Clay's (1975) principles of writing. Children discover that writing consists of repeating the same set of marks over and over again. Children who are working on the recurring principle will make lines of pseudo cursive writing or repetitive use of a few letters.

Scaffolding: When an adult provides a framework that allows children to stretch their play to a higher level.

Semantics system: The science of word meaning.

Script: A term often used to describe the action pattern of children's pretend play. They will often generate a series of actions that are used whenever they are "cooking," "going to the store," or doing some other action. These scripts can then be combined into larger stories.

Social director: One of the teacher's roles for facilitating dramatic play. As social director, the teacher helps children to enter play, assists them in finding a role, and draws other children into the play when needed.

Sociodramatic play: Dramatic play involving two or more children. Children are pretending with regard to actions, objects, and/or characters as they interact with each other in the imaginary story they are creating.

Solitary play: One of Parten's (1932) four types of social interaction. This occurs when children are engaged in their own activities with little regard for others, for example, a child playing mother feeds her baby without noticing other children around her.

Stage manager: One of the teacher's roles for facilitating dramatic play. This term was first used by Jones and Reynolds (1992). As stage manager, the teacher sets the stage for pretend play by arranging the area and providing props.

Story box: A box containing a series of small props to retell the story of a book.

Symbolic play: Play in which actions or objects are used to represent other actions or objects: A doll can represent a baby, a stick can represent a magic wand, or sitting on a chair can represent a bus trip.

Symbolic representation: Using an action, object, visual symbol, or word to represent something else.

Symbolic thought: Also called abstract thought. It is the ability to create and manipulate images mentally. The emergence of symbolic thought can be seen as children begin engaging in symbolic play, where they use an action or object to represent another action or object.

Symbolic transformation: The process of using imagination to change one object to another, for example, pretending a cylindrical block is a cup.

Syntax: The rules for combining words and phrases into sentences and paragraphs.

Teacher as scribe: One of the teacher's roles for facilitating dramatic play. This is a term coined by Jones and Reynolds (1992). As scribe the teacher records children's play interactions. The written version of their play is shared with parents, posted in the room, and read back to the children.

Timeout: A technique used in disciplining children. Children are asked to sit and calm down when their behavior is inappropriate. The child and teacher can then discuss the behavior once the child is calm. Time out is meant to be a natural consequence of the behavior; unfortunately, it is often misused. In many cases it becomes a negative interaction, without helping children to understand why their behavior is inappropriate, or how they might accomplish their goals in a more appropriate way.

Written language: Using print to record words or ideas or communicate with others.

References

Athey, I. (1988). The relationship of play to cognitive, language, and moral development. In D. Bergen (Ed.), *Play as a medium for learning and development: A handbook of theory and practice* (pp. 81–101). Portsmouth, NH: Heinemann.

Baretta-Lorton, M. (1976). *Math their own way: An activity centered mathematics program for early childhood education.* Menlo Park, CA: Addison Wesley.

Beckwith, L. (1986). Parent-infant interactions and infant's social-emotional development. In A. Gottfried & C. Brown (Eds.), *Play interactions: The contribution of play materials and parental involvement to children's development* (pp. 279–292). Lexington, MA: D.C. Heath and Company.

Bentzen, W. (1993). *Seeing young children: A guide to observing and recording behavior.* Albany, NY: Delmar Publishers.

Bergen, D. (Ed.) (1988). *Play as a medium for learning and development: A handbook of theory and practice.* Portsmouth, NH: Heinemann.

Bowman, B. (1990). Play in teacher education: The U.S. perspective. In E. Klugman & S. Smilansky (Eds.), *Children's play and learning: Perspective and policy implications* (pp. 97–111). New York: Teachers College Press.

Bredekamp, S. (Ed.) (1987). *Developmentally appropriate practice in early childhood programs serving young children birth through age 8.* Washington, DC: NAEYC.

Bretherton, I. (1986). Representing the social world in symbolic play: Reality and fantasy. In A. Gottfried & C. Brown (Eds.), *Play interactions: The contribution of play materials and parental involvement to children's development* (pp. 119–148). Lexington, MA: D.C. Heath and Company.

Bruner, J.S. (1983). *Child's talk.* New York: Norton.

Bundy, B. (1991). Fostering communication between parents and preschools. *Young Children, 46*(2), 12–17.

Calkins, L. (1986). *The art of teaching writing.* Portsmouth, NH: Heinemann.

Caplan, F. & Caplan, T. (1977). *The second twelve months of life.* New York: Grosset & Dunlap.

Carlsson-Paige, N. & Levin, D. (1987). *The war play dilemma: Balancing needs and values in the early childhood classroom.* New York: Teachers College Press.

Carlsson-Paige, N. & Levin, D. (1990). *Who's calling the shots? How to respond effectively to children's fascination with war play and war toys.* Santa Cruz, CA: New Society Publishers.

Cazden, C. (Ed.) (1981). *Language in early childhood education.* Washington, DC: NAEYC.

Chomsky, C. (1972). Stages in language development and reading exposure. *Harvard Educational Review*, *42*, 1–33.

Christie, J. (Ed.) (1991). *Play and early literacy development*. Albany, NY: State University of New York Press.

Christie, J. (1995). Literacy play interventions: A review of empirical research. In S. Reifel (Ed.), *Advances in early education and day care, Vol. 16*, 3–24. CN:JIA Press

Christie, J. & Wardle, F. (1992). How much time is needed for play? *Young Children*, *47*(3), 28–32.

Clay, M. (1975). *What did I write*. Aukland, New Zealand: Heinemann.

Curry, N. & Bergen, D. (1988). The relation of play to emotional, social and gender/sex role development. In D. Bergen (Ed.), *Play as a medium for learning and development: A handbook of theory and practice* (pp. 107–131). Portsmouth, NH: Heinemann.

Daiute, C. (Ed.) (1993). *The development of literacy through social interaction: New direction for child development, No. 61*. San Francisco: Jossey-Bass Publishers.

Davidson, J. (1989). *Children and computers together in the early childhood classroom*. Albany, NY: Delmar Publishers.

Dimidjian, V. (Ed.) (1992). *Play's place in public education for young children*. Washington, DC: National Education Association.

Dowhower, S. (1989). Curriculum dilemma: The early reader "Mom, I never read in school." *Reading Horizons*, *30*(1), 41–51.

Dyson, A. (1993). From prop to mediator: The changing role of written language in children's symbolic repertoires. In B. Spodek & O. Saracho (Eds.), *Language and literacy in early childhood education* (pp. 21–41). New York: Teachers College Press.

Fein, G. (1981). Pretend play in childhood: An integrative review. *Child Development*, *52*, 1095–1118.

Fein, G. (1986). The affective psychology of play. In A. Gottfried & C. Brown (Eds.), *Play interactions: The contribution of play materials and parental involvement to children's development* (pp. 31–49). Lexington, MA: D.C. Heath and Company.

Fein, G. & Rivkin, M. (Eds.) (1986). *The young child at play: Reviews of research, Vol. 4*. Washington, DC: NAEYC.

Fein, G. & Schwartz, S. (1986). The social coordination of pretense in preschool children. In G. Fein & M. Rivkin (Eds.), *The young child at play: Reviews of research Vol. 4* (pp. 99–111). Washington, DC: NAEYC.

Feitelson, D. & Ross, G. (1973). The neglected factor—play. *Human Development*, *16*, 202–223.

Fenson, L. (1984). Developmental trends for action and speech in pretend play. In I. Bretherton (Ed.), *Symbolic play: The development of social understanding* (pp. 249–270). New York: Academic Press.

Fenson, L. (1986). The developmental progression of play. In A. Gottfried & C. Brown (Eds.), *Play interactions: The contribution of play materials and parental involvement to children's development* (pp. 53–65). Lexington, MA: D.C. Heath and Company.

Ferreiro, E. & Teberosky, A. (1982). *Literacy before schooling*. Trans. by K. Castro. Portsmouth, NH: Heinemann.

Ford, S. (1993). The facilitator's role in children's play. *Young Children, 48*(6), 66–69.

Fox, B. & Saracho, O. (1990). Emergent writing: Young children solve the written language puzzle. *Early Child Development and Care, 56*, 81–90.

Freyberg, J. (1973). Increasing the imaginative play of urban disadvantaged kindergarten children through systematic training. In J. Singer (Ed.), *The child's world of make-believe: Experimental studies in imaginative play* (pp. 74–103). New York: Academic Press.

Garvey, C. (1990). *Play.* Cambridge, MA: Harvard University Press.

Genishi, C. (1988). Children's language: Learning words from experience. *Young Children, 44*(1), 16–23.

Genishi, C. (1989). Observing the second-language learner: An example of teacher's learning. *Language Arts, 66*(5), 509–515.

Gibson, L. (1989). *Literacy learning in the early years: Through children's eyes*. New York: Teachers College Press.

Giffin, H. (1984). The coordination of meaning in the creation of a shared make-believe reality. In I. Bretherton (Ed.), *Symbolic play: The development of social understanding* (pp. 73–100). Orlando, FL: Academic Press.

Glazer, S. (1989). Oral language and literacy development. In D. Strickland & L. Morrow (Eds.), *Emerging literacy: Young children learn to read and write* (pp. 16–26). Newark, DE: International Reading Association.

Goffman, E. (1974). *Frame analysis: An essay on the organization of experience*. New York: Harper and Row.

Goldenberg, C. (1989). Making success a more common occurrence for children at risk for failure: Lesson for Hispanic first graders learning to read. In J. Allen & J. Mason (Eds.), *Risk makers, risk takers, risk breakers* (pp. 48–79). Portsmouth, NH: Heinemann.

Goodman, K. (1986). *What is whole in whole language*. Portsmouth, NH: Heinemann.

Gottfried, A. & Brown, C. (Eds.) (1986). *Play interactions: The contribution of play materials and parental involvement to children's development*. Lexington, MA: D.C. Heath and Company.

Griffing, P. (1983). Encouraging dramatic play in early childhood. *Young Children, 38*(4), 13–22.

Gutierrez, K. (1993). Biliteracy and language-minority children. In B. Spodek & O. Saracho (Eds.), *Language and literacy in early childhood education* (pp. 82– 101). New York: Teachers College Press.

Haight, W. & Miller, P. (1993). *Pretending at home: Early development in a sociocultural context.* Albany, NY: State University of New York Press.

Hall, N. (1991). Play and the emergence of literacy. In J. Christie (Ed.), *Play and early literacy development* (pp. 3–25). Albany, NY: State University of New York Press.

Harste, J. & Woodward, V. (1989). Fostering needed change in early literacy programs. In D. Strickland & L. Morrow (Eds.), *Emerging literacy: Young children learn to read and write* (pp. 147–159). Newark, DE: International Reading Association.

Hatch, J. & Freeman, E. (1988). Kindergarten philosophy and practices; perspectives of teachers, principals, and supervisors. *Early Childhood Research Quaterly, 3,* 151–166.

Heath, S. (1983). *Ways with words: Language, life and work in communities and classrooms.* NY: Cambridge University Press.

Heidemann, S. & Hewitt, D. (1992). *Pathways to play: Developing play skills in young children.* St. Paul, MN: Redleaf Press.

Heim, N. & Davidson, J. (1993, November). The place of teacher talk in children's play. Paper presented as part of a preconference session on play at the NAEYC conference, Anahiem, CA.

Henderson, A.T. (1988). Parents are a school's best friend. *Phi Delta Kappa 70*(2), 149–153.

Hendrick, J. (1992). *The whole child.* New York: Macmillian.

Hiebert, E. (1981). Developmental patterns and interrelationships of preschool children's print awareness. *Reading Research Quarterly, 16,* 236–260.

Hirsch, E. (Ed.) (1984). *The block book.* Washington, DC: NAEYC.

Holdaway, D. (1979). *The foundations of literacy.* Syndey: Ashton Scholastic.

Hutt, C. (1971). Exploration and play in children. In R. Herron & B. Sutton-Smith (Eds.), *Child's play* (pp. 231–251). New York: Wiley.

Isaacs, S. (1930). *Intellectual growth in young children.* London: Routledge & Kegan Paul.

Johnson, J. (1990). The role of play in cognitive development. In E. Klugman & S. Smilansky (Eds.), *Children's play and learning: Perspective and policy implications* (pp. 213–234). New York: Teachers College Press.

Johnson, J., Christie, J., & Yawkey, T. (1987). *Play and early childhood development.* Glenview, IL: Scott, Foresman and Company.

Jones, E. & Reynolds, G. (1992). *The play's the thing: Teachers' roles in children's play.* New York: Teachers College Press.

Klugman, E. & Smilansky, S. (Eds.) (1990). *Children's play and learning: Perspective and policy implications.* New York: Teachers College Press.

Kostelnik, M., Soderman, A., & Whiren, A. (1993). *Developmentally appropriate programs in early childhood education.* New York: Macmillan.

Levin, D. (1994). *Teaching children in violent times.* Cambridge, MA: Educators for Social Responsibility.

Linder, T. (1990). *Transdisciplinary play based assessment: A functional approach to working with young children.* Baltimore: Paul. H. Brooks Publishing Company.

Martinez, M., & Roser, N. (1985). Read it again: The value of repeated readings during story time. *The Reading Teacher, 38,* 782–786.

Mason, J. (1980). When do children begin to read: An exploration of four-year-old children's letter and word reading competencies. *Reading Research Quarterly, 15,* 203–227.

Masonheimer, P., Drum, P., and Ehri, L. (1984). Does environmental printing identification lead children into word reading? *Journal of Reading Behavior, 14,* 257–271.

McCracken, M., & McCracken, J. (1972). *Reading is only the tiger's tail.* San Rafael, CA: Leswing Press.

McElmeel, S. (1993). *McElmeel booknotes: Literature across the curriculum.* Englewood, CO: Teacher's Ideas Press.

McLane, J. & McNamee, G. (1990). *Early literacy.* Cambridge, MA: Harvard University Press.

McLoyd, V. (1986). Scaffolds or shackles? The role of toys in preschool children's pretend play. In G. Fein & M. Rivkin (Eds.), *The young child at play: Reviews of research, Vol. 4* (pp. 63–77). Washington, DC: NAEYC.

McNeill, D. (1966). Developmental psycholinguistics. In F. Smith & G. Miller (Eds.), *The genesis of language: A psycholinguistic approach* (pp. 15–84). Cambridge, MA: MIT Press.

Monighan-Nourot, P. (1990). The legacy of play in American early childhood education. In E. Klugman & S. Smilansky (Eds.), *Children's play and learning: Perspective and policy implications* (pp. 59–85). New York: Teachers College Press.

Morrow, L. (1989). Designing the classroom to promote literacy development. In D. Strickland & L. Morrow (Eds.), *Emerging literacy: Young children learn to read and write* (pp. 121–134). Newark, DE: International Reading Association.

Morrow, L. (1993). *Literacy development in the early years: Helping children read and write.* Boston: Allyn & Bacon.

Myhre, S. (1993). Enhancing your dramatic-play area through the use of prop boxes. *Young Children, 48*(5), 6–11.

Nathenson-Mejia, S. (1989). Writing in a second language: Negotiating meaning through invented spelling. *Language Arts, 66*(5), 516–526.

National Association of Elementary School Principals (1990). *Early childhood education and the elementary school principal: Standards for quality programs for young children*. Alexandria, VA: Author.

National Association of State Boards of Education (1988). *Right from the start*. Alexandria, VA: Author.

Nelson, K. (1973). Structures and strategies in learning to talk. *Monographs of the Society for Research in Child Development, 38*(1–2, serial No. 149).

Nelson, K. (1985). *Making sense: The acquisition of shared meaning*. New York: Academic Press.

Neuman, S. & Roskos, K. (1991). The influence of literacy-enriched play centers on preschoolers' conceptions of the functions of print. In J. Christie (Ed.), *Play and early literacy development* (pp. 167–187). Albany, NY: State University of New York Press.

Nicholich, L. (1977). Beyond sensorimotor intelligence: Assessment of symbolic maturity through analysis of pretend play. *Merrill-Palmer Quarterly, 23*, 88–99.

Ninio, A. (1980). Picture-book reading in mother-infant dyads belonging to two sub-groups in Israel. *Child Development, 51*, 587–590.

Ninio, A. & Bruner, J. (1978). The achievement and antecedents of labelling. *Journal of Child Language, 5*, 5–15.

Paley, V. (1990). *The boy who would be a helicopter: The use of story telling in the classroom*. Cambridge, MA: Harvard University Press.

Parten, M.B. (1932). Social participation among preschool children. *Journal of Abnormal Psychology, 27*, 243–269.

Pellegrini, A. (1986). Communicating in and about play: The effect of play centers on preschoolers' explicit language. In G. Fein & M. Rivkin (Eds.), *The young child at play: Reviews of research, Vol. 4* (pp. 79–91). Washington, DC: NAEYC.

Piaget, J. (1962). *Play, dreams and imitation in early childhood*. New York: Norton. Originally published 1945; trans. C. Gategno & F.M. Hodgson, (1951). London: Routledge and Kegan Paul.

Piaget, J. (1974). *Language and thought of the child*. New York: New American Library.

Pica, R. (1995). *Experiences in movement with music, activities and theory*. Albany, NY: Delmar Publishers.

Powell, D. (1989). Families and early childhood programs. *Research monographs of the National Association for the Education of Young Children, Vol. 3*. Washington, DC: NAEYC.

Pulaski, M. (1973). Toys and imaginative play. In J. Singer (Ed.), *The child's world of make-believe: Experimental studies in imaginative play* (pp. 74–103). New York: Academic Press.

Raines, S. & Canady, R. (1989). *Story S-T-R-E-T-C-H-E-R-S: Activities to expand children's favorite books*. Mt. Rainier, MD: Gryphon House.

Raines, S. & Canady, R. (1991). *More story S-T-R-E-T-C-H-E-R-S: Activities to expand children's favorite books*. Mt. Rainier, MD: Gryphon House.

Rasinski, T. (1989). Reading and empowerment of parents. *The Reading Teacher, 43*, 226–231.

Rogers, C. & Sawyers, J. (1988). *Play in the lives of children*. Washington, DC: NAEYC.

Rogers, F. & Sharapan, H. (1992). Some thoughts about play. In V. Dimidjian (Ed.), *Play's place in public education for your children* (pp. 73–78).Washington, DC: National Education Association.

Rubin, K., Fein, G., & Vandenberg, B. (1983). Play. In P. Mussen (Ed.), *Handbook of child psychology, 4th Ed.* (pp. 693–774). New York: Wiley.

Rubin, K. & Howe, N. (1986). Social play and perspective-taking. In G. Fein & M. Rivkin (Eds.), *The young child at play: Reviews of research, Vol. 4* (pp. 113–125). Washington, DC: NAEYC.

Saltz, R. & Saltz, E. (1986). Pretend play training and its outcomes. In G. Fein & M. Rivkin (Eds.), *The young child at play: Reviews of research, Vol. 4* (pp. 155–173). Washington, DC: NAEYC.

Saracho, O. & Spodek, B. (1993). Introduction. In B. Spodek & O. Saracho (Eds.), *Language and literacy in early childhood education* (pp. vii–xiii). NY: Teachers College Press.

Schickedanz, J. (1986). *More than the ABCs*. Washington, DC: NAEYC.

Schickedanz, J. (1989). The place of specific skills in preschool and kindergarten. In D. Strickland & L. Morrow (Eds.), *Emerging literacy: Young children learn to read and write* (pp. 96-106).

Schickedanz, J. (1990). *Adam's writing revolutions: One child's literacy development from infancy through grade one*. Portsmouth, NH: Heinemann.

Schickedanz, J. (1993). Designing the early childhood classroom environment to facilitate literacy development. In B. Spodek & O. Saracho (Eds.), *Language and literacy in early childhood education* (pp. 141–155). NY: Teachers College Press.

Schickedanz, J., York, M., Stewart, I., & White, D. (1990). *Strategies for teaching young children*. Englewood Cliffs, NJ: Prentice Hall.

Schweinhart, L. (1993). Observing young children in action: The key to early childhood assessment. *Young Children, 48*(5), 29–33.

Shantz, C. (1983). Social cognition. In J. Flavell & E. Markman (Eds.), *Handbook of child psychology: Vol. 3. Cognitive development* (pp. 495–555). New York: Wiley.

Shipley, D. (1993). *Empowering children: Play-based curriculum for life long learning*. Scarborough, ONT: Nelson Canada.

Skinner, B. (1957). *Verbal behavior*. Boston: Appleton-Century-Crofts.

Slaughter, J. (1992). *Beyond story books: Young children and the shared book experience.* Newark, DE: International Reading Association.

Smilanski, S. (1968). *The effects of sociodramatic play on disadvantaged preschool children*. New York: Wiley.

Smilansky, S. (1992, July). Are peers able to facilitate sociodramatic play of younger children? Paper presented at *Play and Cognitive Ability: The Cultural Context* Workshop. Boston: Wheelock College

Smilansky, S. & Shefatya, L. (1990). *Facilitating play: A medium for promoting cognitive, socioemotional and academic development in young children.* Gaithersburg, MD: Psychosocial & Educational Publications.

Smith, P. & Vollstedt, R. (1985). On defining play: An empirical study of the relationship between play and various criteria. *Child Development, 46,* 1042–1050.

Snow, C. (1983). Literacy and language: Relationships during the preschool years. *Harvard Educational Review, 53,* 165–189.

Snow C. & Ninio, A. (1986). The contracts of literacy: What children learn from learning to read books. In W. Teale & E. Sulzby (Eds.), *Emergent literacy: Writing and reading* (pp. 116–138). Norwood, NJ: Ablex.

Snow, C. & Tabors, P. (1993). Language skills that relate to literacy development. In B. Spodek & O. Saracho (Eds.), *Language and literacy in early childhood education* (pp. 1–20). New York: Teachers College Press.

Spodek, B. & Saracho, O. (1993). Language and literacy programs in early childhood education: A look to the future. In B. Spodek & O. Saracho. (Eds.), *Language and literacy in early childhood education* (pp. 196–200). NY: Teachers College Press.

Strickland, D. & Morrow, L. (Eds.) (1989). *Emerging literacy: Young children learn to read and write.* Newark, DE: International Reading Association.

Sulzby, E. (1988). A study of children's early reading development. In A. Pellegrini (Ed.), *Psychological bases for early education* (pp. 39–75). Chichester, ENG: Wiley.

Sulzby, E. (1989). Assessment of children's writing and of children's language while writing. In L. Morrow & J. Smith (Eds.), *The role of assessment and measurement in early literacy instruction* (pp. 196–200). Englewood Cliffs, NJ: Prentice-Hall.

Sulzby, E. (1991). The development of the young child and the emergence of literacy. In I. Flood, J. Jensen, D. Lapp, & J. Squire (Eds.), *The handbook of research in the teaching of english language arts* (pp. 273–285). NY: Macmillan.

Sulzby, E., Barnhart, J., & Hieshima, J. (1989). Forms of writing and rereading from writing: A preliminary report. In J. Mason (Ed.), *Reading and writing connections* (pp. 31–50). Needham Heights, MA: Allyn and Bacon.

Sulzby, E. & Teale, W. (1985). Writing development in early childhood. *Educational Horizons, 64,* 8–12.

Taylor, D. (1983). *Family literacy: Young children learn to read and write.* Exeter, NH: Heinemann.

Taylor, D. (1986). Creating family story: "Matthew! We're going for a ride!" In W. Teale & E. Sulzby (Eds.), *Emergent literacy: Writing and reading* (pp. 139–155). Norwood, NJ: Ablex.

Taylor, D. & Dorsey-Gaines, C. (1988). *Growing up literate: Learning from inner city families.* Portsmouth, NH: Heinemann.

Taylor, D. & Strickland, D. (1989). Learning from families: Implications for educators and policy. In J. Allen & J. Mason (Eds.), *Risk makers, risk takers, risk breakers* (pp. 251–277). Portsmouth, NH: Heinemann.

Teale, W. (1984). Reading to young children: Its significance for literacy development. In H. Goelmann, A. Oberg, & F. Smith (Eds.), *Awakening to literacy* (pp. 110–121). Portsmouth, NH: Heinemann.

Teale, W. (1986). The beginnings of reading and writing: Written language development during the preschool and kindergarten years. In M. Sampson (Ed.), *The pursuit of literacy: Early reading and writing* (pp. 1–29). Dubuque, IA: Kendall/Hunt.

Teale, W. (1987). Emergent literacy: Reading and writing development in early childhood. In J. Readance & R. Baldwin, (Eds.), *Thirty-sixth yearbook of the National Reading Conference, 36,* 45–74. Rochester, NY: National Reading Conference.

Teale, W. & Sulzby, E. (1986). Emergent literacy: A perspective for examining how young children become writers and readers. In W. Teale & E. Sulzby (Eds.), *Emergent literacy: Writing and reading* (pp. iv–xxv). Norwood, NJ: Ablex.

Teale, W. & Sulzby, E. (1989). Emergent literacy: New perspectives. In D. Strickland, & L. Morrow (Eds.), *Emerging literacy: Young children learn to read and write* (pp. 1–15). Newark, DE: International Reading Association.

Temple, C., Nathan, R., Temple, F., & Burris, N. (1993). *The beginnings of writing.* Needham Heights, MA: Allyn and Bacon.

Vandeberg, B. (1986). Play theory. In G. Fein & M. Rivkin (Eds.), *The young child at play: Reviews of research, Vol. 4* (pp. 17–27). Washington, DC: NAEYC.

Van Hoorn, J., Nourot, P., Scales, B., & Alward, K. (1993). *Play at the center of the curriculum.* New York: Merrill.

Veitch, B. & Harmes, T. (1981). *Cook and learn.* Menlo Park, CA: Addison Wesley

Voss, M. (1988). "Make way for applesauce": The literate world of a three year old. *Language Arts, 65*(3), 272–278.

Vygotsky, L. (1967). Play and its role in the mental development of the child. *Soviet Psychology, 12,* 62–76.

Vygotsky, L. (1978). *Mind in society: Development of higher psychological processes.* Cambridge, MA: Harvard University Press.

Wells, G. (1985). Preschool literacy-related activities and success in school. In D. Olson, N. Torrance, & A. Hildyard (Eds.), *Literacy, language and learning: The nature and consequences of literacy* (pp. 229–255). Cambridge: Cambridge University Press.

Werner, H. & Kaplan, B. (1963). *Symbol formation*. New York: Wiley.

Wittmer, D. & Honig, A. (1994). Encouraging positive social development in young children. *Young Children, 49*(5), 4–12.

Wood, D., McMahon, L., & Cranston, Y. (1980). *Working with under fives*. Ypsilanti, MI: High/Scope Press.

Woodward, C. (1984). Guidelines for facilitating sociodramatic play. *Childhood Education, 60*, 172–177.

Bibliography of Children's Books and Software

Ahlberg, J. & Ahlberg, A. (1979). *Each peach pear and plum: An "I spy" story.* New York: Scholastic Books.

Aliki (1969). *My visit to the dinosaurs.* New York: Harper and Row.

Baker, K. (1993). *Hide and snake.* New York: Trumpet Club, Inc.

Barrett, J. (1978). *Cloudy with a chance of meatballs.* New York: Macmillian.

Barrie, J. M. (1911). *Peter Pan.* London: Hodder & Stoughton.

Barton, B. (1981). *Building a house.* New York: Greenwillow Books.

Berenstain, S. & Berenstain, J. (1981). *Berenstain bears' moving day.* New York: Random House.

Blos, J. (1984). *Martin's hats.* New York: Morrow.

Bridwell, N. (1963). *Clifford the big red dog.* New York: Scholastic Books.

Brown, M. (1947). *Goodnight moon.* New York: Harper and Row.

Burton V. L. (1937). *Choo Choo the runaway engine.* New York: Scholastic Books.

Burton, V. L. (1939). *Mike Mulligan and his steam shovel.* Boston: Houghton Mifflin.

Butterworth, N. (1986). *Jill the farmer and her friends.* London: Walker Books Ltd.

Campbell, R. (1982). *From the zoo.* New York: Four Winds Press.

Carle, E. (1975). *The mixed-up chameleon.* New York: Harper and Row.

Carle, E. (1977). *The grouchy lady bug.* New York: Thomas Y. Crowell.

Carle, E. (1981). *The very hungry caterpillar.* New York: Philomel Books.

Cartwright, S. & Zeff, C. (1983). *Find the piglet.* London: Usborne Publishing Ltd.

Civardi, A. (1985). *First experiences: Moving house.* Tulsa, Oklahoma: EDC Publishing.

Color Me. Software. Chicago, IL: Mindscape.

Cook, B. (1956). *The little fish that got away.* New York: Scholastic Books.

Demi (1985). *Demi's find the animal ABC.* New York: Trumpet Club, Inc.

Dubanevich, A. (1983). *Pigs in hiding.* New York: Scholastic Books.

Dwight, R. (1972). *Bert's hall of great inventions.* New York: Golden Books.

Ehlert, L. (1987). *Growing vegetable soup.* San Diego: Harcourt Brace Jovanovich.

Expolore-a-story. Software. Lexington, MA: D.C. Heath.

Freeman, D. (1954). *Beady Bear.* New York: The Viking Press.

Freeman, D. (1968). *Corduroy.* New York: The Viking Press.

Freeman, D. (1978). *A pocket for Corduroy.* New York: Puffin Books.

Galdone, P. (1972). *The three bears.* New York: Scholastic Books.

Galdone, P. (1973). *The little red hen.* New York: Clarion Books.

Galdone, P. (1975). *The gingerbread boy.* New York: Clarion Books.

Gauch, P. (1971). *Christina Katerina and the box.* New York: Coward, McCann & Geoghegan.

Guilfoile, E. (1957). *Nobody listens to Andrew.* Follett Publishing.

Hall, D. (1979). *Ox-cart man.* Viking Press.

Handford, M. (1987). *Where's Waldo?* Boston: Little Brown and Company.

Heller, R. (1981). *Chickens aren't the only ones.* New York: Grosset and Dunlap.

Henrietta, (1991). *A mouse in the house.* New York: Dorling Kindersley, Inc.

Hill, E. (1980). *Where's Spot?* New York: Putnam.

Houtzig, D. (1985). *A visit to the Sesame Street hospital.* New York: Random House.

Johnson, C. (1955). *Harold and the purple crayon.* New York: Harper and Row.

Kalan, R. (1981). *Jump, frog, jump!* New York: Scholastic Books.

KidPix. Software. Novato, CA: Broderbund.

Knight, H. (1964). *Where's Wallace?* New York: Harper and Row.

Kowitt, H. (1991). *The Fenderbenders get lost in America.* New York: Scholastic Books.

Krauss, R. (1945). *The carrot seed.* New York: Harper and Row.

LeSieg, T. (1965). *I wish I had duck feet.* New York: Random House.

LeSieg, T. (1966). *Come over to my house.* New York: Random House.

Lionni, L. (1968). *Swimmy.* New York: Pantheon.

Marzollo, J. (1992). *I spy : A book of picture riddles.* New York: Scholastic Books.

McCloskey, R. (1941). *Make way for ducklings.* The Viking Press.

McGovern, A. (1971). *Too much noise.* New York: Scholastic Books.

Martin, B. (1963). *The three billy goats gruff: A Norwegian folk tale with wood cuts.* New York: Holt, Reinhart and Winston.

Micklethwait, L. (1991). *An alphabet in art.* New York: Greenwillow Books.

Numeroff, L. (1985). *If you give a mouse a cookie.* New York: Harper and Row.

Potter, B. (1902). *The tale of Peter Rabbit.* New York: Fredrick Warne & Company.

Ray, H.A. (1941). *Curious George.* Boston: Houghton Mifflin.

Raskin, E. (1966). *Nothing ever happens on my block.* New York: Trumpet Club, Inc.

Sendak, M. (1963). *Where the wild things are.* New York: Harper and Row.

Slobodkina, E. (1940). *Caps for sale.* New York: Harper and Row.

Small, D. (1985). *Imogene's antlers.* New York: Crown Publishers.

Steig, W. (1969). *Sylvester and the magic pebble.* New York: Simon and Schuster.

Tarturi, N. (1984). *Have you seen my duckling?* New York: Greenwillow Books.

Tallarico, A. (1990). *Where are they? Search for Susie.* Chicago: Kids Books Inc.

Ungerer, T. (1964). *One, two where's my shoe?* New York: Harper and Row.

Wadsworth, O. (1986). *Over in the meadow.* New York: Puffin.

Wilder, L. I. (1932). *Little house in the big woods.* New York: Harper and Row.

Wilson, A. (1990). *Look! The ultimate spot-the-difference book.* New York: Trumpet Club, Inc..

Yektai, N. (1989). *What's silly?* New York: Trumpet Club, Inc.

Subject Index

Active role play center, 54
Activities, 60–61, 111, 201, 209–210, 246–248, 257
Adult roles in children's pretend play, 47–69
  common questions adults ask, 72–77
  getting started as play facilitator, 69–72
  interpreter, 67–68
  mediator, 66–67
  observer, 47–49, 70
  player, 61–66
  social director, 68–69
  stage manager, 49–61
Aggressive behavior, 4, 19, 29–30, 66–67, 171, 177
Aggressive themes and characters, 75–76
All-encompassing integration, 107, 108–114, 213, 217, 221–222, 224–226
Alphabet, 242
Alphabet in Art, An (Micklethwait), 204, 305
Art, 158, 163, 179–183, 246–247
Associative play, 21–22, 23–24

Beady Bear (Freeman), 219, 304
Berenstain Bears' Moving Day, The (Berenstain & Berenstain), 220, 221, 304
Bert's Hall of Great Inventions (Dwight), 220, 304
Billy Goats Gruff, The (Martin), 200, 217, 225, 305
Blocks, 14, 157, 158, 160–179

Book ideas as source of dramatic play, 219–222
Books
  activities based on, 175, 201, 209–210
  children's, 189–226
  homemade, 183, 254
  home reading, 190–194, 206
  and pretend play, 175, 194, 211–226
  reading in school, 194–210
  rereading, 192, 196, 194–205
  times for reading, 195–196, 201–205
Book sharing, 206–207
Book time, 203–205
Building a House (Barton), 175
Bulletin board, 253–254

Caps for Sale (Slobodkina), 213, 217, 224, 305
Carrot Seed, The (Krauss), 222, 305
Characters as source of book play, 216
Chickens Aren't the Only Ones (Heller), 222, 305
Child-initiated integration, 107, 124–128, 215, 216, 219, 223
Choo Choo the Runaway Engine (Burton), 175, 304
Christina Katerina and the Box (Gauch), 126, 220, 305
Clifford the Big Red Dog (Bridwell), 216, 304
Cloudy with a Chance of Meatballs (Barrett), 190, 219, 304

Cognitive development, and dramatic play, 5–6, 9, 31–36
Color Me (Mindscape), 248, 304
Come Over to My House (LeSieg), 175, 305
Communication
  forms of, 170–172, 267, 268, 271, 275–284
  with administrators, 284–286
  with children, 42–47, 61–69
  with parents, 235, 267, 268, 271–275, 277–282
  with teachers, 284–286
Conflict, 4, 19, 36, 66–67, 68, 177
Constructive play, 14
Continuity between home and school, classroom and classroom, 262–287
  building partnerships with administrators and other professionals, 284–286
  building teaching/parent partnerships, 270–275
Cooperative play, 22
Coplayer, 62–63
Corduroy (Freeman), 209, 210, 304
Creative movement, 247
Curious George (Ray), 216, 305

Decentration, 26
Decontextualization, 31
Demi's Find the Animal (Demi), 204, 304

Development, and dramatic play
  cognitive, 5–6, 31–36
  language, 6, 37–39, 101–102
  physical, 6–7
  social emotional, 3–4, 20–30
Developmental differences in children's pretend play, 15–20
Dramatic Play: An Integrative Process (film), 34, 45
Dramatic play
  definition, 11–15
  with books, 211–226
  with blocks, 165–166
  and literacy, 6, 98–104, 105–128, 159–161, 170–176, 182–183, 185
  with manipulatives, 183–186
  outside, 186–187
  providing time and space for, 8–10
  supervising, 3, 19, 22–40, 41–77, 176–179, 181
  themes for, 23, 34–36, 129–155, 158–159
  value of, 3–7, 20–30, 31–36, 37–39, 98–104
Dramatic play area, 8

Each Peach Pear and Plum; An "I Spy" Story (Ahlberg & Ahlberg), 203, 304
Egocentric children, 67
Emergent literacy
  communicating about, 85–86, 102
  defined, 79
  development of written language, 79, 87–98, 231–232
  and dramatic play, 6, 98–104, 105–128, 159–161, 170–176, 182–183, 185
  modes of integrating into dramatic play, 105–128

and oral language, 79–86, 249–251
  support of, 98–104, 230–261
English as a second language, 38, 86
Enrichment integration, 107, 114–122, 214, 217, 220–221
Environment. *See* Literacy-rich environment
Environmental print, 91, 100, 240–244
Evaluating dramatic play, 140–141
  versus play, 12–13
Exploration, 12–13, 163, 179–180
Explore-a-Story (computer program), 181, 304

Family storybook reading, 191, 206
Feltboard stories, 160, 196–197, 201
Fenderbenders Get Lost in America, The (Kowitt), 204, 305
Find the Piglet (Cartwright & Zeff), 203, 304
First Experiences: Moving House (Civardi), 204, 304
Five-year-olds at play, 18–20, 26, 79, 95, 105, 189, 262
Flexibility principle, 95
Four-year-olds at play, 1–2, 14, 16–18, 24–29, 33, 38, 43, 78, 89, 96, 105, 114–115, 123, 125, 130–131, 165, 190, 210, 213, 236, 252, 262
From the Zoo (Campbell), 175, 220, 304

Generative principle, 93
Gingerbread Man, The (Galdone), 209, 305
Goodnight Moon (Brown), 208–209, 219, 304

Grouchy Lady Bug, The (Carle), 207, 304
Group book culture, 207–210
Growing Vegetable Soup (Ehlert), 209, 304

Harold and the Purple Crayon (Johnson), 200, 305
Have You Seen My Duckling? (Tarfuri), 203, 204, 306
Hide and Snake (Baker), 203, 304
House boxes, 166

If You Give a Mouse a Cookie (Numeroff), 197, 305
Imaginative play, 11
Imogene's Antlers (Small), 217, 305
Incidental integration, 107, 123–124, 126–128, 214–215, 217, 219–220, 224
Individualization, as related to communicating with families, 271–272
Initiating play, 28–30
Interpreter, of children's play, 67–68
Intervention in child's pretend play, 41–47
I Spy: A Book of Picture Riddles (Marzollo), 204, 305
I Wish I Had Duck Feet (LeSiegs), 222, 305

Jill the Farmer and Her Friends (Butterworth), 189, 304
Jump, Frog, Jump! (Kalan), 213, 305

KidPix (computer program), 181, 305
Knowledge base, child's, 34, 36, 265

Language as a social symbol system, 86–87

Language development and dramatic play, 6, 37–39, 101–102
Lap reading, 191
Listening to children, 77, 85
Literacy. *See* Emergent literacy
Literacy-rich environment, 227–261
  creating, 239–251
  unit based learning, 252–261
Literacy themes, 110, 118–119
Little Fish That Got Away, The (Cook), 209, 304
Little House in the Big Woods (Wilder), 1, 306
Little Red Hen, The (Galdone), 193, 194, 305
Look! The Ultimate Spot-the-Difference Book (Wilson), 204, 306

Make Way for Ducklings (McCloskey), 193, 194, 305
Manipulation of objects, 13, 161, 163
Manipulatives, 161, 163, 183–186
Maps, 173–174, 182
Martin's Hats (Blos), 200, 214, 304
Master players, 2, 20, 63–65, 70, 72, 159
Math activity, 257
Math Their Own Way (Baretta-Lorton), 257, 294
Mediator, of children's play, 66–67
Message board, 229–230
Metacommunication, 102
Metalinguistic awareness, 86
Metalinguistic skills, development of, 102
Mike Mulligan and His Steam Shovel (Burton), 175, 304
Mixed-up Chameleon, The (Carle), 213, 214

Mouse in the House, A (Henrietta), 204, 305
Movement, 247
Movies, as source of stories, 223
Moving Day (Tobias), 221
My Visit to the Dinosaurs (Aliki), 262, 304

Narrative, 102, 176
Newsletters, 278–280
Nobody Listens to Andrew (Guilfoile), 200, 305
Nothing Ever Happens on My Block (Raskin), 204, 305
Novice player, 159, 164, 168

Object-as-actor play, 161–163
Observation of children, 13, 30, 33, 40, 48, 69–70, 158, 233
Observer, of children's play, 47–49
One, Two Where's My Shoe? (Ungerer), 204, 306
Oral language, 79–86
  development of, 80–82
  and dramatic play, 101–102
  uses of, 81
Outside play, 158, 186–187
Over the Meadow (Wadsworth), 269, 282, 306
Ox-Cart Man (Hall), 193, 195, 207, 305

Parallel play, 21
Parallel player, 61–62
Parent conferences, 283
Parent handbook, 278
Parent meetings, 282
Parents
  communication with, 235, 267, 268, 271–275
  expectations, 266–267
  support of literacy, 191–194, 264
Peers
  as play tutors, 34
  social interaction with, 21–22

Personal involvement, level of, 162
Perspective taking, 24–28
Peter Pan (Barrie), 193, 304
Phonetic spelling, 90
Phonologic system, 82
Physical development, and dramatic play, 6
Pictorial symbols, 234–235, 248
Pigs in Hiding (Dubanevich), 204, 304
Play
  associative, 21–22
  characteristics of, 12
  constructive, 14
  cooperative, 22
  initiating, 28–30
  parallel, 21
  Piaget's three levels of, 12
  solitary, 21
  versus exploration, 12–13
Player, as adult role in children's play, 61–66
  coplayer, 62–63
  parallel player, 61–62
  play tutoring, 63–66
Playing pretend, 2
Play-training, 42
Play tutoring, 63–66
Plot, as source of book play, 222–226
Pocket for Corduroy, A (Freeman), 216, 304
Policy statements, 278
Pragmatic system, 82, 97
Pretend play. *See* Dramatic play
Props, 2, 9, 33–34, 40, 51–53, 121
  in block area, 166–168, 169
  choosing familiar, 36, 168
  in dramatic play outside, 186–187
  literacy-related, 141, 143, 145, 147, 149, 151, 154, 182
  for nonhouse play, 57–58

Props (*cont.*)
  written materials as, 173–175
Psychoanalytic theory of play,
  41
Puppets, 197–198, 199

Reading at home, 190–194
  and benefits to young
    children, 191
  development of family
    reading interactions,
    191–192
  special family book events,
    193–194
  special qualities of lap
    reading, 191
  value of playing about
    books, 194
Reading readiness model,
  98–99
Recipes, 247
Recurring principle, 92
Role playing, and perspective
  taking, 26

Scaffolding, 42–45
Schema, 5–6
Scripts, 2, 170
Settings, as sources of book
  play, 217–219
Semantic system, 82
Sensory play, 158, 163
Signs and labels, 170–172, 242
Silliness, 30, 75, 251
Social development and
    dramatic play, 20–30
  and complexity of dramatic
    play, 30
  initiating play, 28–30
  level of social interaction
    with peers, 21–22
  taking the perspective of
    others, 24–28

teacher support of different
    levels of play, 22–24
Social director, of children's
    play, 68–69
Social emotional development
    and dramatic play, 3–4
Social interaction with peers,
    21–22, 162
Sociodramatic play, 11, 12
Solitary play, 21, 162
Stage manager, of children's
    play, 49–61
Stories
  creating, 180–182, 250–251
  and discussion, 60–61
Story box stories, 198, 200
Swimming (Lionni), 209, 305
Sylvester and the Magic Pebble
    (Steig), 160, 305
Symbolic play, 11
Symbolic representation, 234
Symbolic thought, 31–33
Symbolic transformation, 31
Symbols, and emergent
    literacy, 234–235
Syntax, 82

Tale of Peter Rabbit, The (Potter),
    216, 305
Teacher as scribe, 68
Teacher roles
  and application of
    knowledge of cognitive
    development, 34–36
  as "artist apprentice," 56
  building partnerships with
    administrators and
    other professionals,
    284–286
  fostering language
    development, 38–39
  corresponding with families,
    281

as play facilitator, 69–72
  building rapport with
    others, 270–271
  supporting different levels
    of play, 22–24
Three Bears, The (Galdone), 200,
    305
Three-year-olds at play, 15–16,
    26, 42, 44, 61–62, 79, 118,
    130, 165, 169, 189
Time-out, 66
Too Much Noise (McGovern),
    197, 200, 225, 305
Transitional spelling, 90
Treasure hunts, 247–248
Trips, 60
TV as source of stories, 223
Two-year-olds at play, 15, 23,
    26, 189, 208

Unit based learning, 252–261
Unit blocks, 165

Very Hungry Caterpillar, The
    (Carle), 197–198, 304
*Visit to the Sesame Street
    Hospital, A* (Houtzig),
    189, 217, 305

What's Silly? (Yektai), 204, 306
Where Are They? Search for Susie
    (Tallarico), 204, 306
Where's Spot? (Hill), 216, 305
Where's Waldo? (Handford),
    203, 204, 305
Where's Wallace? (Knight), 204,
    305
Where the Wild Things Are
    (Sendak), 216, 284, 305
Writing center, 244–246

Author Index

Alward, K., 14, 38, 39, 47, 56, 65, 68, 302
Athey, I., 5, 6, 294

Baretta-Lorton, M., 257, 294
Barnhart, J., 109, 114, 301
Beckwith, L., 4, 294
Bentzen, W., 47, 294
Bergen, D., 3, 37, 294, 295
Bowman, B., 8, 294
Bredekamp, S., 266, 267, 270, 271, 284, 294
Bretherton, I., 5, 31, 32, 294
Brown, C., 3, 296
Bruner, J., 42, 191, 294, 299
Bundy, B., 272, 294
Burris, N., 87, 89, 90, 92, 94, 95, 102, 241, 302

Calkins, L., 264, 294
Canady, R., 211, 300
Caplan, F., 81, 294
Caplan, T., 81, 294
Carlsson-Paige, N., 76, 294
Cazden, C., 84, 294
Chomsky, C., 191, 295
Christie, J., 6, 34, 41, 42, 47, 59, 61, 63, 295, 297
Clay, M., 91, 92, 93, 95, 96, 97, 295
Cranston, Y., 61, 303
Curry, N., 3, 295

Davite, C., 99, 295
Davidson, J., 38, 248, 295, 297
Dimidjian, V., 3, 295
Dorsey-Gaines, C., 96, 272, 302
Dowhower, S., 232, 295
Drum, P., 91, 298

Dyson, A., 80, 114, 233, 234, 295

Ehri, L., 91, 298

Fein, G., 2, 3, 4, 31, 102, 295, 300
Feitelson, D., 33, 295
Fenson, L., 26, 32, 295, 296
Ferreiro, E., 92, 296
Ford, S., 49, 296
Fox, B., 265, 296
Freeman, E., 8, 297
Freyberg, J., 33, 296

Garvey, C., 12, 296
Genishi, C., 38, 82, 296
Gibson, L., 86, 87, 99, 191, 296
Giffin, H., 6, 102, 296
Glazer, S., 80, 81, 101, 296
Goffman, E., 54, 296
Goldenberg, C., 268, 296
Goodman, K., 98, 296
Gottfried, A., 3, 296
Griffing, P., 47, 56, 296
Gutierrez, K., 38, 86, 87, 297

Haight, W., 2, 297
Hall, N., 101, 297
Harmes, T., 247, 302
Harste, J., 120, 233, 297
Hatch, J., 8, 297
Heath, S., 96, 297
Heidemann, S., 33, 48, 297
Heim, N., 38, 297
Henderson, A.T., 264, 297
Hendrick, J., 267, 297
Hewitt, D., 33, 48, 297
Hiebert, E., 191, 297
Hieshima, J., 109, 114, 301

Hirsch, E., 297
Holdaway, D., 191, 206, 297
Honig, A., 4, 67, 303
Howe, N., 3, 300
Hutt, C., 13, 297

Isaacs, S., 41, 297

Johnson, J., 34, 41, 42, 47, 59, 61, 63, 297
Jones, E., 2, 8, 20, 45, 47, 49, 58–59, 65, 68, 251, 297

Kaplan, B., 31, 303
Klugman, E., 3, 298
Kostelnik, M., 54, 60, 80, 267, 271, 281

Levin, D., 76, 241, 294, 298
Linder, T., 39, 43, 298

Martinez, M., 192, 298
Mason, J., 91
Masonheimer, P., 91, 298
McCracken, J., 191, 298
McCracken, M., 191, 298
McElmeel, S., 211, 298
McLane, J., 194, 211, 298
McLoyd, V., 34, 57, 298
McMahon, L., 61, 303
McNamee, G., 194, 211, 298
McNeill, D., 84, 298
Miller, P., 2, 297
Monighan-Nourot, P., 42, 298
Morrow, L., 6, 80, 84, 86, 201, 246, 298, 301
Myhre, S., 34, 52, 298

Nathan, R., 87, 89, 90, 92, 94, 95, 102, 241, 302

Nathenson-Mejia, S., 87, 298
National Association of
    Elementary School
    Principals, 266, 299
National Assocation of State
    Boards of Education,
    266, 299
Nelson, K., 83, 84, 299
Neuman, S., 6, 299
Nicholich, L., 32, 299
Ninio, A., 42, 191, 299, 301
Nourot, P., 14, 38, 39, 47, 56, 65,
    68, 302

Paley, V., 251, 299
Parten, M.B., 21, 299
Pellegrini, A., 6, 102, 299
Piaget, J., 12–13, 14, 26, 31, 42,
    67, 299
Pica, R., 247, 299
Powell, D., 264, 267, 268, 299
Pulaski, M., 34, 299

Raines, S., 211, 300
Rasinski, T., 268, 300
Reynolds, G., 2, 8, 20, 45, 47, 49,
    58–59, 65, 68, 251, 297
Rivkin, M., 3, 295
Rogers, C., 3, 6, 14, 31, 33, 300
Rogers, F., 3, 300
Roser, N., 192, 298
Roskos, K., 6, 299
Ross, G., 33, 295
Rubin, K., 3, 300

Saltz, E., 3, 33, 300
Saltz, R., 3, 33, 300
Saracho, O., 98, 99, 103, 265,
    296, 300, 301
Sawyers, J., 3, 6, 14, 31, 33, 300
Scales, B., 14, 38, 39, 47, 56, 65,
    68, 302
Schickedanz, J., 84, 86, 91, 201,
    202, 206, 233, 240, 243,
    246, 300
Schwartz, S., 3, 295
Schweinhart, L., 47, 300
Shantz, C., 26, 300
Sharapan, H., 3, 300
Shefatya, L., 33, 301
Shipley, D., 54, 300
Skinner, B., 84, 301
Slaughter, J., 212, 301
Smilansky, S., 3, 12, 14, 15, 33,
    34, 42, 63, 298, 301
Smith, P., 14, 301
Snow, C., 81, 85, 88, 89, 96, 97,
    98, 102, 103, 191, 192,
    301
Soderman, A., 54, 60, 80, 267,
    271, 281, 298
Spodek, B., 98, 99, 103, 300, 301
Stewart, I., 84, 86, 300
Strickland, D., 6, 265, 301, 302
Sulzby, E., 79, 96, 97, 98, 99,
    109, 114, 120, 301, 302

Tabors, P., 81, 85, 88, 89, 96, 97,
    98, 102, 103, 301

Taylor, D., 96, 191, 265, 272,
    302
Teale, W., 79, 87, 89, 91, 96, 98,
    99, 109, 114, 120, 191,
    192, 206, 302
Teberosky, A., 92, 296
Temple, C., 87, 89, 90, 92, 94,
    95, 102, 241, 302

Vandenberg, B., 3, 13, 300, 302
Van Hoorn, J., 14, 38, 39, 47, 56,
    65, 68, 302
Veitch, B., 247, 302
Vollstedt, R., 114, 301
Voss, M., 193, 302
Vygotsky, L., 3, 31, 42, 103, 302

Wardle, F., 59, 295
Wells, G., 191, 303
Werner, H., 31, 303
Whiren, A., 54, 60, 80, 267, 271,
    281, 298
White, D., 84, 86, 300
Wittmer, D., 4, 67, 303
Wood, D., 61, 303
Woodward, C., 54, 303
Woodward, V., 233, 297

Yawkey, T., 34, 41, 42, 47, 59,
    61, 63, 297
York, M., 84, 86, 300

Author Index-Children's Books

Ahlberg, A., 203, 304
Ahlberg, J., 203, 304
Aliki, 262, 304
Baker, K., 203, 304
Barrett, J., 190, 219, 304
Barrie, J.M., 193, 304
Barton, B., 175, 304
Berenstain, J., 220, 221, 304
Berenstain, S., 220, 221, 304
Blos, J., 200, 214, 304
Bridwell, N., 216, 304
Brown, M., 208–209, 219, 304
Burton, V.L., 175, 304
Butterworth, N., 189, 304
Campbell, R., 220, 304
Carle, E., 197–198, 207, 213, 304
Cartwright, S., 203, 304
Civardi, A., 204, 304
Cook, B., 209, 304
Demi, 204, 304
Dubanevich, A., 204, 304
Dwight, R., 220, 304

Ehlert, L., 209, 304
Freeman, D., 209, 210, 216, 219, 304
Galdone, P., 193, 194, 200, 209, 305
Gauch, P., 126, 220, 305
Guilfoile, E., 200, 305
Hall, D., 193, 195, 207, 305
Handford, M., 203, 204, 305
Heller, R., 222, 305
Henrietta, 204, 305
Hill, E., 215, 305
Houtzig, D., 189, 217, 305
Johnson, C., 200, 304
Kalan, R., 213, 305
Knight, H., 204, 305
Kowitt, H., 204, 305
Krauss, R., 222, 305
LeSieg, T., 175, 222, 305
Lionni, L., 209, 305
Martin, B., 200, 217, 225, 305
Marzollo, J., 204, 305

McCloskey, R., 193, 194, 305
McGovern, A., 197, 200, 225, 305
Micklethwait, L., 204, 305
Numeroff, L., 197, 305
Potter, B., 216, 305
Raskin, E., 204, 305
Ray, H.A., 216, 305
Sendak, M., 216, 284, 305
Slobodkina, E., 213, 217, 224, 305
Small, D., 217, 305
Steig, W., 160, 305
Tallarico, A., 204, 306
Tarfuri, N., 203, 204, 306
Tobias, T., 221
Ungerer, T., 204, 306
Wadsworth, O., 269, 282, 306
Wilder, L.I., 1, 306
Wilson, A., 204, 306
Yektai, N., 204, 306
Zeff, C., 203, 304